The Musical Migration
and Ernst Toch

The Musical Migration and Ernst Toch

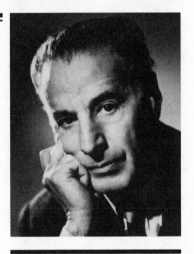

DIANE PEACOCK JEZIC

IOWA STATE UNIVERSITY PRESS / AMES

Diane Peacock Jezic taught music literature at Towson State University, Towson, Maryland, until her death in 1989.

© 1989 Iowa State University Press, Ames, Iowa 50010
All rights reserved

Composed by Iowa State University Press
Printed in the United States of America
♾ This book is printed on acid-free paper

First edition, 1989
International Standard Book Number: ISBN 0–8138–0322–5

Library of Congress Cataloging-in-Publication Data

Jezic, Diane.
    The musical migration and Ernst Toch / Diane P. Jezic.—1st ed.
        p.   cm.
    Bibliography: p.
    Includes index.
    ISBN 0–8138–0322–5
    1. Toch, Ernst. 1887–1964. 2. Composers—Biography. 3. Music—United States—European influences. 4. Music—United States—20th century—History and criticism. I. Title.
ML410.T54J5   1989
780′.92—dc20   89–11224
[B]

To my loving and devoted husband,
DRAGAN V. JEZIC, M.D.,
another distinguished émigré.

―――――――――

Contents

Musical Examples

Preface

With the decade of the 1980s marking the fiftieth anniversary of the fascist-imposed European migration to America, and with 1987 marking the centennial of the birth of émigré composer Ernst Toch, this book seeks to honor both occasions within a single framework—that which I have termed "the musical migration." In presenting the life, times, and works of Ernst Toch, whose story is representative of a whole generation of creative exiles, the book seeks to document Toch's and other émigré composers' contributions to twentieth-century musical America. Thus, *The Musical Migration and Ernst Toch* is also a tribute to the generation of Americans who absorbed the émigrés into the mainstream of their lives. The subsequent combining of foreign and American talents and cultures is an event that deserves to be studied from the perspective of half a century later.

It is said that we arrive at an understanding of the present by studying the past. Having immersed myself in the music and writings of Toch, I am convinced that his life represents a historic epoch worth retelling; that his compositions and writings represent a cultural epoch worth reevaluating; and that his life and works comprise an essential link in the socio-political and cultural chain that began fifty years ago. In the case of a transplanted composer such as Toch, the cultures of two continents merge, clash, and combine in a fascinating progression of twentieth-century musical thought and expression.

In their book *The Intellectual Migration—Europe and America, 1930–1960,* Donald Fleming and Bernard Bailyn comment upon the need for continuing scholarship on those individuals who participated in the migration:

> [Biographies] deserve to be written under any one of three conditions: if the [person] is a man of great achievements; if, due to his position, he has been in contact with many important people or important events; or, if by external circumstances, he can be considered a case representing a situation or development of interest.[1]

Ernst Toch qualifies for all three conditions. Not only are his compositions and writings representative of a man of great achievements, but his life story is interwoven with some of the most momentous events and most celebrated names in twentieth-century cultural history: Thomas Mann, Bertolt Brecht, Lion Feuchtwanger, Arnold Schönberg, Wilhelm Furtwängler, Erich Kleiber, Erich Leinsdorf, Elizabeth Sprague Coolidge, George Gershwin, Thornton Wilder, to name but a few.

One of the problems in writing about the migration is that the number of surviving participants in it, or witnesses to it, has greatly diminished. A primary source since the beginning of my research on Toch was the composer's widow, Lilly Toch (1892–1972). From the time we first visited together in Pittsburgh, to hear William Steinberg's performance of Toch's Second Symphony, until her sudden death in Santa Monica, April 1972, Mrs. Toch was an ardent correspondent and a vibrant link with a past that I had only read about.

Several weeks before her death, Mrs. Toch completed a series of interviews that, transcribed posthumously, are a fascinating social and historical documentary of the times in which the Tochs lived. Because she kept copies of all correspondence, writings, essays, and speeches, Mrs. Toch's contribution to the research on Toch is enormous.

Mrs. Toch was essentially responsible for the establishment of the Ernst Toch Archive at UCLA. Founded in 1967, the Toch Archive has since been expanded and further organized through the dedicated work of several persons. The composer's oldest grandson, Lawrence (Ren) Weschler, is most responsible for making the archive the workable tool that it is today. His work on behalf of his grandfather's legacy has also included the publication of a biographical essay, reprinted as the Introduction to Toch's *The Shaping Forces in Music* (Dover Edition, 1977), and the presentation of a series of "Talks on Toch," in 1974 for the tenth anniversary commemoration of the composer's death.

Toch's late daughter, Franzi Toch Weschler (1928–1988), was continually supportive. She opened her Santa Monica home to me and provided photographs and other memorabilia, in addition to detailed reminiscences of what it was like to grow up in a distinguished, though displaced, family.

Dr. Charlotte Erwin, chairperson of the 1987 Toch Centennial in Los Angeles, has been particularly helpful in securing current information about Toch performances and publications both here and abroad.

I am also indebted to the following people: Marsha Berman, associate music librarian at UCLA, who enabled me to do West Coast research on the East Coast; Dr. Konrad Wolff, pianist and author, an émigré from Berlin, who encouraged the project from the beginning, and who proofread the manuscript; Dr. Edith Borroff, composer, musicologist, and author, who insisted that I assess the musical migration from the American point of view as well as the European; Dr. Elliott Galkin, author and professor, who encouraged me to research the life and works of Toch; and Dr. Margaret Zassenhaus, author and physician, who proofread, with my sister, Marilyn Stranahan, the final version.

Special thanks are also due Konrad Hopkins, publisher of Wilfion Books, Paisley, Scotland, whose belief in the project included long-distance editing; Gerald Donnelly, of Paisley, Scotland, who proofread an earlier draft of the book; and Laurie Harper-Blake and Janet Kozlay for their early preparations of the typescript.

Dr. Dragan V. Jezic, my husband and an émigré from Croatia, Yugoslavia, has not only provided moral support, but a living example of what it is like to adopt, be adopted by, and adapt to a new country.

Thanks are due the following institutions and organizations: The UCLA Foundation; the Ernst Toch Archive, Music Library, UCLA; the Center for Research of the German-Speaking Emigration, State University of New York, Albany; the Peabody Institute Library of the Johns Hopkins University; and the Enoch Pratt Library in Baltimore.

Particular acknowledgment is due Jack Docherty, again of Paisley, Scotland, for compiling the Filmography that appears in the appendix of the book, and for contributing the information on Toch's film music which is presented in Chapter 4. Likewise, grateful acknowledgment is due Alyson McLamore of UCLA for her preparation of the Discography and the updated Worklist of Toch's Compositions, a revision of the 1977 catalog of works compiled by Dr. Charles Johnson.

Special thanks are also due Richard Kinney, director of the Iowa State University Press, Bill Silag, managing editor of the Press, and my editor, Gavin Lockwood, for their care and special attention in making this book a reality.

Lutherville, Maryland
Spring 1989

The Musical Migration
and Ernst Toch

─ 1

The Musical Migration

On the surface, the fate of the musician forced to emigrate seems less onerous than that of an actor, writer or scientist. [After all], a musician with his instrument in hand, can play and be understood in Paris, New York, or Rio . . . [But] composers are more difficult to transplant: there are subtle differences in musical tastes and customs. BORIS SCHWARZ

━━━ During the 1920s, American and European composers regularly crisscrossed the Atlantic in a mutually enriching cultural exchange. American composers went to Europe: Aaron Copland, Roy Harris, Walter Piston, Virgil Thompson, Ross Lee Finney, Ben Weber, Mark Brunswick, George Gershwin, and Roger Sessions in Paris; and Marc Blitzstein, Adolph Weiss, George Antheil, Henry Cowell, and Roger Sessions (also) in Berlin. European composers visited America: Darius Milhaud, Béla Bartók, Sergei Prokofieff, and Igor Stravinsky, who brought to the New World the New Music from postwar Europe. Earlier, Frederick Delius had been in Florida (1884–1886), Antonín Dvořák in New York (1892–1895), Richard Strauss in New York (briefly in 1904), and Gustav Mahler also in New York (1907–1911). Moreover, for years, American performers, whose finishing school was Europe, and European virtuosos and conductors lured to America by higher fees and greater fame, had been making the transatlantic passage, which had come to resemble a rite of passage.

In 1933, however, when Hitler became chancellor of Germany, the flood gates of a momentous migration were opened, but this time it was entirely one-way. Among the performers who sought refuge in America were pianists Artur Schnabel and Rudolf Serkin, violinists Adolf Busch and Joseph Szigeti, cellists Gregor Piatigorsky and Emanuel Feuermann, the Budapest Quartet, the Roth Quartet, the Kolisch Quartet, and the Albeneri Trio. Among the exiled conductors were

Bruno Walter, George Szell, William Steinberg, Pierre Monteux, Erich Leinsdorf, Julius Rudel, Maurice Abravenel, Efrem Kurtz, Antal Dorati, Paul Paray, Max Rudolf, Dmitri Mitropoulos, and Arturo Toscanini. European musicologists, whose discipline was in its infancy in this country, flocked to America: Curt Sachs, Alfred Einstein, Karl Geiringer, Hugo Liechtentritt, Paul Nettl, Willi Apel, Emanuel Winternitz, Leo Schrade, Felix Salzer, Manfred Bukofzer, Hans Tischler, Hans Theodore David, Eric Werner, Hans Moldenhauer, Hans Nathan, and Frederick Dorian, among others. What an impressive list of musical talent! Add to these luminaries the thirty-five composers listed in this book, and one can hardly disagree with the commonly held belief that

> of all the waves of immigrants that have landed on American shores since the pilgrims, the European refugees who fled Hitler in the 1930s may qualify as the best and the brightest. An entire civilization could be reconstructed from the writers, artists, musicians, philosophers, and scientists in their desperate ranks.[1]

What is of prime importance to this study is the fact that for the first time in this country's music history, American and European composers, sharing the same territory, were thrust into real competition for audiences, recognition, and commissions. From 1933 on, the situation for émigré composers, more than that of their supporting casts of performers, conductors, and musicologists, was entirely different from what it had been in earlier years.

Before studying this new situation, it will be helpful to review the key political and musical events (Table 1.1) that both precipitated and complicated the musical migration.

Table 1.1. Events Leading to Migration

Date	Event
January 30, 1933:	Adolf Hitler becomes chancellor
March 11, 1933:	Producer Carl Ebert and conductor Fritz Siedry are dismissed from their posts at the Berlin Municipal Opera
March 15, 1933:	Berlin Radio issues an absolute ban on Negro jazz
April 10, 1933:	Nazi minister of propaganda, Dr. Göbbels, rejects Furtwängler's and American conductors' pleas for Jewish conductors and performers to be heard in Germany

May 10, 1933:	The burning of *Kulturbolshevists'* and leftist intellectuals' books and musical scores
May 31, 1933:	American composers form their own Composers' Protective Society, protesting their inferior social position, and citing attitudes of Americans against modern music
October 31, 1933:	Arnold Schönberg arrives in America at the age of 59
February 8, 1934:	Virgil Thompson's opera (with Gertrude Stein) *Four Saints in Three Acts* premiered at the New York Metropolitan
February 10, 1934:	Howard Hanson's opera *Merry Mount* is produced at the Metropolitan Opera House
March 6, 1934:	Walter Piston conducts the premiere of his *Concerto for Orchestra,* Boston Symphony
October 1934:	Ernst Toch (age 47) begins his American career teaching at the New School for Social Research in New York City
December 6, 1934:	Göbbels denounces the "moral decay of atonal composers"
December 12, 1934:	Roy Harris's *When Johnny Comes Marching Home* premiered by Eugene Ormandy in Minneapolis
December 20, 1934:	Ernst Toch's *Big Ben Variations* premiered by Boston Symphony
October 30, 1935:	The Federal Music Project, a branch of Roosevelt's WPA, is created to provide work for American composers
April 10, 1937:	Paul Hindemith (age 42) performs his *Viola Sonata* at Elizabeth Coolidge's eighth Festival of Chamber Music, Washington, D.C.
December 19, 1937:	Forty-eight representative American composers establish the American Composers' Alliance in New York City to protect the performing rights of American composers.

By 1938, musical America was in a difficult position as far as modern music was concerned. On the one hand, American composers were demanding their fair share in performances. On the other hand, the presence of an illustrious corps of European composers in America could help the fundamental cause of making American audiences more receptive to twentieth-century music.

According to Boris Schwarz, quoted at the beginning of this chapter, "composers are apt to dry up when they are removed from their native land."[2] Transplantation had a profound effect on most of the émigré composers, Ernst Toch among them. They were affected by having to adapt to an American public not much interested in imported modern music, or to the film industry in Hollywood, which gained the most from the émigré talent, or to American colleges and universities, which sometimes had to be coerced into taking on distinguished foreign composers.

Questions of how the émigré composers viewed America and themselves in America, and how America viewed them, become intertwined. When these composers, already bereft of their publishers and public, had to earn their living in work other than composing, while trying to create in styles still being defined, the reciprocal effects of transplantation begin to blur. It is impossible to discuss "subtle differences in musical tastes and customs" or "drying up" without first putting the émigré composers into a larger context.

The larger context involves knowing, specifically, how some of the more renowned émigré composers fared in America and, generally, what kind of problems the creative émigrés encountered as a group. Without this background on the cultural-intellectual migration, it would be difficult, if not impossible, to evaluate the experiences and contributions of Ernst Toch as composer, teacher, and writer in America.

According to postwar statistics, as they appear in Maurice Davie's *Refugees in America,* no fewer than sixty-nine composers came to America between 1933 and 1941.[3] The lives of the well-known composers—such as Stravinsky, Bartók, Schönberg, Hindemith, and Weill—have been richly documented in biographies and music histories. Several of the lesser known composers have also been the subject of specialized biographies: Eisler, Krenek, Korngold, Zeisl, and Kahn. However, the lives and works of many composers known to have emigrated to America remain confined to doctoral dissertations and scholarly music journals, although nearly all appear in the major music dictionaries and encyclopedias. What is missing is a master list of the sixty-nine, which may not ever be possible to compile.[4]

They came from various parts of Europe: Arthur Honegger (b.

France, but a Swiss national all of his life), Igor Stravinsky (b. Russia), and Alexandre Tansman (b. Poland) from Paris; Béla Bartók and Miklós Rózsa from Hungary; Bohuslav Martinu and Jaromír Weinberger from Czechoslovakia; Mario Castelnuovo-Tedesco from Italy; the Russian-born composers Nicolai Lopatnikoff and Dmitri Tiomkin from Berlin, along with Friedrich Holländer (b. in London) and Karol Rathaus (b. Poland), also from Berlin. But, by far, most of the composers were either Austrian or German by birth.

For the most part, these émigré composers were employed either in Hollywood film studios or at educational institutions, and some worked in both places. Appendix A chronicles the names, ages, places of settlement, and principal American employment of twenty-five German-Austrian composers whose migration began fifty years ago.[5]

Many of these composers crossed paths with Ernst Toch at some point, in Vienna, Mannheim, Donaueschingen, Baden-Baden, Berlin, New York, Hollywood, or Los Angeles. Their worlds in Europe and America were rather small, and many of the composers were acquainted with one another. After all, most of the transplanted composers, and, for that matter, transplanted intellectuals as a group, shared a common fate.

The problems of resettling intellectuals and creative artists were complex. In 1933, the Academic Assistance Council in London formed the Committee on Displaced Scholars, which acted as a clearing house, helping refugees get a guarantee of employment in the United States—a prerequisite to receiving a permanent entry visa.

In that British universities could not begin to accommodate all the scholars, the council formed a counterpart group in the United States called the Emergency Committee in Aid of Displaced Foreign Scholars. Made up of presidents of American universities and other professional institutions, this committee was supported by both Jewish and non-Jewish funds. Mindful of American scholars' unemployment, the committee offered refugees teaching positions lasting from one to three years, contributing grants of approximately two thousand dollars a year to universities that hired a refugee.

However, in 1937, the Emergency Committee urged the Academic Assistance Council not to send more refugee scholars, when American colleges and universities became too crowded, and younger American faculty members opposed hiring the foreigners. Nevertheless, the council bypassed the American request, giving the intellectuals travel expenses and letting them scout out their own opportunities in America. As the number of scholars increased, the committee decreased its grants, with the result that by 1940, over 6,000 persons had appealed to them, but they were able to help only 355.

Nevertheless, as late as 1940–1941, the Emergency Committee, through its young hero Varian Fry, succeeded in rescuing hundreds of refugees trapped in Marseilles and southern France. Among those that Fry rescued, and who, quite literally, caught the last boats to America, were the artists Marc Chagall, Marcel Duchamp, and Henri Matisse, and the writers Thomas and Heinrich Mann, Lion Feuchtwanger, Alfred Döblin, Franz Werfel, and his wife Alma Mahler. The Emergency Committee worked in close collaboration with the Institute for Advanced Study in Princeton and with the New School for Social Research in New York City.

Another committee that rescued intellectuals was the Emergency Society of German Scholars Abroad, an organization in Switzerland established by German refugees. Publishing lists of nearly fifteen hundred Germans who had lost their academic posts, this organization received assistance from the Rockefeller Foundation in America.

In fact, many private organizations came to the relief of the oppressed, and virtually every religious organization participated: the American Jewish Joint Distribution Committee, the American Friends Service Committee, the War Relief Services of the National Catholic Welfare Conference, and the Unitarian Service Committee, among many others.

The American rescue committees fell into two categories: general refugee services and professional relocation agencies. One of those in the first category was the National Refugee Service, founded in 1938. With its own social service department, it provided a wide range of services, including financial relief, education for naturalization, a retraining division, and a service for social and cultural adjustment. By 1939, this network extended to more than nine hundred local community organizations throughout America. Rescue committees in the second category tried to find employment for specific professional groups. The American composer Mark Brunswick, having returned from thirteen years of study in Europe, was appointed chairman of that service's National Committee for Refugee Musicians (1938–1943).

Perhaps the most noteworthy project to employ the displaced scholars in America was the New School for Social Research, soon to be known as the "University in Exile," founded by Dr. Alvin Johnson. The faculty of this university consisted almost entirely of Europeans, many of whom found that their employment at the New School led, within a short time, to university and college appointments elsewhere in the country. Ernst Toch and Hanns Eisler were among several musicians helped by Johnson's humanitarian efforts. Countless letters of recommendation were written to the New School, such as this one from Bruno Walter on Toch's behalf.[6]

Hotel Savoy-Plaza
New York, N.Y.

October Twenty-first
1933

Henry Cowell, Esq.
New School for Social Research
66 West 12th Street
New York City

Dear Mr. Cowell:

Ernst Toch is a well-known German composer whose works have been played by the leading musical societies and organizations in Germany.

The last time I heard a Toch composition was at the Zurich Music Festival under the baton of Doctor Volkmar Andreae in 1932.

Ernst Toch is an interesting musician with a distinct profile and his coming to this country would certainly be a cultural acquisition.

Sincerely Yours,

BRUNO WALTER

Three days after the Nazi book burning on 10 May 1933, the *New York Times* announced that the New School for Social Research was expanding to become a "University in Exile." A huge fund-raising campaign began. Prior to 1933, Alvin Johnson, who had founded the New School in 1921, tried to attract some notable German scholars to teach there, and they refused. Now they were clamoring for the jobs.

As Laura Fermi remembers the German scholars' view of American culture:

While they lived in Germany, many of the future émigrés, especially those outside the field of the natural sciences, did not think much of American culture. They had such a very positive opinion of their *Kultur* that they just didn't pay any attention to an intellectual society as young as the American, which committed the sin of still being preoccupied with practical matters. German scholars were then convinced, as some admitted later, that there was only one humanism, one philosophy, and one way to look at social questions—the German way.[7]

The optimism of her further claim that "this attitude, shared by most learned Germans, was awesome and impressive to American scholars," seems somewhat naive. No doubt she is right about American scholars not competing with the Germans teaching in disciplines still in their infancy, such as musicology, or in disciplines obviously in need of imported talent. She might also be referring to the awe in which some American students may have held their famous émigré teachers. For instance, as a teenager, Schönberg's pupil (and later distinguished scholar on him) Dika Newlin observed:

I find Schönberg a VERY inspiring teacher. He is 64 and does not enjoy the best of health, but he is vigorous both in mind and body. Very self-centered, of course, as one might expect; very few people of his reputation can escape being egocentric. . . . I believe he has little sentimental leanings . . . as can be deduced from his music [which is] intellectual gymnastics. . . . He teaches very concisely and very methodically."[8]

In general, however, the evidence on the attitudes of American scholars toward their foreign colleagues, especially as co-workers on the same college or university faculty, is contradictory, as in these two opinions of American academics on their foreign colleagues:

He's as good as, but no better than, the American teachers. If I had to choose between letting him go and letting one of the Americans go, I'd let him go.

and

He's too good for the college. He has more music in his little finger than all the rest of the faculty put together.[9]

The academic salaries paid to exiled composers were scandalously low. In 1943, Toch earned fifteen hundred dollars a year for occupying the Alchin Chair in Composition at the University of Southern California. On the one hand, faculties liked to boast the presence of eminent

European scholars whom they employed, but on the other hand, they were not prepared to pay them higher salaries for the privilege of being affiliated with a university or college, which was a necessity for a composer in America even at that time. The salaries were low because

> the depression hit the young in the academic world more than those already well established in their careers. . . . Alvin Johnson estimated that 5,000 American Ph.D.'s were unemployed [in the mid-thirties]. To them, the foreigners seemed unfair competition and they often vigorously opposed their appointments. Colleges and universities could not disregard the Americans' feelings. . . . It was not unusual to consider yourself lucky to obtain a teaching position paying $1500 a year.[10]

In a chapter included in *The Cultural Migration: The European Scholar in America* (1953) art historian Erwin Panofsky noted the situation in many American universities that employed émigré scholars in his subject:

> No art historian has, to the best of my knowledge, ever displaced an American-born. The immigrants were either added to the staffs of college or university departments already in being, or were entrusted with the teaching of art history where it had previously been absent. . . . In either case, the opportunities of American students and teachers were widened rather than narrowed.[11]

What is central here are the extensive adjustments that the émigrés had to make as they faced new cultural and teaching problems.

Of course the major problem was language. The German scholars, in particular, tended to express themselves in "the abstract language of cultivation," as Laura Fermi calls it. This language, complex and philosophical, clashed with the less intellectual vocabularies of American students and academic administrators.

Furthermore, in Europe, the Herr Professor Doktor was revered within the university and esteemed within the community. In America, however, the émigré had to teach different kinds of students, who had neither the exposure to nor the curiosity about the highly cultivated subjects on which the professor was an expert, and who, consequently, often seemed disrespectful.

In his chapter "The Academic Welcome," Anthony Heilbut characterizes some of the displaced academics.

> Academics were surprised at the switch in emphasis here. American colleges were "student-centered"; instead of required courses, students were

allowed "electives." In Europe the professor was king, but in democratic America, the students elected him. One historian, after forty years here, still says, "They're so unequipped I've never had one student from whom I learned a thing." Hannah Arendt continually referred to her students as "her children". . . . Wilhelm Reich was so correct that in his laboratory he would even call his wife by her academic title.[12]

The problem of having to make themselves understood in practical terms and simplified language forced some of the émigré composers to invent new ways of teaching their tradition to the American students, which resulted in the publication of a number of influential textbooks. Among these were Schönberg's *Fundamentals of Musical Composition,* Hindemith's *Elementary Training for Musicians,* Krenek's *Modal Counterpoint,* and Toch's *The Shaping Forces in Music.*

For all these émigré writers, the linguistic and communication problems were not easily solved, as Henry Pachter observed:

> Working in a language which is not the language of one's dreams is to miss many over- and under-tones, ambiguities, and poetic notions, the spontaneousness, and even the silences. Dimensions of thought and feeling must be replaced by a technique of significations, using spoken words in prefabricated, studied sequences, which threaten to impoverish that which they set out to enrich. Uneducated people quickly learn to make small talk in canned phrases. Intellectuals learn slowly and tend to speak "translatese," painfully aware that it is one flight below the level they would like to inhabit intellectually.[13]

Living, working, and composing in a foreign culture, which was sometimes friendly, sometimes not, exerted a continual psychological pressure on the émigrés and may have affected their creativity.

But the greatest psychological pressure on them was caused by their agony over Europe's suffering during the war years, resulting in a drying up of inspiration to compose. Toch, for instance, added only one new work to his catalog during the war years (*Poems to Martha,* Op. 66, 1942), not counting his film scores.

Shortly before his suicide, Stefan Zweig, sorrowful over the "creative death" of Rainer Maria Rilke, begged to know: "Will such lyricism again be a possibility in this era of turbulence and universal destruction? Is it not a lost tribe that I am bemoaning?"[14]

Few émigrés were immune to anxiety over the whereabouts of their friends and relatives still in Europe, and over ways they might be helped to escape. And many of the refugees, safe in America, felt guilty about those who had been left behind. As Bruno Walter explained:

"Anxiety concerning the fate of friends we had left behind in Europe and the welfare of those who were forced to build up a new existence in the U.S. was our constant companion during the first years of our settlement in America."[15]

Creativity could not flourish in such anxious circumstances, aggravated by requests from friends and relatives who needed affidavits of support, which were required for visas. Toch expended a great deal of energy making enough money to provide these affidavits. Where America had earlier favored those refugees whose skills might be useful to the country, by 1939–1940 the refugees themselves had to assume the financial burden of supporting friends and relatives.

Related to their anxiety about the dispersion of their families was the refugees' own uncertainty about where they should settle. For many émigrés, New York City was their first American home, but they might not remain there for long. Few, if any, wanted to move elsewhere, after "inventing their lives" (Laura Fermi) with stopovers in Paris, London, or Switzerland, before eventually arriving in New York. That city, besides having the largest émigré population in America, was the city geographically closest to Europe. For in the minds of many émigrés was the hope that they might go back to Europe once the war was over.

Many of those who did leave New York, with the assistance of private foundations and service networks, went to Los Angeles, which by 1945 had the second largest émigré population in the United States. The main attraction there was Hollywood, where employment of émigré talent was substantial. And with the arrival in 1941 of the Feuchtwangers, the Brechts, the Manns, the Kafkas, and the Werfels, Los Angeles became the center for literary giants in exile. The musical opportunities, however, in spite of the presence of such illustrious performers as Gregor Piatigorsky, Sergei Rachmaninoff, and Jascha Heifetz, could not rival those of New York. Los Angeles had a philharmonic orchestra, conducted until 1940 by Otto Klemperer, but in the late 1930s and early 1940s the city lacked both a resident opera and a ballet, which the émigrés considered a serious cultural deficiency.

The émigrés developed observable personality traits that many Americans could scarcely comprehend and, therefore, sometimes misinterpreted. As Anthony Heilbut explains in his preface to *Exiled in Paradise:*

> After the political shocks of emigration, they could not trust any form of sanctuary. Thus, though they knew enough to take advantage of almost

any situation, they also knew too much to feel completely comfortable or safe. . . . The émigré tone is witty and impious . . . sharp and biting. . . . Although the refugees were often magnificently forthright, emigration had trained them in the arts of concealment . . . a bit like the old court Jews, they exerted great authority in some areas, but in other places they remained vulnerable.[16]

In America, where class lines were less sharply drawn than in Europe, people could become annoyed with the émigrés' *bei uns* (where we live) mentality, contrasting their present way of life with that they had enjoyed in Europe. Perhaps expecting the émigrés to show humility or gratitude for being given the opportunity to teach in America, college faculty members sometimes voiced their irritation, as this professor expressed:

> In spite of the fact that he has lived in this country for seven years or more, he has a distinctly foreign appearance and speaks with a strong accent. This prejudices some people against him, because . . . they feel there is an occasional arrogance in his manner. . . . He does have a rather heavy Germanic way of presenting a topic which tends to make some people feel that there is not as much in the topic as the difficulty in following him would suggest.[17]

Xenophobia was a fact of life in America from the postdepression through the postwar years. Some evidence of its existence has already been cited, but this particular instance seems close to unbelievable today.

> When it became known in 1932 that Albert Einstein planned to come to America, the Women's Patriotic Corporation tried to prevent his entry. In December 1932, the *New York Times* published an article calling Einstein "a German *Bolshevist* . . . his theory has no scientific value . . . not understandable because there was nothing to understand" . . . to which Einstein replied in the newspaper, "Wouldn't it be funny if they wouldn't let me in? Why, the whole world would laugh at America!"[18]

One last account from an émigré musician, a college teacher, reveals the deeper aspect of America's covert fear of foreigners. Writing in 1945, he reflected:

> I have found that in those two fields [music and college teaching], the main obstacles will arise from a certain FEAR of the native-born musicians and teachers that the immigrants are better or at least considered better by students and the public.[19]

Anti-Semitism was also a reality in America. The Jewish and non-Jewish Americans feared that as the number of Jewish immigrants continued to rise, anti-Semitism would increase. In that two-thirds of the more than three hundred thousand émigrés admitted to the United States by 1941 were Jewish, these fears tended to grow proportionately.

It is against this background of historical events, cultural differences, xenophobia, anti-Semitism, and personal problems caused by the migration that the case of Ernst Toch can be presented. By examining Toch's life and times, and his musical compositions and writings, in both their European and American settings, an attempt can be made to assess the strength, depth, and character of the impact of the migration on twentieth-century music in America.

=2

Introducing Ernst Toch

===== **It seems that only my musical jokes have taken root.**
—Ernst Toch to Lilly Toch, c. 1960

There may be some truth in Toch's comment on the fate of his music.[1] If someone familiar with the composer's name were asked, "Do you remember what he wrote?" the answer might be *The Geographical Fugue.* Another person might answer, "I recall a funny piano piece . . . *The Juggler,* and also the *Big Ben Overture."* Someone else might have heard of the fanciful opera *The Princess and the Pea,* or perhaps *Pinocchio,* or *Peter Pan,* or the lighter pieces for woodwinds, such as *Five Pieces for Wind Instruments and Percussion* or the *Sonatinetta for Flute, Clarinet and Bassoon.* Still others acquainted with Toch the composer for Hollywood films might recall the romantic love theme in *Peter Ibbetson,* or the eerie mood music in *The Cat and the Canary,* or the scary chase music in *Dr. Cyclops.*

By "musical jokes" Toch probably meant his lighter works. The slowdown in performances of his more substantial compositions, such as his first three symphonies, composed between the ages of sixty-three and sixty-seven, his string quartets, and his piano and cello concertos, was a bitter blow to him. The lighter works, which were easy to write, seemed to appeal more to American audiences. Why? Did Americans just want to be entertained?

As a successful composer of sixteen Hollywood films, Toch regretted that his film writing reputation outweighed that of serious composer. After all, in Europe he had also composed incidental music for fifteen stage and radio plays and four film scores, but there he had been known as a first-class composer of concert music.

With over 145 extant works in his catalog, 49 of which remain unpublished, Ernst Toch yearned, quite rightly, to be taken seriously. He composed for the stage, for the concert or recital hall, for the opera house, for amateur music makers, and for the screen. Some of his works are certainly entertaining; some are profound statements from a profound thinker; many are noteworthy contributions to twentieth-century music.

▬▬ I am the forgotten composer of the twentieth century.
—Toch to Nicolas Slonimsky, 1962

Though hardly a new complaint among composers of this century, Toch's pessimistic self appraisal in 1962 is gripping, because just six years earlier, his Third Symphony had won the Pulitzer Prize, and, in fact, America had not done badly by this particular émigré composer.[2] Serge Koussevitsky, William Steinberg, George Szell (once a pupil of Toch's in Vienna), Antal Dorati, Erich Leinsdorf, and Otto Klemperer, among the émigré conductors, had premiered many of his American works. Furthermore, the American patrons, Mrs. Elizabeth Sprague Coolidge and Mrs. Marian MacDowell, had commissioned important works from him. Without their support, there would have been no Piano Quintet Op. 64, fewer performances of his chamber music, no Fourth Symphony, and no peaceful respites at the MacDowell Colony in Peterborough, New Hampshire.

It is tempting to dismiss the forgotten composer lament as the grumbling of an old man of seventy-five. But Toch, who was "simply enormously unwilling to talk about himself" (Mrs. Toch), really did see himself sinking deeper and deeper into oblivion. It had been almost thirty years since he had left Germany. What did the young postwar Germans or Austrians know or care about him?

If Toch were truly convinced that his adopted country or his homeland had forgotten him in 1962, he probably discounted the fact that his name appeared, as it still does, in the major music dictionaries, encyclopedias, and books on film and twentieth century music. But if he were predicting the constantly changing musical tastes that could bypass so much of his music during the years after his death, Toch's pessimism seems to have validity.

Recognized though Toch was during his American years, being elected to the American National Institute of Arts and Letters, in the same year as his Pulitzer Prize, 1956, or winning an American Grammy Award in 1960 or receiving an honorary doctorate or being offered guest lectureships at prestigious American universities, including delivering the Charles Elliot Norton lecture at Harvard in 1943, was not the kind of recognition for which he yearned.

What he probably wished for was a return to the days of some thirty-five years before. In the Weimar Republic, Toch's music had been championed by such internationally known conductors as Erich Kleiber, Wilhelm Furtwängler, and Hermann Scherchen. The Rosé and the Amar Quartets had performed his string quartets all over Europe, and by 1929, at the age of forty-two, Toch had already entered into the hallowed pages of *Riemann's Musik-Lexikon.*

> As a composer, Toch is one of the most versatile and inventive talents of the New Music. Full of fresh and spirited music-making, he has no trace of negative parody in his style, and has succeeded in making the transition from initial "music to please" to always freer and more secure expressive music.[3]

The *Berliner Tageblatt* and the *Frankfurter Zeitung* had carried reviews of his music, and had also featured articles by him, usually about the New Music, or on such fads as "Music for Mechanical Instruments," "Music for the Radio," or "Music for Sound Film." In the newspapers and the contemporary music circles in the late 1920s and 1930s, he had shared the limelight with his friends and acquaintances Paul Hindemith, Arnold Schönberg, Paul Dessau, Hanns Eisler, and Kurt Weill. He had, in fact, become so well-known in Europe that in 1932 he was invited by the American *Pro Musica* to tour the United States. Altogether those were impressive achievements for a fifteen-year career (1918–1933) in Germany!

Having been so prominent during his European years, Toch, in his old age, probably preferred to remember his past selectively, perhaps giving in to the *bei uns* syndrome. Or perhaps he was finally realizing that he could never recover what he had lost.

Only now, almost twenty-five years after his death, are some of his buried works being resurrected. At the time of this writing, Toch's Centennial has been officially celebrated in Los Angeles, with radio broadcasts and live performances at the University of Southern California and UCLA. Elsewhere, *Pinocchio* was performed by the National Symphony Orchestra under Rostropovich in Washington, D.C., and the Violin Sonata, Op. 21, was performed by Eudice Shapiro in Pittsburgh.

However, Germany seems to have done more in honoring the Centennial, with radio broadcasts, live performances, and lectures. As part of the Berlin Festspiel in September 1987, performances have included the vocal chamber work *There is a Season for Everything,* the Cello Concerto, Op. 35, and the String Trio, Op. 63. Performances in Mannheim, where Toch lived from 1919–1929, have included a solo piano recital of Toch's German piano music, an all-Toch chamber music program, an all-Toch recital of vocal and instrumental works, and a special Toch Centennial program of orchestral, solo, and chamber works, presented at the Musik Hochschule. Performances in Munich have included the one-act opera *The Princess and the Pea* and the vocal chamber piece *The Chinese Flute,* at the Richard Strauss Conservatory, and members of the Munich Philharmonic have programmed a concert of Toch's chamber music. Considering the renewed interest in Toch's less prolific compatriots E. W. Korngold and Alexander Zemlinsky, one likes to believe that a revival of Toch's music is just beginning.

I am a wanderer, a pilgrim on earth—but are you anything more?

—Goethe, *The Sorrows of Young Werther*

Einstein referred to himself as a "bird of passage"; Toch preferred the word "wanderer" for himself. Whatever the impact of emigration had on his personality or creativity, Ernst Toch, before and much more after emigration, was a philosopher—not just a musical philosopher, as evidenced in his two books and many of his articles, but a philosopher of the human condition. Appropriately, he identified with and dedicated his Second Symphony to "the lonely seer in a time of darkness, the only victor in a world of victims, Albert Schweitzer."

As a wanderer, Toch was hardly immune from feelings of depression and loneliness. Confiding in his dear friend Mrs. Elizabeth Sprague

Coolidge in 1943, he wrote that "response and reassurance have come up all along the way in the old world. I felt I reached people's heart and mind, there was a living process of communication, justifying any work and endearing it to myself. I never questioned the *raison d'être* of my doings. Here I feel terribly lonesome."[4]

No doubt countless letters expressing the same isolation were written by all but the most fortunate or optimistic émigrés.

But ten years later, after a summer spent at the MacDowell Colony, Toch wrote: "This visit has planted another magic island within the magic island; it restored and fortified my faith in mankind, in human spirit and willpower, and in my blessed adopted country."[5]

Similarly, Toch dedicated his *Shaping Forces in Music* "to the country which gave me shelter when shelter was taken from me . . . in everlasting gratitude."

Interwoven with his sense of gratitude is the composer's apparent humility. His friend the pianist Jakob Gimpel observed that "he watched the ever changing world outside him with a kindness and humility, born of wisdom which is the mark of the great."[6]

The composer himself often wrote or spoke with obvious humility. Upon the occasion of his seventy-fifth birthday celebration in Los Angeles, whose organizational committee had included such luminaries as Jack Benny, Jascha Heifetz, and Gregor Piatigorsky, Toch responded:

> Another drain on my capacity to express myself comes from you; from your overwhelming kindness to show me by your presence that you consider what I have done in my life has not been too bad. May I quote Hans Sachs who says in Wagner's *Die Meistersinger,* "Words, right to you, bow me to earth; your praise is far beyond my worth."[7]

and, upon an earlier occasion he wrote:

> Was I a flea, a mouse, a little nothing when I compared what I did with what Mozart did?[8]

Here, Toch was describing how he taught himself composition, by studying and copying the string quartets of Mozart; his self-effacing humility thus appears to have been with him since childhood.

Wie herrlich dass Sie Musiker und Philosoph sind! **How wonderful that you are both a musician and a philosopher!**
—Albert Schweitzer to Toch, 1953

Whether Toch is regarded as a neo-Romantic composer-writer, waxing eloquent with mottos attached to his symphonies, or as a writer of books and journal articles on such subjects as "The Forms of Musical Expression in the Course of Changing Times," the philosophical aspect of his creative work cannot be ignored. "Good music has its roots in the ever ancient, ever new, ever timeless human soul . . . it is the seat of naivete, the womb of spontaneous conception, of inspiration," he wrote.[9]

I do not press, I am pressed; I do not write, I am written.
—Last note from Ernst to Lilly Toch, 1964

Ernst Toch was such an inspired composer that he kept a lighted pen and manuscript paper next to his bed for that moment of inspiration when it came. Furthermore, when he sat down to work at his desk, the idea already in his mind, he never wrote other than the full score—no condensed copy to be orchestrated later. A good example of his inspired music is the orchestral piece *Notturno,* composed after an evening's walk in the woods at the MacDowell Colony. "In art and nature alike, first comes creation . . . then, observation," he said.[10]

If a composer is so much guided by inspiration, he probably does not care much for traditional musical analysis. Toch's opinions here never varied. "It is said that composition of the past arrived at some forms or frames FOR GOOD REASONS. Let us try to investigate these reasons instead of the forms; the sources and forces at work below the surface, instead of the surface."[11]

He said it over and over: "The composer wrestles with his only purpose; to clarify in his own mind some concepts which possessed him beyond his will."[12]

> About this troubling state of affairs . . . there is an intricate component lodged in Ernst's personality.
>
> —Dr. Toni Stolper, letter to the author

Although referring to the forgotten composer question, Dr. Stolper, a lifetime friend of the Tochs, hinted that the composer's complex personality may have contributed, indirectly,

> to the slowdown in performances during his last years: I understood him to be a very private, introvert type, not the virile type of an instinctive public relations actor with the gift of acting the right way at the right time to the right person. . . . He might impress sundry confreres and persons of influence with his creative and human eminence. But to other contenders in the field of publicity, it might appear as a touch of awkward arrogance.[13]

Other close acquaintances confirm the composer's introverted personality. "I saw him as a gentle, self-contained being, sometimes withdrawn . . . absolutely genuine in everything he did or said, single-minded in his devotion to his chosen field."[14]

He mostly preferred to be alone and so he missed some significant opportunities, such as meeting the new conductor of the Los Angeles Philharmonic, Zubin Mehta. "Even if they play like God himself, it cannot compare to the music I hear in my head," he insisted (Mrs. Toch). Although in Germany Toch had participated in European contemporary music festivals, he was never keen on going to concerts. "For me, the highest form of musical enjoyment consists in the quiet reading of a score . . . an attic room, the basic necessities of life, a piano, and *The Well-Tempered Clavier.*[15]

Confirming his preference to stay home rather than attend concerts, Toch's daughter, Franzi Weschler, recalled that her "parents only rarely went out together socially themselves. Occasionally they went to concerts if a work of my father's was being played."[16]

However, when the composer did venture out, in the company of close friends, his presence was keenly felt. The widow of composer Eric Zeisl, a close friend of Toch's, related the following episode:

> He (Toch) came over to us at night and we had talks and visited with each other. One of the highlights for everybody was in the late afternoon, right before dinner. When everybody had finished with work, they used to go to the swimming pool . . . and everybody was waiting when Ernst Toch came out and made his *salto mortale* into the water. It was just fantastic because he was already seventy at the time, and really so acrobatic.[17]

Alongside the public introvert was the private extrovert. Marta Feuchtwanger, one of the pillars of the Los Angeles émigré community, observed that "in public life, Toch seemed aloof, an attitude caused by his extreme shyness. But he knew laughter and joy in a circle of devoted friends."[18]

Toch's daughter recalled how her father could entertain the guests invited to their Santa Monica home.

> Mother would make large dinner parties bearable for him by seating him at a small round table in an adjoining area with just two or three special friends, who knew his sensitive ears and respected his special need for protection from what was, for him, auditory bedlam. Still, meek and withdrawn as my father was most of the time, he was also often the life of the party, having both rooms in stitches over his famous mimicking acts and clowning antics which . . . he could sometimes be prevailed upon to perform. He was a master teller of long narrative jokes and stories of funny personal experiences, and he would sometimes pop up with great spontaneous witticisms and an unexpected quick repartee.[19]

Social, but unsociable, depending. Laughter and joy? Certainly these were also Toch's companions, as evidenced by the titles of the lighter compositions mentioned earlier. Added to the list should be, among others, the *Comedy for Orchestra,* Op. 42, and the *Circus Overture* of 1954. A circus fan all his life, Toch wrote the overture to depict circus clowns, performers, acrobats (which he was, himself), and the beasts and animals. One could presume that he may have felt more at home with animals, including his pet dachshunds, especially considering the text of his 1961 choral work *Song of Myself,* based on Walt Whitman's "I think I could turn and live with animals," from *Leaves of Grass.*

Very serious, he could also be almost sarcastic, in a tone typical of ex-Berliners. When queried by an interviewer upon the occasion of Toch's performing his Piano Concerto with the Boston Symphony in 1932, "And what direction do you expect music to take in the future?" Toch's curt reply was, "the right direction." When asked by a friend to write out an analysis of the Violin Sonata Op. 44, Toch scribbled a letter to the violinist.

> One of the most original things about this sonata is that it is written for the violin, as most violin sonatas are, in contrast to a Heckelphone Sonata, which, without exception, is written only for the heckelphone. Not uninteresting is also the fact that here the bow and pizzicato are employed, in contrast to the Bass Tuba, which can only be played with the mouth, and only very seldom, as it mostly happens in contemporary music, with the behind.[20]

And so, the reticent music philosopher could also be satirical.

He was Jewish by birth, but as an adult he did not observe the rituals of his faith. "Good art is religious," he said. But in remaining true to his credo of a universal religion, Toch may have been misunderstood by those who espoused one religion or another. After reading a campaign plea for building a Jewish Community Center in Santa Monica, Toch penned the following reply:

> My answer is decidedly, emphatically, ardently, and passionately "no." Would your prospective building show the inscription "Devoted to the Brotherhood of Mankind" or "Human Community Center" or "World Community Center" or anything of this sort, your enterprise would have my wholehearted collaboration.[21]

He was apolitical, but was so convinced about the threat of Hitler that he unequivocally announced to his wife on 30 January 1933, "We're leaving"—and they did so, that same year. He was by nature peace loving, perhaps even a pacifist, but in 1914 he did his patriotic duty and signed up for the Austrian army.

He was open-minded and yet incredibly stubborn. Even after hearing all the criticisms of the cumbersome libretto he had chosen for his last opera, *The Last Tale,* Op. 88, he steadfastly held on to Melchior Lengyel's version of *Scheherazade,* translated into English from the Hungarian. The opera has yet to be performed.

He was both naive and practical. When conducting a rehearsal of one of his works in Germany, he was genuinely unaware that the musicians' union controlled the clock. When reminded, "Mr. Toch, it's already 12:00," he demurred, "Oh, I'm not so particular, I don't mind" (Mrs. Toch). But he also wrote to Mrs. Coolidge in 1943 that he had heard Arnold Schönberg was thinking of retiring from UCLA, and could she perhaps suggest that *he* replace his friend and neighbor?[22]

He was, unquestionably, devoted to his wife Lilly, and unquestionably devoted singularly to his work. Sometimes he would praise Lilly publicly, such as on the occasion of his seventy-fifth birthday celebration, "I have the good fortune to have a wonderful wife." Similar praise was apparent in this newspaper report of a visit with the Tochs:

> When I approached his house I saw the maestro in deep concentration. . . . He was having his daily chess game with his charming wife Lilly. "That is the only thing I can do better than Lilly," he said, "and sometimes she beats me."[23]

Toch's daughter, however, reflected upon her father's workaholic behavior which often excluded those people closest to him.

> My father would sequester himself in his study for days and weeks on end, refusing to come out even when mother pleaded with him to take a certain special call or to read a letter she had written before she took it to the post office. "I implore you" ("Ich bitte dich"), she used to cry, "just this once" . . . reaching out her arms with upturned hands as though to try to draw him physically to her, a scenario that repeated itself so frequently, so dramatically, it still surfaces in my mind's eye today . . . as if mother's supplications were at this moment ringing through the house.[24]

To be sure, Ernst and Lilly Toch were the products of a bygone generation, when it was assumed that the wife would devote herself to protecting and promoting her husband. In retrospect, one must give enormous credit where it is due, to Lilly Toch, for facilitating so much, as described by their daughter Franzi:

> Mother had a single-minded purpose: to protect my father from intrusion from the outside world, to provide him the conditions necessary for his work, and to deal with the practical aspects of his creative life that he would never have been able to address on his own, and from which deficiency he might have starved to death without her. For mother, it was a perennial conflict: nurturing of my father's physical and emotional needs, while yet looking out for the practical requisites of his creative professional existence.[25]

"The Teaching of Music Composition is Futile"
—Toch, 1954

How could he write such a thing? To believe it, in private, was one thing, but to openly disclaim what the universities paid their composers to do was another. What would his former students, who were becoming composers, themselves, think?

A dedicated teacher who could spend an entire afternoon sequestered in his studio teaching one student, and whose book *The Shaping Forces in Music* was selling well, Toch seemed to be saying that all his pedagogical efforts had been useless. Perhaps he was being true to his own experience as a self-taught composer. Or, perhaps, in retrospect, he felt he had given too much of himself to efforts that had cost him dearly in a heart attack in 1948. Whatever his reasons were, his controversial statement, on first glance, might be viewed as another instance of a rather paradoxical personality.

Writing of a string quartet was a sublime delight before the world knew of the atom bomb.

−Ernst Toch to Coolidge, 1946

If there is one musical constant, a thread which weaves through an incredibly diverse musical output, including four concertos, four operas, sixteen film scores, seven symphonies, more than ten orchestral pieces, several songs, numerous piano pieces and other instrumental solos and sonatas, *Gebrauchsmusik,* music for speaking chorus, among many other works, that constant is the string quartet, and he wrote fourteen of them in all. They were the metier of a lifetime.

To group Toch's music into customary stylistic periods−early, middle, and late−does not really work. True, the chamber music of his pre−World War I years sounds different from that written after 1918, but not only Toch the composer had changed−so also had the world, and its music.

What is almost uncanny, though, is that Toch's career as a composer divides itself symmetrically, not only between the continents, with thirty years in Europe and thirty years in America, but also into four subdivisions of fifteen years each, as illustrated in Table 2.1.

Table 2.1. Ernst Toch's Composing Career

Place	Years	Total Years	Compositions (No.)
Europe	1903−1933	30	Op. 9−61 (52)
Vienna	1903−1918	15	Op. 3−25 (22)
Germany	1918−1933	15	Op. 26−61 (25)
America	1934−1964	30	Op. 62−98 (36) plus 16 films
New York & Los Angeles	1934−1949	15	Op. 63−71 (8)
[Brief sojourn in Europe]	1949−1950	1	Op. 72−73 (2)
Return to Los Angeles	1950−1964	14	Op. 74−98 (25)

A gifted composer and a creative thinker, Ernst Toch was a man of his times. As a participant in the musical migration, he demonstrated repeatedly his versatility in adapting to a new culture and the demands it made upon him, while he also retained his independence of thought and creativity.

His is a story of two worlds and two cultures, and, in a way, he was two men: one, a participant in, and the other, an observer-critic of a long, exciting, but often difficult and bewildering journey through this century's musical history.

His story begins in Vienna.

═ 3

Toch's Life, Times, and Music — Europe

═══ **Homage to Tradition, 1887–1919**

In Nicolas Slonimsky's words, Ernst Toch was a "child of Vienna who inherited the double tradition that was Vienna's."[1] More accurately, the city had a wealth of traditions by the time Toch took notice of the music world around him, and that was comparatively late in his musical development.

The "double tradition" was the classical tradition of Mozart and the romantic tradition of Brahms. But in defining Toch's inherited tradition a dilemma arises in that several so-called romantic traditions were represented in Vienna at the turn of the century. Bruckner had died in 1896, Brahms in 1897, but the controversy that the romantic music of these two composers had generated continued unabated. Eduard Hanslick, the reigning music critic who championed Brahms, had four more years of life in which to vent his hostility toward Wagner, for what he considered decadent, emotion-laden music dramas.

Hanslick's successor at *Die Neue Freie Presse,* the brilliant critic Julius Korngold, despised new works, especially those by Schönberg. The Viennese press and public were so conservative that even Gustav Mahler had a difficult tenure as director of the Hofoper during his last years there. Mahler had restored uncut versions of Wagner's operas to

Viennese audiences, who were still engrossed in Wagnermania, but programming new works was less acceptable to them.

In addition to Johann Strauss the Younger and the romantic legacy of operettas, there were the so-called post-romantic composers. Among them were Alexander Zemlinsky (1871–1942), whose early chamber works had been praised by Brahms, but who had later joined his brother-in-law Schönberg in his Society of Composers; Franz Schmidt (1874–1939), who would have studied with Bruckner at the Vienna Conservatory if the older composer had not fallen ill and taken a leave of absence; and the most famous of all, Franz Schreker (1878–1934), whose opera *Der ferne Klang* (1912) impressed Schönberg and influenced Berg in *Wozzeck,* while his opera *Der Schatzgräber* (1920) established him as a leader of the avant-garde. The youngest of this group of composers, Erich Wolfgang Korngold (1897–1957), the son of Julius Korngold and a pupil of Zemlinsky, won acclaim for his operas *Violanta* (1916) and *Die tote Stadt* (1920), both examples of the romantic-verismo style. This assortment of classical and romantic traditions coexisted in a Vienna whose political climate Carl Schorske described in his book *Fin-de-Siècle Vienna:* "[In 1897] the Christian Social demagogues began a decade of rule in Vienna which combined all that was anathema to classic liberalism. . . . [The liberals] had been crushed by modern mass movements, Christian, anti-Semitic, socialist and nationalist."[2]

And yet, as the musicologist Mosco Carner observed, "a new spirit of adventure and exploration existed in the prewar Vienna of Mahler and Schönberg, of Hofmannsthal, Zweig, Karl Kraus, Otto Wagner and Freud."[3]

Concerning musical performances during the prewar years, the opera programmed Richard Strauss's *Feuersnot, Salomé,* and *Elektra* and Puccini's *Tosca,* but *Salomé* and *Elektra* were rejected by the board's censors. The "spirit of adventure and exploration" was more in evidence in performances sponsored by private societies such as *Die Vereinigung Schaffender Tonkünstler,* which premiered Schönberg's *Pelleas und Mélisande* and some of Mahler's works; moreover, the Rosé Quartet had survived protests over their performances of Schönberg's *Verklärte Nacht* in 1910.

In 1905, the Rosé Quartet performed a string quartet by an unknown young Viennese composer, Ernst Toch. It was a traditional work, combining Mozartian clarity of form with Brahmsian harmonic language. It caused no controversy or protest, and so it went unnoticed, as did the composer himself for the first sixteen years of his life.

What were those formative years like, in the life of Ernst Toch? The two principal sources of biographical information on Toch's formative years are his wife, Lilly Zwack Toch (1892–1972), and his sister Elsa Toch Roman (1884–1973), who was in her nineties by the time she amended Lilly's transcribed reminiscences. In that the composer himself provides few details about this period, a biographer has to rely heavily on the secondhand accounts.

Ernst Toch, born on 7 December 1887, was the second child of Gisela and Moritz Toch; his sister Elsa preceded him by three years. Moritz Toch had been the second of nine children, all of whom were raised in the Jewish quarter of Nikolsburg, Moravia, now Czechoslovakia, where his parents had owned a *Wechselstube* (a money exchange). Moritz had struggled hard to establish himself in Leopoldstadt, the Jewish quarter in Vienna, and was proud of the relative financial security he had obtained as a merchant, selling unprocessed leather for shoes.

Piano lessons began for the Toch children when Ernst was eight and Elsa eleven. Elsa Roman recalls that her brother never practiced and never studied much, that he was always composing; Mrs. Toch states that the young Toch felt compelled to hide his composing from his parents, who could not comprehend his absorption in such trivia.

For his bar mitzvah, Toch received the gift of books, ones by Schiller and Goethe among them. Raised in Jewish rituals and able to read both Greek and Hebrew, he was required to attend Temple and Hebrew school on Saturday and to observe all the holiday rites, although this religious observation ceased after Moritz Toch died in 1904.

After his father's death, Toch moved with his family from the third district in Vienna to the twelfth district, to the home of Toch's maternal aunt. Apparently Toch did not live there very long, as he soon moved in with the Joseph Amlinger family during his last year of Gymnasium in 1905. About this time he began giving piano lessons, tutoring boys in school, and coaching the young prodigy George Szell.

As a composer, Toch was completely self-taught and described his musical education as follows:

> I have not studied with anybody. . . . I was left on my own and managed to acquire at length what I learned in a completely autodidactic way. I made the decisive discovery that pocket scores existed. The quartet I happened to see in the window of a music shop was one of the so-called

10 famous quartets of Mozart. I bought it. I was carried away when reading this score. Perhaps in order to prolong my exaltation, I started to copy it, which gave me deeper insight. By and by, I bought and copied all ten scores. But, I did not stop after that. After copying three or four, I started to copy the fifth. I decided I would only continue with my copying up to the repeat sign, and then try my hand at making that part myself, which leads back to the original key. Then I compared mine with the original. I felt crushed.[4]

Toch was an extremely gifted youth, although uncertain and insecure about his hobby of composing. Mrs. Toch attributed his youthful feelings of insecurity to his earliest childhood sense of "engaging in a worthless activity," which he felt "he had to hide."

Like Schönberg, Toch learned from the great masters. But unlike Schönberg, the only response Toch ever had on his composing abilities came when he was sixteen, from Arnold Rosé, who had received Toch's quartet through an intermediary, Joseph Fuchs, one of Toch's young schoolmates. According to Mrs. Toch, Joseph Fuchs was simply a practical joker, but he apparently had a real interest in promoting Toch's music, as can be seen in this letter to Fuchs from B. Schott, the music publishers in Mainz, written in 1906:

Herr Joseph Fuchs: We received the sonata, also the compositions listed above (string quartet, Ständchen and Praeludium for piano, and "Bitte" for singer and piano) . . . with great interest felt for the author, but, even so, we find these new things are not ready for publication.[5]

The works referred to are the Sonata for Piano in D Major, Op. 7 (c. 1905), one of the string quartets from his earliest compositions, "Ständchen" (Serenade), the first piece of the Melodische Skizzen (Melodic Sketches) Op. 9, "Praeludium" (Prelude) from Drei Praeludien (Three Preludes) Op. 10, and the vocal piece. All except the piano pieces are lost.

Although two decades later Schott did publish Toch's music, Toch's first publisher was Paul Pabst of Leipzig, who issued his piano works Op. 9, 10, and 11 in 1908.

Between 1902 and 1905, Toch composed five string quartets (Op. 1–5), a piano trio, two sets of piano pieces, a piano concerto, and an impromptu and a scherzo for piano. Then came the Quartet in A Minor, Op. 6; a Sonata in D Minor, Op. 7; a Sonata for Clarinet and Piano, Op. 8; Stammbuchverse (Album Verses) Op. 13; and one piece for solo voice and piano, "Bitte" (Please). Everything from the earlier period, Op. 1–9 (through 1905), was lost in a most tragic way. Toch had given the works to Mlle. Mikolas, the daughter of his piano teacher, with whom he was infatuated, and the young woman, trapped in Vienna after the *Anschluss,* perished during the war. The only compositions extant from that period are the piano works Op. 9, 10, and 11, published by Pabst in 1908, and the manuscript for the String Quartet in A Minor, Op. 12, performed by the Rosé Quartet. The opening measures of this early quartet, as they appear in the first violin part of the composer's manuscript, are representative of Toch's Brahmsian style, with its long, spun-out melodies at the beginning, and their subsequent motivic invention. Although the full score is not available, the very tonal harmonic vocabulary is implied in the melody. (Musical Example 3.1.)

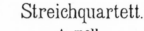

Streichquartett.

Violine 1   A-moll.

Ernst Toch.

Musical Example 3.1. String Quartet in A Minor, Op. 12, mt. 1, mm. 1–37. Source: Original manuscript, Toch Archive.

Sometime between 1906 and 1908, Toch noticed an announcement at the Vienna Conservatory for a composing competition for the Mozart Prize, which was held every four years. The compositions, with only mottoes attached, were to be submitted anonymously, a stipulation that appealed to Toch. Toch submitted a string quartet, perhaps Op. 12 or Op. 15, and his *Kammer Symphonie* (Chamber Symphony) in F for 10 instruments (c. 1906), for which the motto was *Immer strebe zum*

Ganzen (Always Strive for the Whole). The prizewinner would be required to spend a year in Frankfurt, Germany, although the stipend covered four years, at twenty-five hundred dollars a year in German marks. One of the announced jurors in addition to Max Reger was Ludwig Thuille, who died in 1907, about the time Toch must have submitted his work, although the prizewinner was not announced until 1909. By 1908, Toch had not yet ventured into anything daring, and the conservative German jury found his traditionalism and craftsmanship impressive. He won the prize and, officially abandoning his medical studies at the University of Vienna, headed for Frankfurt.

There, at the Conservatory, he presented himself to the composition teacher, Iwan Knorr, who commented, "You wanted to study with me? But I was going to ask if you would allow me to study with you."[6] This remark from Knorr is particularly meaningful when one considers that at the time Knorr was one of the most revered teachers of composition in Germany. The English composer Cyril Scott (1879–1970) recalled what it was like to study with Knorr.

> I begged my father to let me return to Frankfurt in order to study with Iwan Knorr who was reputed to be one of the finest composition teachers then known. . . . He was no cut-and-dried German music professor; he had lived many years in Russia and had been able to count Tchaikowski among his friends. . . . One of the secrets of Knorr's excellence as a teacher was that he never discouraged originality if it was in good taste.[7]

Toch studied piano with Willy Rehberg, who demonstrated quite an interest in his talented student, and the young Toch began practicing the piano seriously for the first time in his life. He also decided to take violin lessons, which is rather amusing in that he had already composed seven string quartets, a piano trio, a chamber symphony, and three pieces for violin and piano, "Vom sterbendem Rokoko" (From the Dying Rococo). According to Mrs. Toch's memoirs, the Violin Duos, Op. 17, were written in Frankfurt while Toch was studying the violin, although the publication date in the catalog is 1909. This composition is notable for its humorous didacticism, as described in Cobbett's *Cyclopedic Survey of Chamber Music*.

> Toch's Duos, Op. 17, are cleverly written instructive pieces for beginners, the second violin playing exclusively on open string, leaving all the melodic development to the first violin, which has a very effective part of moderate difficulty.[8]

His first year in Frankfurt also produced another string quartet, Op. 18, in D-flat Major, dedicated to the Grand Duke of Hessen. A five-movement, thirty-minute work, it is considerably more expansive than his earlier quartets. Perhaps it was the change of atmosphere, as Toch moved from Vienna to Frankfurt, that was responsible for the different style.

Another significant composition during Toch's year in Frankfurt was incidental music for a play by Marie Waldeck, *Der Kinder Neujahrstraum (The Children's New Year's Dream)*, Op. 19. His next work in this medium came fifteen years later, when he scored background music to Berthold Viertel's version of *Bacchae* of Euripides. But at twenty-three, he had his first taste of the exciting possibilities of writing music for the stage.

In general, the Frankfurt years, 1910–1912, might be called the "violin years," regardless of the fact that he had written string quartets earlier. First came a perfunctory "Romanze" (1910), an arrangement for violin and piano of the fourth piece of that title from the piano pieces published in *Melodische Skizzen (Melodic Sketches)*, Op. 9; then the Serenade for Three Violins, Op. 20 (1911); and his Violin Sonata, Op. 21 (1912). This last work sounds so Brahmsian that Toch, in later years, called it "Brahms's Fourth Violin Sonata." The Sonata in E Major, a three-movement work, and twenty-eight minutes long, is similar to the earlier String Quartet Op. 12, in that it contains little harmonic or melodic audacity. (Musical Example 3.2.)

The Frankfurt years were interrupted by Toch's compulsory military service in Austria. Normally, this would have occurred in 1908, when he was twenty-one, but because he was enrolled in medical school at the time, he was granted a three-year deferment.

It was during one of his returns to Vienna, about 1913, that he met his wife-to-be, Lilly Zwack. This is her account of their first meeting:

> He really was a very attractive person. . . . We came, my sister, my parents and I, and when we entered the living room [of the Amlinger home in Vienna], he sat on the piano bench with Father Amlinger and played four hands. And they didn't interrupt when we came. . . . He was immensely happy.[9]

Toch, however, spent most of his time in Germany until 1914. He had been awarded a four-year stipend, he had been given a job at the Mannheim Conservatory in 1913 by his piano teacher Willy Rehberg,

Musical Example 3.2. Violin Sonata in E Major, Op. 21, mt. 1, mm. 1–17. Source: Original manuscript, Toch Archive.

then director in Mannheim, and, apart from composing and teaching, he was writing a book for his composition students, entitled *Die Melodielehre (Treatise on Melody)*.

But with the outbreak of World War I, Toch was back in Vienna ready to fight for Austria. Just before leaving Mannheim, he had composed a patriotic work, *An Mein Vaterland (To My Homeland)*, which is scored for large orchestra, including organ, soprano solo, and mixed and boys' choruses. However, this work was never performed. On the subject of Toch's early patriotism, Mrs. Toch explained that

> he was nationalistic, and he saw it also the duty of a man to stand for his country. He saw that it was inevitable, and he loved at that time the idea

of Austria. He didn't love the practice of Austria. But it was his country and he didn't consider that in the heart of Europe any country could stand without its military force. . . . The motto of our emperor was "If you want peace, prepare for war." But he considered it something to have a schooling of discipline . . . as hard as possible, in order to achieve the utmost results.[10]

A few months before their marriage in July 1916, Lilly Zwack had confided to her Uncle Sigmund, the husband of her mother's younger sister, that she was interested in a young composer who had received orders to fight on the Italian front. Sigmund was the editor of an important journal in Zurich, the *Internationale Rundschau,* noted for its liberalism. After the young woman poured out her worries and related the life story of Ernst Toch, Uncle Sigmund stunned her by querying, "And you permit a man like this just to become cannon fodder?" And he went on:

A man of that category, a man of such capacity, a man of such extraordinary gifts should and can be exempted from that kind of military duty. . . . There is nothing wrong to make a try, to put it before the authorities who he is and how he has shown such extraordinary gifts and achievement.[11]

Spurred to action, Lilly Zwack collected letters attesting to the importance of that life for Austria. The first was from Arnold Rosé, then the director of the Vienna Conservatory, and the second from Austrian composer Julius Bittner (1874–1939), who was also a lawyer and the president of the Tonkünstlerverein in Vienna. Meanwhile, Uncle Sigmund set the machinery in motion to rescue Toch from the trenches.

On a furlough in July 1916, Ernst Toch married Lilly Zwack and then returned to duty on the Italian front while Lilly remained with her parents. Several months later, the rescue letter arrived, stating that Toch was to report for another physical examination. The result was his reassignment to Galicia, a region in lower Austria, where Lilly could visit him and they could wait out the end of the war together.

After he had been recalled to the front and was preparing to return to Vienna, he happened to notice, in an Italian bookstore, a picture entitled "Serenade" by the Bavarian artist Karl Spitzweg (1808–1885). He bought the painting, which was an idyllic and peaceful representation of a castle with some musicians in the foreground. The contrast between his life in the trenches and the placid scene in the picture was so striking that he wrote the "Spitzweg" Serenade, Op. 25, against

the sounds of war in the background. This one movement, Trio for Two
Violins and Viola in G Major, is distinguished by its lilting six-eight
meter. Again, there is little melodic or harmonic innovation. (Musical
Example 3.3.)

The Serenade proves that Toch's composing abilities were still intact. In its meandering melodies, sometimes symmetrically phrased, sometimes not, mostly tonal, this beautiful poem provides a glimpse of what would emerge from the German Toch two years later. It also marks the end of Toch's apprenticeship to the double tradition of classicism and romanticism that Vienna had bestowed upon him.

Although Toch had been awarded the Austrian State Prize every year between 1914 and 1918, at the end of the war he prepared to leave Austria. By this time, he was considerably disillusioned with a bloody war that had brought the dissolution of the Austro-Hungarian Empire and the establishment of the republic of Austria. However, Toch's restlessness and desire to leave can be traced to the conservatism of Vienna's musical life. Ernst Krenek described it this way:

> A most peculiar attitude of hedonistic pessimism, joyful skepticism touching on morbid sophistication became the dominant trait in Vienna's intellectual climate. . . . Every outstanding personality brought up in the peculiar atmosphere lived ever after in a dialectical syncretism of love and hatred for that city which offered splendid potentialities for highest accomplishments as well as the most stubborn resistance to their realization.[12]

Mrs. Toch's Uncle Sigmund phrased it another way: "Marry a composer? Well, whenever I hear something modern I leave the hall."[13]

It was the right time for Toch to leave Vienna. He had a wife to support, and his teaching position was still open to him in Mannheim. The emerging modernist would now make his home in Germany. Toch had already incorporated much that was German into his music, for, after about 1906, the music of Richard Strauss, Max Reger, and perhaps Hans Pfitzner had certainly exerted an influence over him.

Toch's homage to tradition had been notable for its craftsmanship and attention to musical form. But during his three years in Germany, the harmonies and contrapuntal textures of his works expanded, often bordering on Straussian or Mahlerian harmonic language.

Toch had made his mark as a composer of chamber music—eight string quartets, violin duos, the "Spitzweg" Serenade, and a chamber symphony. He had written incidental music for a play and was a published composer of piano solos. He now had a firm grounding in the craft of composition, even if his formal instruction had been confined to two years in Germany.

It would be tempting to compare his Brahmsian works to those of his Viennese contemporaries Zemlinsky, Schmidt, Schreker, and Korngold, but such comparisons are only speculative at best. At any rate, the era of pre–World War I Viennese romanticism was coming to an end.

He needed to leave—to find a new audience, to discover his true voice. Although his one champion in Germany, Max Reger, was dead, he had a job waiting for him at the Mannheim Conservatory, and so it was farewell, Vienna, and its classical and romantic traditions.

The Emerging Modernist, 1919–1929

"It was the only place we could have a job and get housing," Lilly Toch emphasized. That is why they had not gone to Berlin, as many composers, artists, dramatists, and writers would soon do. Mannheim itself was a very musical city, and Heidelberg, with Max Weber and the intelligentsia, was just a short ride away.

In 1918–1919, people in Germany and Austria who were in a position to contemplate traveling were not yet fully aware that Berlin would be the place to go. Schönberg, an intermittent visitor to Berlin since 1901, stayed in Vienna for a while, then exited permanently for Berlin in 1925; Franz Schreker went there in 1920; Hans Pfitzner, opera director in Munich, was in Berlin temporarily to conduct one master class before Busoni came out of exile in Switzerland and returned to Berlin to become the reigning composition teacher at the Musik Hochschule; and around 1920 Kurt Weill led the long line of young composer-students who would make their way to Berlin.

Although performances of so-called modern music in Germany still concentrated on the compositions of Pfitzner, Reger, and Strauss, it was not long before the new voices from the postwar composers were being heard. The spirit of the New Music was pervasive, not only in Berlin or at the first Donaueschingen Festival in 1921, or at the International Society for Contemporary Music (ISCM), but throughout Europe. Just as the early members of the Novembergruppe had declared that "the future of art, and the seriousness of this hour forces us revolutionaries of the spirit toward unity and close cooperation," so Europe's young composers were struggling with new modes of artistic expression.

Before the war, the painter Wassily Kandinsky had embraced a radically different form of art, expressionism, which was characterized by vivid colors and exaggerated perspectives. After 1918, expressionism was a term that applied also to certain kinds of music. These statements from Kandinsky and Schönberg illustrate what expressionism meant to both prewar painters and postwar composers:

> The refusal to employ the habitual form of the beautiful leads one to admit as sacred all the procedures which permit the artist to manifest his own personality (Kandinsky). The artist does not create what others think as beautiful, but what his innermost urges compel him to create . . . advancing as far as the exploration of tone color for its own sake (Schönberg).[14]

After the war, both Austria and Germany went through periods of economic and political turmoil. The Austro-Hungarian Empire was dismembered into several independent states. In Germany, the November 1918 Revolution was followed by civil unrest, assassinations of important political and cultural leaders like Rosa Luxemburg, Gustav Landauer, and Walter Rathenau, and astronomical inflation. Not even the most committed romantic or traditionalist artist or composer could remain unaffected by these events, and many of the postwar intellectuals felt the need to break with the cultural traditions of the past.

Toch was one of those who felt the need. For Christmas 1919 he composed his Ninth String Quartet, which began in C Major but in the last movement broke free of a discernible key center. It had been almost ten years since his last quartet and three years since the "Spitzweg" Serenade. Now he was entering a new phase that might be called "toward the New Music," as later practiced by Hindemith. Commenting on Toch's stylistic evolution, Nicolai Lopatnikoff observed that

> a clear stylistic cleavage distinctly appears between the music written before the First World War . . . and the first major work of 1919, the Ninth String Quartet, Op. 26. . . . This work, together with the Tenth Quartet, Op. 28 . . . seems to have been a milestone making the turning point which led him to an idiom reflecting the more adventuresome voice and atmosphere of the twenties.[15]

The emerging modernist's style exhibits many characteristics of *Die Neue Musik,* particularly in its emphasis on linear counterpoint. The result? — expanded melodic lines, huge intervallic skips, accented dissonances, and harmonic clashes. (Musical Example 3.4.)

Musical Example 3.4. String Quartet, Op. 26, C Major, mt. 1, mm. 1–6. Source: Leuckhart. Used by permission of AMP/G. Schirmer.

Even though Toch did not yet know Hindemith, who was ten years his junior, he was writing in a style that would link him permanently with the younger disciple of the New Music. Like Hindemith, Toch moved from a type of atonal expressionism in the early twenties, to neoclassicism in the mid-twenties, to semi-*Gebrauchsmusik* at the end of the twenties.

But from 1919–1923, Toch was teaching by day and composing by night and, with such a schedule, managed to compose only five new works in four years. However, he seemed content with his routine that, although not allowing enough time for composing, at least offered him lecturing engagements, the chance to write occasional articles for newspapers, and, above all, the chance to cultivate friends in Heidelberg, some of whom were to influence his career.

One who did so was Wilhelm Furtwängler, one year older than Toch, but already well on his way to becoming a major musical figure. As the composer of chamber works, one symphony, and a seventeen-movement setting of Goethe's *Walpurgisnacht,* Furtwängler was excellent company for Toch. And Furtwängler was also becoming known as one of the leading German conductors of New Music. He apprenticed with Pfitzner at the Strasbourg Opera and then became director of the Lübeck Opera (1911–1915). His tenure at the Mannheim Opera (1915–1920) overlapped Toch's stay in that city long enough for the two men to become friends. Over the next decade, Furtwängler premiered Toch's *Comedy for Orchestra,* Op. 42, and his *Little Theater Suite,* Op. 54, in Leipzig. But more importantly, he introduced Toch's music to the conductors Erich Kleiber, Fritz Busch, and Hermann Scherchen, who also became, within the decade, champions of Toch's New Music.

Apart from Furtwängler, Toch had only a few musical friends in Mannheim. Two of them were the duo-pianists Hans Bruch, who premiered several of Toch's piano pieces, especially the *Burlesques,* and his wife, Lena Weiler Bruch.

But in spite of this couple's willingness to perform duo-piano music, if Toch would only consent to write some, he did not do so until the end of his life. This reluctance to exploit the sonority of his own instrument in combination with either piano or other instruments is curious. Even when hungry for commissions and performances during his first years in America, Toch initially refused Mrs. Elizabeth Sprague Coolidge's commission to write a Piano Quintet (1938), trying to persuade her that some other medium might suit him better. Eventually he did give in and composed the work.

In 1920, Toch, challenged by the sound-timbre possibilities of a full orchestra, composed *Phantastische Nachtmusik* (*Fantastic Night Music*), Op. 27. His first work of program music, it depicted a sleepwalker experiencing a wide range of sensations. The premiere took place in Mannheim, and it was performed frequently in Germany from 1925 to 1927, and once in Chicago. The significance of this one-movement tone poem is that it forecast the mysterious music that Toch wrote for such Hollywood films as *The Ghost Breakers* and *None Shall Escape*.

A year later, Toch returned to his favorite medium, the string quartet. This one, subtitled "Bass," Op. 28, was unique in that it was based on a set of musical anagrams. Written and dedicated to his cousin John Bass, who had given Toch his most treasured possession, the complete works of Mozart, the "Bass" Quartet starts each movement with the pitches B(B-flat)—A—Es(E-flat)—Es(E-flat).

The quartet is written without a key signature and makes abundant use of the interval of the fourth and the tritone. This twenty-five minute, four-movement quartet contains other new devices: in the third movement, Toch calls for the sound effects of *Katzenhaft schleichend* (sneakingly, catlike), and in that same Scherzo and Trio he breaks into unrestrained changes of meter. Throughout the work, melodic development is linear, with the melodic and rhythmic taking precedence over the harmonic, thereby making the work sound dissonant and rhythmically disjointed. (Musical Example 3.5.)

The first performance of the "Bass" Quartet was given just before the Donaueschingen Festival in Kassel, Germany, by the Hans Lange Quartet from Frankfurt, in the same year that the International Society for Contemporary Music was founded (1922) and a year after Toch met Hindemith. When Hindemith became one of the program directors of the Donaueschingen Festival, he commissioned Toch to write another quartet, his eleventh, Op. 34 (1924).

Toch's music has often been compared with Hindemith's, perhaps because they were both composing at the same time, in the same place. Furthermore, each of the summer music festivals was dedicated to a specific theme, one year to chamber music, the next to music for military bands, and in 1926, to electronic or mechanical instruments. Naturally

Meinem lieben Vetter und Freund Hans Bass.

Streichquartett
auf den Namen „Bass."

I.

Ernst Toch, Op. 28.

Energisch. ♩ = 100 - 108.

Violine I.

Violine II.

Viola.

Cello.

Eigentum und Verlag
Tischer & Jagenberg, G. m. b. H., Cöln.   T. & J. 724.   Stich und Druck von
Breitkopf & Härtel in Leipzig.

Musical Example 3.5. String Quartet, Op. 28, mt. 1, mm. 1–7. Source: Leuckhart. Used by permission of AMP/G. Schirmer.

the compositions commissioned for these festivals were similar in genre, if not in techniques.

The year 1923 was a turning point for Toch, for he became "Herr Doktor" Toch. Before the war, when he had taught music theory and composition in Mannheim, he had written his own textbook subtitled, in English translation, "A History and Inquiry into the Subject of Melody," in 1912 and 1913. He had entrusted it to his wife's safekeeping during the war and had all but forgotten it after the war. When Mrs. Toch's Uncle Sigmund learned of the treatise, he suggested that this document might suffice as a doctoral thesis. The wheels of academic machinery turned in Toch's favor, thanks to two of Toch's friends in Heidelberg, Emil Lederer, distinguished professor of economics, and Theodor Kroyer, musicologist. With the years of medical study at the University in Vienna counting toward the doctoral requirements, Toch was informed that his treatise would qualify him to take the final exams. These were administered by his Heidelberg friends, and in June 1923 the title of "Doktor der Philosophie" was conferred upon him. This title proved one of his most valuable assets when, years later, he sought a university teaching post in America.

Die Melodielehre was published in 1923 by Max Hesse in Berlin and was translated into Russian and Spanish. Lilly Toch recalls that Toch received many congratulatory letters from composers and teachers, among whom were Ferruccio Busoni, Hugo Leichtentritt, and Hans Pfitzner. Mrs. Toch also recalls that upon receiving the publisher's check for the book, Toch rushed out to buy two shirts, trying to beat the inflation that would render such purchases impossible within hours!

The years 1923 to 1933 comprise one of the most prolific periods, with over thirty-two works, from Op. 29 to Op. 61. Perhaps the most decisive event for Toch was his securing a publisher in 1923. This was B. Schott Söhne, in Mainz, who became his exclusive publisher until he left Germany in 1933. Not only did Schott commission new works but they also offered him relative financial security, thus freeing him from heavy teaching responsibilities.

The Chinese Flute, Op. 29, and the *Dance Suite,* Op. 30, composed in 1922, were the first works by Toch that Schott published. *The Chinese Flute* was premiered by Scherchen in Frankfurt on 29 June 1923 and was subsequently performed at contemporary music festivals in Prague and Zurich, at the International Society for Contemporary Music, and in Chicago conducted by Rudolph Ganz in 1932. Subtitled

"Chamber Symphony with Soprano Solo," it is a series of mood pictures inspired by Chinese poems, from the same collection by Hans Bethge which Mahler used in his *Das Lied von der Erde.* Orchestrated for fourteen instruments, including two flutes, two clarinets, strings, celesta, and percussion, *The Chinese Flute* is "not constructed on a number of songs but rather it is conceived as an instrumental composition to which the human voice is added as a link to interpret the words."[16]

Also in 1923, Toch composed a set of three piano pieces entitled *Burlesques,* Op. 31, the third of which was inspired by an actual circus performer. This very picturesque, almost programmatic piece appealed immediately to the sizable market of amateur pianists. After the initial publication of the collection, Schott issued a separate sheet music edition of the single piece called "The Juggler." Probably one of Toch's most popular works for solo piano, this piece was reported to have been performed even in Nazi Germany, with the composer's name omitted, and, as Lilly Toch confirmed, it earned more sustained royalties over the years than almost any other of Toch's compositions. The popular theme in C Major is programmatic, and it does not display any of the harmonic, melodic, or rhythmic audacity found in some of his other works dating from this period. (Musical example 3.6.)

III
(Der Jongleur)

Musical Example 3.6. Toch—*Burlesken,* Op. 31, "Der Jongleur" (The Juggler) mm. 1–14. Copyright by B. Schott's Soehne, Mainz, 1924. Copyright renewed Schott & Co. Ltd., London, 1952. All rights reserved. Used by permission of European American Music Distributors Corporation, sole U.S. and Canadian agent for B. Schott's Soehne, Mainz.

Up to 1920, Toch had composed mainly for string quartet, solo piano, and small chamber ensemble, with the exception of the unpublished *An Mein Vaterland* (1913) and the *Phantastische Nachtmusik*, Op. 27, for orchestra (1920–1921). In 1924, however, he began his transition from chamber music to concerto, opera, operetta, and, at the turn of the decade, incidental music for radio plays and sound films.

With the commission of Five Pieces for Chamber Orchestra, Op. 33, for the International Music Festival in Prague, where it was premiered by Erich Kleiber, Toch's reputation was firmly established. The premiere of the String Quartet No. 11, Op. 34, by the Amar Quartet occurred at the 1924 Donaueschingen Festival, followed by numerous performances, including the String Quartet of the Dresden Philharmonic in Berlin and the Vienna String Quartet touring Germany.

The years 1925 and 1926 were stellar ones for Toch and the New Music. Emanuel Feuermann premiered the Concerto for Cello and Chamber Orchestra, Op. 35, at the Deutsches Tonkünstlerfest in July 1925. Over the next seven years, Feuermann, the most famous cellist of the time, performed the concerto more than sixty times with major orchestras, including Klemperer's in Berlin and Pierre Monteux's, the Concertgebouw, in Amsterdam. Over fifty concert reviews of the work are on file in the Toch Archive. Typical is this one from the noted musicologist Alfred Einstein, in the *Berliner Tageblatt:*

> This enchanting and felicitous work in which the solo instrument is the primus inter pares and, yet dominates, is new in expression and old in form. It renounces neither sentiment nor humor, and shows the spirit of invention in every note.[17]

That same year, Toch was awarded the Schott Prize for his Cello Concerto. Steadily gaining national recognition, he was encouraged by Schott to keep his name in front of the public. From then on, not only reviews of performances of his works but also articles written by him appeared regularly in the newspapers and music journals throughout Germany. Scored for a chamber orchestra of flute, oboe, clarinet, bassoon, horn, percussion, and string quartet, the Cello Concerto is difficult not only in its required virtuosity but also in its profusion of twentieth century techniques: accidentals everywhere, changing meters, large intervallic skips, rhythmic complexity, and predominance of the linear over the harmonic. (Musical Example 3.7.)

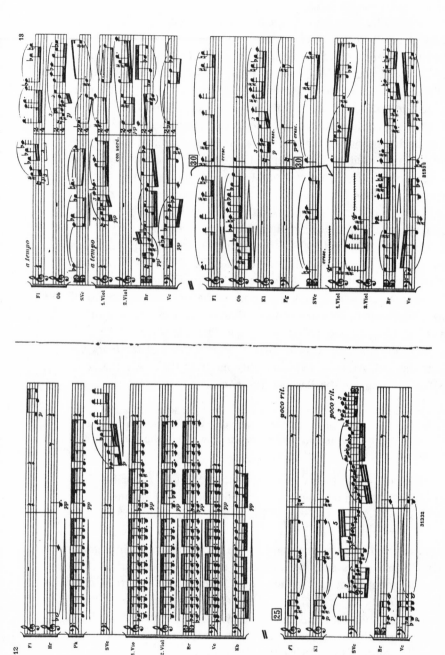

Musical Example 3.7. Toch—*Konzert Für Violoncell Und Kammerorchester* (Concerto for Violoncello and Chamber Orchestra), Op. 35. Copyright 1925 by B. Schott's Soehne, Mainz. Copyright renewed. All rights reserved. Used by permission of European and American Music Corporation, sole U.S. and Canadian agent for B. Schott's Soehne, Mainz.

In the spring of 1926, Walter Gieseking premiered Toch's Piano Concerto No. 1, Op. 38, in Düsseldorf. This led to a performance, which had no less than seventeen rehearsals, by the Swiss pianist Walter Frey, under Hermann Scherchen, at the International Society for Contemporary Music and a performance by the German pianist Elly Ney with Wilhelm Furtwängler conducting the Leipzig Gewandhaus Orchestra. The concerto was also performed in Berlin and other European cities by Gieseking, Frey, and Ney. In London, it was performed by Edwin Fischer, and in New York, in 1928, by Elly Ney. This virtuoso work is distinguished by its powerful opening statement in the piano, "Molto Pesante," in fortissimo octaves. It is followed by an orchestral fanfare, then a fiery piano cadenza that ushers in the allegro first movement. (Musical Example 3.8.)

As the Piano Concerto became more popular, so did the smaller pieces for solo piano, *Drei Klavierstücke* (Three Piano Pieces), Op. 32, and Capricetti, Op. 36, composed in 1925–1926. During the years 1926 to 1931, Toch's reputation as a composer of modern piano literature grew simultaneously with his rise to prominence as a first-rate pianist.

Shortly after the success of the Piano Concerto in 1926, a friend in Heidelberg suggested to Toch that it really did not make sense for famous pianists to make money with his concerto on concert engagements, when he, the composer, could perform the work just as well. When Toch protested that the concerto was too difficult for him, his friend challenged him to try to play it. After a few months of intensive practice and preparation, Toch debuted as a piano virtuoso, appearing first with radio orchestras and later as soloist and accompanist all over Germany. The Piano Concerto No. 1 remained a staple of his repertoire, and in 1950, at the age of sixty-three, Toch performed it with the Vienna Philharmonic under Herbert Haefner.

Also composed in 1926, the two Divertimenti for String Duo, Op. 37, No. 1 for Violin and Cello and No. 2 for Violin and Viola, were premiered by members of the Kolisch Quartet in Vienna and later performed in Germany, as well.

The Donaueschingen Festival of 1926 featured original works especially composed for mechanical instruments, a new field of electronic experimentation years ahead of its time, for which Toch's contribution was three original pieces for the *Welte-Mignon Klavier*. This electric instrument was manufactured by the Welte-Mignon factory in Freiburg, which, tragically, was bombed during the war. However, as a result of

Konzert
für Klavier und Orchester

Musical Example 3.8. Toch—Piano Concerto, Op. 38, mt. 1, mm. 1–12. Copyright 1926 by B. Schott's Soehne, Mainz. Copyright renewed. All rights reserved. Used by permission of European American Music Distributors Corporation, sole U.S. and Canadian Agent for B. Schott's Soehne, Mainz.

the interest and publicity provoked by the Festival, the name of Ernst Toch soon became associated with the avant-garde of the late twenties in Germany.

Toch's writings of this period reflect his fascination with the possibilities for tone color in the new technology. However, the new direction that Toch saw for himself was not in the realm of mechanical instruments or electronic music, but in opera.

In the early 1920s, Toch had composed a one-act opera, *The Princess and the Pea,* Op. 43, based on a fairy tale of Hans Christian Andersen, adapted by Benno Elkan. When the invitation came to participate in the 1927 Donaueschingen Festival, whose theme was to be one-act operas, Toch put the finishing touches on his fairy tale work and submitted it. Performed in Baden-Baden, the Festival's new home, where the audiences and publicity increased considerably, it was conducted by Scherchen, whose wife sang the soprano role. Hindemith's *Hin und Zurück* was also performed at the 1927 Festival, as was Kurt Weill's *Mahagonny* and Milhaud's *L'Enlèvement d'Europe.* Toch's opera enjoyed numerous other performances in Europe as well as America. This forty-eight-minute, one-act opera, *The Princess and the Pea,* is not easy to perform, with its emphasis on linear and rhythmic counterpoint. The independence of the vocal lines, with seeming disregard for harmony, is complicated with either difficult skips or a profusion of chromaticism that may temporarily obscure any tonal center. (Musical example 3.9.)

A new era of one-act chamber operas had begun in Germany. This genre, whether performed in municipal opera houses or by radio orchestras and singers, gave composers new opportunities for both musical and political expression. Toch, however, for the most part apolitical in his musical expression, preferred the lighter, less serious texts as vehicles for opera composition. His 1928 one-act opera *Egon und Emilie,* Op. 46, based on a farcical text by Christian Morgenstern, foreshadowed the type of work that he would later undertake in scoring radio dramas in Berlin.

After the Donaueschingen Festival transferred to Baden-Baden, under Hindemith's direction, two genres, *Gemeinschaftmusik* (Community Music) and *Gebrauchsmusik* (Utility Music), were featured. In 1928, the Festival was devoted to film music, with experiments in synchronization. Along with Hindemith, Milhaud, Paul Dessau, and George Antheil, Toch was commissioned to compose synchronization

Musical Example 3.9. *The Princess and the Pea,* Op. 43, mm. 72–83: excerpts from the ending of the one-act opera. Used by permission of AMP/G. Schirmer.

music for the film *Die Kinderfabrik* (*The Children Factory*). This was Toch's first experience in composing for the new sound films, a challenge that he apparently enjoyed immensely: "This gave him, in the beginning, such a tremendous joy. If he was given a free hand, some music came out which was quite remarkable."[18]

He had begun to compose for radio as early as 1927. The commission for the *Comedy for Orchestra* of that year came about through Hindemith's brother-in-law, Dr. Flasch from Frankfurt, who was in charge of the Ministry of Culture and Education, the agency that determined the programs of radio broadcasts. As a result of this connection, Hindemith had been influential in getting much of the New Music performed by radio orchestras. Composed specifically for radio, Toch's *Bunte Suite* (*Motley Suite*) of 1928 was widely broadcast over German radio stations. This entertaining collection of six dance movements, including a "Carousel" and a "Marionette Dance," was composed for the purpose of teaching listeners to recognize the instruments of the orchestra and, as such, became quite a success.

Other significant works composed during Toch's last years in Mannheim include the didactic or *Gebrauchsmusik* piano pieces, *Kleinstadtbilder* (*Pictures of a Small Town*), the vocal pieces for soprano solo and piano, Neun Lieder (*Nine Songs*), Op. 41, based on poems by Rilke, Christian Morgenstern, and Wilhelm Busch, and the neoclassical Sonata for Violin and Piano, Op. 44. In 1928, Toch's only organ work, a concerto for organ and orchestra, was published under the title *Fanal* (*Beacon*), Op. 45.

Mrs. Toch cites *The Princess and the Pea* along with the Cello Concerto, the Piano Concerto, and *The Juggler* as the works primarily responsible for Toch's rise to fame in Germany. The wave of performances of the first chamber opera and then of its successor, *Egon und Emilie,* brought Toch's name to the forefront of modern German composers. It was time to move on, this time to Berlin.

On 7 August 1928, Toch became a father at age forty-one, when his only child, his daughter Franzi, was born in Heidelberg. The then mayor of Mannheim, a Dr. Heinrich, tried to dissuade the family of three from leaving his city and even went so far as to offer the family their own private apartment in the castle!

Mrs. Toch confirms that by 1928 "his income was already very excellent, by many performances and by the income of performing rights which were starting to flow . . . with even some monthly payments by

Schott in the contract, guaranteeing [Toch] a life [in Germany] without any kind of worries," so, with daughter Franzi, in the summer of 1929 the family moved to Berlin.[19]

Berlin, 1929–1933

In the 1920s and early 1930s, Berlin was the mecca for a great many creative artists and intellectuals not only in Germany but also in Austria and other European countries. As Peter Gay confirms in his book *Weimar Culture:*

> To go to Berlin was the aspiration of the composer, the journalist, the actor; with its superb orchestras, its one hundred-twenty newspapers, its forty theaters, Berlin was the place for the ambitious, the energetic, the talented. Wherever they started, it was in Berlin that they became famous.[20]

Schönberg was back in Berlin now; Hindemith went there in 1927. Among the distinguished musical performers there were pianists Artur Schnabel, Edwin Fischer, Carl Friedberg, the young Rudolf Serkin, the young cello virtuoso Emanuel Feuermann, and the members of the Rosé and the Busch Quartets. The conductors working in the city were also remarkable—Erich Kleiber, Otto Klemperer, Wilhelm Furtwängler, and Bruno Walter, who, in his autobiography, described the spirit of Berlin in the brief period of its prosperity before 1933:

> The Philharmonic concerts led by Wilhelm Furtwängler; the Bruno Walter concerts with the Philharmonic Orchestra; a wealth of choral concerts, chamber-music recitals, and concerts by soloists; the State Opera under Erich Kleiber; the Kroll Opera under Klemperer . . . and a number of other institutions matched the achievements of the dramatic state. . . . It was clearly a great epoch in a great city.[21]

Erich Kleiber was the principal conductor of the State Opera; Schönberg was appointed as Busoni's successor at the Prussian Academy of the Arts; and Hindemith, Schnabel, Egon Petri, and Carl Flesch joined the faculty of the Hochschule für Musik, where Franz Schreker had been director since 1920.

When the Kroll Opera was taken over by the Prussian State in 1926, and the Deutsches Opernhaus by the Berlin City Council, there were, together with the State Opera, three subsidized opera houses in Berlin, a circumstance which encouraged the commission of new operatic works.

In 1925, Erich Kleiber premiered Berg's opera *Wozzeck,* followed by Janáček's *Jenufa.* Béla Bartók made guest appearances performing his own works. Kurt Weill, whose *Die Dreigroschenoper,* to a libretto by Bertolt Brecht, was first performed in 1928, had become chief critic for the weekly radio journal *Der Deutsche Rundfunk.* Weill reviewed musical and dramatic programs and wrote several articles about the future of music and radio. And Hanns Eisler, who was busy composing choral works and incidental music for proletarian plays, soon came out against the New Music in the press.

Berlin was also the headquarters for the political cabarets of Otto Reutter and Paul Graetz, whose satires ridiculed German rigidity and made political instability a subject of their art. And Berlin was the center of publishing empires. The firm of S. Fischer, for instance, became renowned by publishing Alfred Döblin's *Berlin Alexanderplatz* as well as the works of Thomas Mann, Hermann Hesse, Gerhart Hauptmann, Carl Zuckmayer, Hugo von Hofmannsthal, and Stefan Zweig.

In a documentary biography of Gustav Stolper's life and career in Weimar Germany, Dr. Toni Stolper, a lifelong friend of the Tochs, observed that

> the characteristic sign of those days was an unparalleled mental alertness. A passionate general concentration upon cultural life prevailed, expressed by the large space devoted to art by the daily newspapers, in spite of the political excitement of the times. . . . German painters, poets, playwrights, psychologists, philosophers, architects, humorists were engaged in an international commerce of ideas.[22]

In a tape-recorded interview, which he calls "Memoirs of a Berlin Concert-Goer," Konrad Wolff talks about the musical vitality of Berlin during his student days there, 1923–1933.

> If we talk about music, the Berlin of those days was everything New York has to offer today. One could subscribe to either Philharmonic series— Walter or Furtwängler—and the dress rehearsals on Sunday mornings were also open to ticket holders. . . . One could really attend a different performance almost every day or night of the week, whether at the Staatsoper, under Kleiber, or the Volksoper [Kroll] under Klemperer, or the Reinhardt Theatre (where Kurt Weill's *Three Penny Opera* had its premiere) . . . from Toscanini to Richard Strauss. . . . Well-known per-

formers were constantly coming to Berlin. . . . Indeed, whoever did not live there, came there. . . . For a creative musician, to live in Berlin then was an incredible experience.[23]

Wolff recalls, among other things, his attendance at the Kleiber dress rehearsal of *Wozzeck,* when the audience threw eggs and tomatoes; the appearance of Klemperer, clad in a Bolshevist-type khaki jacket, conducting Stravinsky's *L'Histoire du Soldat;* Prokofiev conducting his *The Love of Three Oranges;* and Bartók's performance of his Rhapsody for Piano and Orchestra, Op. 1. According to Wolff, the music critic Adolf Weissmann's concert reviews in the *Berliner Tageblatt* represented an artistic spirit in which the new ideas and the old traditions existed side by side for Berlin concert-goers.

Klemperer, with his assistants George Szell and Alexander Zemlinsky, perhaps did more than any other conductor to premiere new works. In addition to the operas already mentioned, Klemperer gave the first Berlin performances of Hindemith's *Cardillac* and *Neues vom Tage,* Milhaud's *Christophe Colomb,* Korngold's *Die tote Stadt,* and the world premiere of two movements from Mahler's Tenth Symphony.

By the end of the 1920s, Berlin was the most cosmopolitan city in Europe. Besides the luminaries of music and literature, Berlin had also attracted Albert Einstein, Erwin Panofsky, Walter Gropius, Wassily Kandinsky, Max Reinhardt, and Paul Tillich, most of whom would soon emigrate to America.

Because Berlin was so hospitable to strangers, the Jewish population there could live comfortably and thrive in their varied pursuits, as Peter Gay explains:

> the overflowing plenty of stimuli of artistic, scientific, commercial improvisations . . . in Berlin of 1918–1933 . . . stemmed from the talents of the Jewish population: its international connections, its sensitive restlessness, and, above all, its absolute instinct for quality.[24]

This was the Berlin into which the Tochs moved in the summer of 1929. Settling near their close friends, the Gustav Stolpers, in Dahlem, a suburb in South Berlin of fine homes and spacious gardens, they were next-door neighbors of Theodor Heuss, who was to become the first president of the Federal Republic of Germany after the war. The house and street immediately appealed to Toch who, always seeking the solitude and peace of mind to compose, observed that "the neighbors are so unmusical, no one will be making music." And so, he established his private studio on the third floor of the house—apart from everyone and everything, except for his dachshund Peter. Daily walks in the fields behind the house led him to the famed Wilhelm Scientific Institute, where the name scientists of the day were working on splitting the atom.

Just twenty minutes away from the Tochs' house lived the novelist Alexander Döblin, on Pottsdammerplatz. In fact, Döblin was one of the first professional friends to call on the Tochs after their arrival in Berlin. A physician before he became a writer, Döblin seemed to have a lot in common with Toch. It was through Döblin the Tochs were introduced to the literary and theatre luminaries of this cultural capital of Europe. Three such notables who became good friends were Max Reinhardt, who had contacted Toch soon after his arrival to ask him to compose incidental music for a play about Mary Baker Eddy; Bertolt Brecht, whose friendship continued in California; and Hanns Eisler's brother, the writer Gerhardt Eisler, who went so far as to proclaim that Toch was "the last inspirational composer of our generation."[25]

From the beginning of their stay in Berlin, the Tochs' circle of friends also included people directly involved in politics, such as Heuss and Stolper, both of whom had served in Parliament as members of the German Democratic party. It was undoubtedly because of his acquaintance with them that Toch was made aware that the political turmoil in Germany was potentially life threatening.

Mrs. Toch relates that the Berlin years were among the happiest of their lives, when Toch composed over fifteen new works, shared the spotlight with the other major creative talents living and working there, and continued to attract attention with his compositions at the New Music Festivals.

With Kurt Weill as music editor of the weekly radio journal, Hindemith's brother-in-law in the Ministry of Culture in Frankfurt, and the tremendous success and influence of the broadcasting industry, it is hardly surprising that the theme of the 1929 Baden-Baden Festival was "Music for Radio." It was a time of rapid technical development in the communications media. The gramophone's recording capabilities were keeping pace with the advances in radio broadcasting, and magnetic recording on iron oxide was being tried out in Germany.

During his remaining years in Germany, Toch was to compose music for radio dramas and for the stage and even write several newspaper articles, such as "Music for the Stage" and "Dramatic Music." His incidental music for stage plays included the movement entitled "Idyll" from his Divertimento for Wind Orchestra, Op. 39, premiered by Hermann Scherchen, which had originally been a pastoral interlude in an expressionist production of Berthold Viertel's version of the *Bacchae* by Euripides. Among his other compositions for the stage were *The Cherry Blossom Festival,* performed in Hamburg in 1928, Shakespeare's *As You Like It,* for the Yiddish Theater in Berlin in 1930, and *The Saint of the U.S.A.,* produced in Berlin in 1931.

Most of the scores for radio plays were composed from 1930 to 1932 for Berlin radio. All of them remain unpublished. They are *Turandot* (1930) for a play by Alfred Wolfenstein, *The Robbers* (1931) based on Friedrich Schiller's *Sturm-und-Drang* play, and two modern versions of Greek tragedies, *Medea* (1931) and *Oedipus Rex* (1931). Of his interest in writing radio scores and incidental music, Mrs. Toch recalls that he certainly enjoyed the assignments, that "it was a kind of substitute for real opera."

Perhaps Toch secretly wished to be through with writing operas at this time because the composing of the three-act opera cappricio, *The Fan,* in late 1929, had practically finished him. Mrs. Toch remembers only too well the "dry spell" her husband experienced while trying to complete the opera. He apparently believed what he told his wife, "I don't think I can ever write another note." Ironically, it was this opera that, four years later, would be dramatically shut down by the Gestapo. During its rehearsal in Cologne, the brownshirts broke in and literally snatched the baton from the conductor, William Steinberg!

But still blissfully unaware of the tragedies that would occur four years later, Toch pulled himself out of his dry spell, and for the next three years, 1930–1933, produced some of his best compositions.

In addition to the incidental music for stage and radio plays, he continued to compose for the piano. After the Piano Sonata, Op. 47, came his five volumes of piano études, *Five Times Ten Etudes,* Op. 55 to Op. 59, published in 1931. His intention was to provide piano students with study pieces utilizing modern techniques in the new harmonic language. As such, they were a first in the New Music in Germany. Encompassing studies in graded order, from the beginning pieces to the most complex virtuoso pieces for the concert performer, these études have been compared to Bartok's set of graded piano pieces in six volumes, the *Mikrokosmos.* Toch's études are certainly among the most significant of his compositions for the piano. The following example comes from "Ten Easy Pieces," Op. 58. (Musical Example 3.10.)

Musical Example 3.10. Toch—Zehn Einfache Etüden (Ten Easy Studies), Op. 58, No. 9, mm. 1–9. Copyright 1931 by B. Schott's Soehne, Mainz. Copyright renewed 1959. All rights reserved. Used by permission of European American Music Distributors Corporation, sole U.S. and Canadian Agent for B. Schott's Soehne, Mainz.

Perhaps Toch's most unexpected success in Berlin came with his *Gesprochene Musik* (Music for Speaking Chorus), 1930, whose third movement, "The Geographical Fugue," Toch had considered a musical joke. In that he did not take the work seriously, he never gave the score to Schott for publication, although it was performed all over Germany by a choral group from the Berlin Hochschule. The work's use of pitchless rhythmical declamation brought Toch considerable publicity, and when it was later presented in America, in English translation, it was equally successful. Perhaps *the* most performed work of Toch, at the time of this writing, is this spoken fugue. (Musical Example 3.11.)

The other major vocal work of this period was written in collaboration with Alfred Döblin, the cantata *Das Wasser* (*The Water*), Op. 53, for tenor, baritone, narrator, and chamber orchestra of strings, flute, trumpet, and percussion, which was premiered at the Berlin Music Festival in 1930. It was performed frequently in Germany, as was *The Little Theatre Suite*, Op. 54, first performed by Furtwängler in Leipzig.

Perhaps one of the most successful performances of Toch's music in Berlin was his *Music for Orchestra and Baritone*, Op. 60, a four movement work based on poetry from Rainer Maria Rilke's *Stundenbuch*. The premiere, conducted by Erich Kleiber in 1932, was one of the last performances Toch was to hear of his music in Germany before he left, permanently. Of its premiere, the noted musicologist Alfred Einstein is said to have remarked, "If there is today any religious music, that is it."[26]

In Toch's German compositions, it is possible to discern patterns that were typical of the musical developments of the times. In Mannheim, he had maintained his original interest in chamber music and music for solo piano. Adhering to the neoclassical trends, his works of the early mid-twenties culminated in the Cello Concerto (1925) and the Piano Concerto No. 1 (1926).

Beginning with the experimental music of the Donaueschingen and Baden-Baden Festivals of 1926–1927, which led to his ventures into incidental music for stage and radio, Toch composed works in collaboration with poets and dramatists after his arrival in Berlin. He did not, however, abandon neoclassicism, the style in which he wrote the Sonatas Op. 44 and Op. 50.

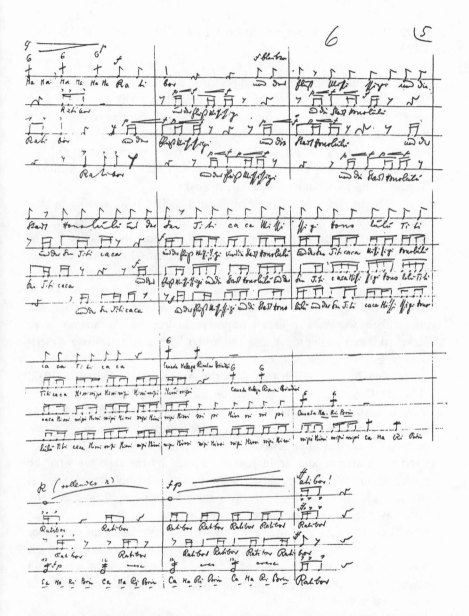

Musical Example 3.11. *The Geographical Fugue.* Source: Original manuscript, Toch Archive.

Preview of America, Return to Berlin, Exodus, 1932–1934

Like many other renowned performers and conductors, Toch was fortunate to get a preview of America in 1932. Invited by the *Pro Musica* society to perform in eight American cities where chapters of the society were located, Toch came to America as a composer-pianist. On his tour he performed his First Piano Concerto with chamber orchestras in Minneapolis, Cleveland, Denver, Seattle, and San Francisco, and with the Boston Symphony, under Serge Koussevitsky.

The background of the *Pro Musica* society is interesting in that Toch was the first and only German to be invited to tour America. The society was founded in Paris by the pianist, author, and teacher E. Robert Schmitz, who had lived in America and established the chapters there, but who preferred to reside in Paris. His purpose was to bring modern composers to America to perform or conduct their works with chamber orchestras and to provide a forum where they could speak about their works. Previous composers invited by the society were Stravinsky and Milhaud, whose tours had helped to introduce Americans to Europe's New Music.

The Tochs were pleased with the America they visited in 1932, although they were rather amused by the provincialism in some communities. Anecdotes are plentiful about the high-cultured Europeans as guests of the friendly, but not always sophisticated Americans. On one occasion Toch was interviewed for a newspaper in Seattle when he arrived there after a long train journey. Asked by the reporter what he preferred to eat, Toch replied, "Raw meat" (possibly steak tartare), which made these headlines in the paper: "Composer from Germany Eats Raw Meat." Two years after the tour, when the Tochs were settled in New York, the story goes that a society woman came up to the composer saying that she remembered him from the *Pro Musica* banquet in his honor in 1932. She then proceeded to reminisce, "It was a wonderful affair, the food, the speeches were wonderful, but didn't you think the music was horrid?"[27]

Nevertheless, the Tochs found America to be a stimulating and vibrant young country, with helpful and friendly people. They were particularly enamored of Southern California, whose beauty made a lasting impression on them. The Tochs especially enjoyed the company of a charming professor, a Dr. Hoffman from Los Angeles, who, a decade later, was convicted of being a German spy! He committed suicide as his only recourse.

During the tour of April–June 1932, Paul Hindenburg was reelected president of Germany, and Mrs. Toch remembers that after this event, the Tochs were invited to a party at the German Consulate in Seattle. When the conversation turned to the election and how it would affect the future of the Weimar Republic, Toch astonished everyone by announcing, "Nothing can be done. The Nazis are going to get power." The arguments against his statement were the familiar ones that the Germans, with their remarkable cultural and intellectual heritage, could never permit such barbarians to seize power. Less than one year later, Toch was making plans for his escape.

Upon return to Germany in the summer of 1932, Toch composed his last German work, his Piano Concerto No. 2, entitled Symphony for Piano and Orchestra, Op. 61. The premiere performance took place in 1933 in London, with the composer playing the solo part and with Sir Henry Wood conducting. The work is neoclassical in its form, and, like a symphony, consists of four movements, but in the order: Allegro (sonata form), Scherzo (a tarantella and a waltz), Adagio (containing a long piano cadenza), and "Zyklus Variabilis," (free variation form, using themes from the other). The solo part in the third movement demands not only a formidable piano technique but also an ability to perform the new techniques inherent in the complexity of the new musical language and style. At the time, Toch, the pianist, and only a handful of other pianists, could have accomplished such a remarkable feat. (Musical Example 3.12.)

While composing this work, Toch came to believe that, in reality, this might be his last year in Germany, and Mrs. Toch relates two ugly incidents that triggered his resolution to leave. The first, in the fall of 1932, occurred as Toch was walking out of Alfred Döblin's house, and the driver of a swerving car that just missed hitting him, called out, "What a pity, there would have been one Jew less."[28] The second incident occurred just one month after Hitler became Chancellor of Germany. The composer was working in his hideaway study on the third floor, when two brownshirts appeared at the front door. Before letting them in, Mrs. Toch made her husband swear not to come out of his room until they were gone. Something of a close call, but who would have predicted that just months later Toch's musical scores and records would be destroyed or blacklisted?

Musical Example 3.12. Toch — Symphonie Für Klavier Und Orchester (Symphony for Piano and Orchestra), Op. 61 mt. I, mm. 30–34. Copyright 1933 by B. Schott's Soehne, Mainz. Copyright renewed. All rights reserved. Used by permission of European American Music Distributors Corporation, sole U.S. and Canadian Agent for B. Schott's Soehne, Mainz.

Although Mrs. Toch was not yet convinced of the necessity to leave, her husband had already devised a plan to get them out. A year before, he had received an invitation from the city of Florence to represent Germany, along with Richard Strauss, at an international music conference. In the spring of 1933, Toch went to Florence to attend the meeting, but instead of returning to Berlin, he went directly to Paris where he telegraphed his wife, "I have my pencil." This was the prearranged signal for her to leave Berlin and join him in Paris. Having entrusted young Franzi to the care of the Gustav Stolpers, who were also preparing to leave, Mrs. Toch arrived in Paris, the first stage of a long journey that would eventually lead them back to America.

Like many of the Europeans fleeing Hitler, the Tochs preferred to remain on the continent, and Paris was the natural choice of a place to stay. But Paris, soon saturated with refugees, could not support the influx of so many homeless and jobless people.

However, one of the bright spots in their situation was the companionship they found among other émigrés. Mrs. Toch recalls a social gathering of refugees from Berlin, when Toch and Schönberg had a serious argument about National Socialism and Judaism. Schönberg vigorously defended his second conversion. Having converted to Catholicism in Vienna, he had recently reclaimed his Judaism in the face of the Nazis' rise to power. However, Toch disagreed with Schönberg's position that one should stand up against the Nazis by reconfirming one's Judaism. Although his premonitions about the danger of Hitler were realistic enough to force him to leave Germany, Toch could not comprehend the necessity to espouse one or another religious doctrine or dogma. His own personal religion was one of tolerance and universalism. In Paris, however, his response to Schönberg was simply, "Why should the Nazis have to tell me that I am a Jew and must be a Jew? I am who I am."[29]

Again, like many other refugees reluctant to leave Europe, the Tochs moved on, this time to London in the fall of 1933. It was during his year there that Toch began his relentless study to perfect his command of English. With the dedication of an artist and a perfectionist, he immersed himself in learning English, making his own dictionaries of definitions and synonyms, a habit that he continued until his last years in America.

It was difficult to find employment in London, but Toch was fortunate in obtaining a work permit to compose the music for three films. The first, *Little Friend,* was produced by the Gaumont-British

Film Studio in London. The second was *Catherine the Great,* produced by London Films-UA, which led to an extension to his work permit. However, after his third film, *The Private Life of Don Juan,* it became clear that life and work in London were not a permanent solution to his economic problems. When Toch realized that his contract with Schott could not be renewed, that his music was, in effect, banned in Germany, he knew that without a publisher it was too risky for him to continue to free-lance in London.

Where to go? Back in Germany music critics penned such insults as, "The performance was rhythmically weak, as unpoetical and mechanical as an etude of Toch on a buzzing phonograph."[30] And former champions of his piano music renounced either him or his music. In her autobiography published in the mid-1930s, Nellie Fey, who had performed Toch's Piano Concerto in Chicago, wrote, "I also played at that time the work of a then contemporary composer." Walter Gieseking, an ardent Nazi, simply dropped Toch's music from his programs.[31]

There was really only one place to go, and that was America. The story of how Toch succeeded in getting the financial backing to emigrate is told by Toni Stolper, who, after arriving in New York in September 1933 with her husband and four children, became one of the thousands of émigrés helping émigrés.

> It became imperative for us to get the Toch family over here as soon as feasible. . . . A teaching position at the New School with an assured academic salary over a couple of years would satisfy the immigration authorities. Alvin Johnson would gladly lend his authority to offering Ernst such a teaching position, provided that the required financial security were forthcoming. . . . Knowing that Ernst had a cousin here in a comfortable financial position, we decided to appeal for his cooperation . . . together he [John Bass] and we procured the wherewithal, and thus in autumn 1934 this project succeeded to everyone's satisfaction.[32]

With the promise of employment, a work permit was assured, as long as he declared his intention to become an American citizen. Thus, in the fall of 1934, well in advance of the filling of the quota on German immigration to the United States, the Tochs joined the swelling numbers of scholars, artists, and intellectuals from Germany and Austria whose new homeland was to be America.

Ernst Toch, c. 1927

Toch with daughter
Franzi, c. 1931

Toch, c. 1937

Toch with daughter
Franzi and wife Lilly, c. 1950

Toch, 1952

Toch with Franzi, Lilly, and grandchildren, c. 1962

4

Toch's Life, Times, and Music — America

On the voyage to New York in 1934 Toch composed *Big Ben: Variation Fantasy on the Westminster Chimes,* Op. 62, which was inspired by the tune of the Westminster chimes he had heard in London. Premiered by the Boston Symphony in December 1934 and later performed by Frederick Stock and the Chicago Symphony, it proved to be one of Toch's most popular works. The composer described how his first "American" work was inspired:

> The theme lingered in my imagination for a long while, and evolved into other forms, somehow still connected with the original one, and finally like the chimes themselves, it seemed to disappear into the fog from which it emerged. I have sought to fix this impression in my variation-fantasy.[1]

In this programmatic work, the Big Ben theme is heard somewhat disguised in the opening, and the variations that follow are of changing moods. The climax of the work is a fugue, concluding with sounds of the chiming clock. It is somewhat ironic that this first American work, which proved very popular, paid tribute to the country that, for one year, had been Toch's other English-speaking homeland.

Once settled in New York, the Tochs renewed their friendship with the Paul Klemperers and they soon became friends with the film producer Lester Cowan and his wife Anne Rinnell, the actor Sam Jaffe, and George Gershwin.

About this time, too, the securing of an American publisher for his works became a major preoccupation. The American affiliate of B. Schott, Associated Music Publishers (AMP), published the *Big Ben Variations* (1935), but with his royalties frozen in Germany and his name blacklisted by Schott in Mainz, Toch did not know where to begin to look for a publisher in the United States. He still hoped that his contract with AMP would eventually help him recoup his royalties for European performances of his works, so when the music publisher G. Schirmer offered to buy his popular orchestral piece, *Pinocchio,* under conditions distinctly unfavorable to the composer, Toch refused.

Gershwin had helped him to gain membership in the American Society of Composers, Authors, and Publishers (ASCAP) in order to be protected by an American performing rights society. But, in the meantime, the rival society of Broadcast Music, Inc. (BMI) had bought AMP. They were reluctant to perform Toch's works, because he was an ASCAP member and they would have to pay performing rights. Furthermore, AMP sold much of their catalog to Schirmer, so Toch was the victim of a publishing house and performing rights breakup that would adversely affect the publication of his music in the years to come.[2]

In spite of the difficulties in finding a single publisher, many of Toch's works were performed during his first years in America. His name was kept before the public, as evidenced in the following review:

> Dr. Ernst Toch is one of the most original creative figures in the music of our time. . . . Those familiar with Dr. Toch know that as a composer he has mounted to pre-eminence . . . that he is assuming, through his more recent works, a position of outstanding significance in contemporary music. . . . His music is modern . . . it is original . . . it is important. Ernst Toch must rank with the foremost creators of modern music, and there are more than a handful of critics who firmly believe that his music will outlive the fierce revolutions of his more famous contemporaries. Among Jewish composers, of whom there exist a prolific number, none promises so much to the future as Ernst Toch.[3]

Toch composed one of the most popular of his American works, *Pinocchio, a Merry Overture,* just one year after coming to America, shortly after he was introduced to the story of Pinocchio at the home of Alvin Johnson, president of the New School for Social Research. The work is appropriately dedicated to Dr. and Mrs. Johnson. Premiered by Otto Klemperer in Los Angeles, *Pinocchio* was also performed by Frederick Stock and the Chicago Symphony (1937), Arthur Fiedler and the Boston Pops Orchestra (1938), Eugene Goosens and the Cincinnati Symphony (1939), Sir John Barbirolli and the New York Philharmonic (1940), Fritz Reiner and the CBS Radio Orchestra (1940), and William Steinberg and the Chicago Symphony (1942), to name a few. This poem appears on the title page of the score:

> Italian lore would have us know
> That gay marionette Pinocchio!
> With deviltry and gamin grace
> He led them all a merry chase.

The popular appeal of the work lies in its programmatic content, making *Pinocchio* a kind of tone poem, as Toch, himself, confirmed: "[Pinocchio] is a sort of brother-in-mischief to the German *Till Eulenspiegel.*"[4] Written in a general tonality of G Major, this seven-minute merry overture sports a waltz theme about midway through. Scored for woodwinds and brass in pairs, percussion, and strings, it is compelling in its rhythmic drive and vitality. The effect is one of rhythmic ostinato, predictive of the famous chase scenes that Toch would soon be scoring for the films. (Musical Example 4.1.)

After their first year in New York (1934–1935), the Tochs made a return trip to Europe in the summer, stopping first in London to pick up Franzi from her boarding school and then going on to Vienna to visit Toch's mother and Lilly's parents. During their stay in Vienna, Toch received a telegram from Paramount Pictures in Hollywood, requesting him to report to their studio within seven days to begin work on the film score for *Peter Ibbetson,* at a salary of $750 a week. Flying from Prague to New York, and then traveling on to California, Toch arrived at the producer's office in exactly seven days. Given lodging and assured that his time would be duly compensated from the date of his arrival, he was also told that his scoring work would not begin for another seven weeks!

George Gershwin is usually credited with launching Toch on his American film scoring career. The quality of their friendship is evident in Gershwin's inscription on the title page of his gift to Toch, the score of *Porgy and Bess:* "for Ernst—with keen appreciation of his music and with warm friendliness—April 1, 1936."[5] Gershwin helped Toch to get his first commission from Warner Brothers, a project that did not mate-

To Dr. and Mrs. Alvin Johnson in cordial admiration

PINOCCHIO
A Merry Overture

ERNST TOCH

Musical Example 4.1. *Pinocchio, A Merry Overture,* mm. 1–5. Used by permission of AMP/G. Schirmer.

rialize. However, the rival studio, Paramount, became interested in securing Toch's talents for their studio. Opening to favorable reviews, including an important one by Olin Downes in the *New York Times,* the film music to *Peter Ibbetson* was a success. Hollywood took notice of their imported talent, and while the studios were deciding how to make best use of these talents, the Tochs returned to New York City and one more year of teaching at the New School (1935–1936).

In the years 1936–1938, Toch was trying to establish himself geographically as well as musically. When Hollywood came through with offers of more permanent employment, the Tochs moved to Pacific Palisades in the fall of 1936, thereby joining a community of distinguished émigrés already settled in Los Angeles.

Shortly after the move to the West Coast, Toch composed his first American chamber work, the String Trio, Op. 63. Written at the request of an acquaintance in Los Angeles who had performed some of Toch's European chamber music, it was not, however, premiered for another ten years. But his reawakened interest in chamber music did lead to his friendship with Mrs. Elizabeth Sprague Coolidge, which lasted until her death in 1953.

Dedicated to promoting performances of chamber music, Mrs. Coolidge frequently commissioned new works from contemporary composers. She subsidized their performances in her concerts at the Library of Congress in Washington, D.C., and at the Berkshire Festival in Massachusetts.

In the fall of 1937 Toch received a commission from Mrs. Coolidge to write a piano quintet, but he was not overjoyed with this assignment, as he did not like to write for piano and strings in combination. Although he informed Mrs. Coolidge that his String Trio, Op. 63, was waiting to be performed, he could not dissuade her from her original request.

Toch's Piano Quintet, Op. 64, was his first and last composition of piano chamber music. Dedicated to Mrs. Coolidge, it was first performed at the Berkshire Festival of Chamber Music in September 1938, with the Roth Quartet and the composer as pianist. Toch's use of nonmusical subtitles for each of the four movements — "The Lyrical Part," "The Whimsical Part," "The Contemplative Part," and "The Dramatic Part" — may, at first glance, look like a simple attempt to communicate moods, or frames of reference, to an audience not overly receptive to what may have been perceived as very atonal music. However, in the end, not even titles proved useful in making this thirty-five minute work more accessible. The piano part is almost as difficult to play as the two preceding piano concertos, and the string parts too often resemble an independent (and difficult) string quartet. (Musical Example 4.2.)

Musical Example 4.2. Quintet, Op. 64, mt. 1, mm. 13–24— for piano, two violins, viola, and cello by Ernst Toch. © Copyright 1947 by Leeds Music Corporation. Rights administered by MCA Music Publishing, a division of MCA Inc., New York, NY 10019. Used by permission. All rights reserved.

It is hardly surprising that Toch would not compose another major instrumental work for ten years!

Meanwhile, back in New York, spurred by President Roosevelt's commitment to finding work for unemployed musicians, a six-week, off-Broadway engagement of *The Princess and the Pea* in an English translation was financed through the WPA. It was subsequently taken up by a number of university and college opera workshops, including those in Los Angeles, under the direction of Toch's friend, the Berlin choral and opera conductor, Hugo Strelitzer.

One of the reviews, written in 1938 by another friend of Toch's, the Austrian émigré composer Paul Pisk, attests to the appeal of this popular work:

> Toch's music is entirely in the vein of light comedy. The chief themes, almost all in rapid tempo, are clearly orchestral. *The Princess and the Pea,* which takes fifty minutes for performance, sparkles with wit and verve, and it has had great success everywhere.[6]

In December 1937, Toch received word of his mother's death in Vienna. Even though he had not formally practiced the observance of religious occasions since the death of his father, he went to a Hollywood synagogue to attend the prayers for the dead. There, Rabbi Sonderling, a member of the German community, discussed with him the possibility of his composing a work that could be performed by the members of the congregation. Choosing the Jewish Exodus from Egypt, as depicted in the Haggadah to be the subject, Toch composed the *Cantata of the Bitter Herbs,* Op. 65. A tonal work, it was performed in the spring of 1938 with instrumentalists from Paramount studios, and among the children in the cast, Toch's nine-year-old daughter, Franzi.

If the String Trio, Op. 63, and the Piano Quintet, Op. 64, were a little too modern for American audiences, Toch's *Pinocchio* and *Big Ben Variations* kept their popularity with the musical public. Commentary in the music journals at this time was optimistic about his "Americanization," as is shown here.

> Ernst Toch, only a few years ago, was one of the most significant figures in contemporary music in Germany. He now belongs to the present-day scene of new music in America. . . . He is never radical . . . he remains always individual and unique . . . the richness of [his music's] emotional content, not excluding his sense of humor, makes his music all-embracing in its appeal.[7]

Beginning with Hitler's invasion of Austria in 1938, the Tochs were consumed with trying to obtain exit visas, with promises of financial support, for friends and relatives caught in Europe. Toch's sister Elsa Roman arrived from Vienna in 1940, about the time that the Toch family moved into their Santa Monica home. Of her aunt's arrival, Franzi recalls:

> I had never had an aunt before . . . suddenly there was an aunt in my life from out of nowhere, but "Tinte" I liked. . . . She moved in with us, with her long black skirts and high button boots and not speaking a word of English. . . . She took over the kitchen, creating all sorts of Viennese magic there.[8]

No doubt similar scenarios were repeated a thousand times over in households throughout America!

With the pressure mounting to provide financial support — i.e., affidavits for visas for other relatives and friends — Toch accepted most of the Hollywood scripts given him to score. As researched by the film critic Jack Docherty, a description of Toch's films follows.

The Hollywood Film Scores, 1935–1945

The 1930s and 1940s in Hollywood were the age of symphonic film music, a style pioneered by the Viennese composer Max Steiner in his score for *King Kong* (1933), and afterwards developed and perfected by another Austrian, Erich Wolfgang Korngold, in his eighteen film scores. Many of the studio composers were, like Steiner, Korngold, and Toch, émigrés from Europe, among them being Mario Castelnuovo-Tedesco, Ingolf Dahl, Paul Dessau, Hanns Eisler, Frederick Hollander, Karol Rathaus, Miklós Rózsa, Dimitri Tiomkin, Franz Waxman, and Eric Zeisl, while young American-born composers, such as Alfred Newman and Bernard Herrman, were also making names for themselves with their own individual scoring styles. Toch's individual style was established in his first Paramount assignment.

Paramount's version of George Du Maurier's fanciful novel *Peter Ibbetson* (1935), originally filmed as *Forever* in 1921, gave Toch his first chance to deal with the kind of subject with which he was to be associated during his years as a composer in Hollywood. The story concerns childhood sweethearts, Peter (Gary Cooper) and Mary (Ann Harding), who meet again as adults, only to be separated once more when Peter is sentenced to life imprisonment for the accidental killing of Mary's husband. Expected to die in his cell, Peter is taught by Mary how to escape to her in his mind. After a lifetime of meeting each other in dreams, they are united in death.

The surrealists claimed *Peter Ibbetson* as a prime example of *l'amour fou*, with André Breton proclaiming it a "triumph of surrealist thought," while Luis Buñuel called it one of the world's ten best films.[9] Yet as Tom Milne has observed, "the film is really a delicate romantic fantasy, shading into uncomfortable arty-crafty mysticism."[10]

Toch approached the subject in his most romantic, almost Mahlerian, manner. According to Mark Evans, "It contained some sensitively scored, highly ethereal dream sequences, and displayed the composer's highly personal style of polyphony and his use of voices for orchestral color."[11] The score earned Toch his first Academy Award nomination, although, as was the practice then, the recipient of it was the studio's music department head, Irvin Talbot, who also conducted. The prolific English-born composer W. Franke Harding also contributed a cue to Toch's score.

In 1936, however, Toch was again summoned to Hollywood to work on another assignment at Paramount. It was an uncredited collaboration on the music for *The General Dies at Dawn* (1936), a very successful feature starring Gary Cooper and Madeleine Carroll, with a screenplay by Clifford Odets, and the first film score by Werner Janssen, who was married to Ann Harding at the time.

As Mark Evans has detailed the procedure followed in preparing the score, Janssen wrote his music while the film was still in production, so inevitably his score did not synchronize with the final edited version.[12] Irving Talbot conducted a proofreading rehearsal at which Toch, Gerard Carbonara, Hugo Friedhofer, and Heinz Roemheld were assigned to edit and revise Janssen's score to make it fit the new timings. In addition, Carbonara and Toch wrote new original cues; Toch's contribution was used again on the soundtrack of the Paramount programmer, *Daughter of Shanghai*, in 1937.

Janssen won an Academy Award nomination for his score, which was one of the best of the period.

Paramount wasted Toch's talent on two B movies: *On Such a Night* (1937) and *Outcast* (1937). The former tells of a houseful of people marooned by flood waters—"so many baffling twists that the thread of narrative is soon lost," judged *Variety*—while the latter concerns a lawyer and a girl aiding an innocent doctor accused of murder and threatened by mob violence.[13] These potboilers did nothing to enhance Toch's reputation as a film composer, and his next three assignments were at another studio, 20th Century-Fox, in Hollywood.

There, musical director Louis Silvers retained Toch to advise him on the latest musical "trends."[14] The first evidence that Toch was at this studio is found in the score of the Shirley Temple film *Heidi* (1937), for which Toch, uncredited, composed part of the score. His cue, "Sledding Away," was published by Movietone Music Corporation for their mood music catalog.[15] The rest of the score was the work of staff composers Charles Maxwell and veteran English-born craftsman Cyril Mockridge.

Silvers also engaged Toch to write the title music, which he did in a style suggestive of the British Raj in India, for John Ford's *Four Men and a Prayer* (1938), the story of four young Englishmen who set out to clear their dishonored father's name.

In 1939, Toch's last project for Silvers at Fox was the stirring title music for *The Story of Alexander Graham Bell,* a respectful but rather dull history lesson in which the Italian-American Don Ameche plays the Scottish inventor of the telephone and marries a deaf girl, played by Loretta Young. The rest of the score was composed by Cyril Mockridge.

Toch's cues for Fox were to find their way onto the soundtracks of such other films as *Suez* (1938), *Everything Happens at Night* (1939), and *The Three Musketeers* (1939).

Back at Paramount, Toch was rewarded with a splendid script, *The Cat and the Canary* (1939), which is "superbly staged, briskly paced, perfectly cast and lusciously photographed. The comedy-thriller par excellence."[16] It had all the elements of a classic in its genre, and Toch responded with vigor to the challenge it presented. His genuinely frightening music adds immeasurably to the picture's atmosphere and suspense, and he never makes the mistake of being less than serious.

Bob Hope makes an engaging hero, helping Paulette Goddard deal with "a rotting mansion in the middle of a swamp, a sinister housekeeper (Gale Sondergaard), a group of frightened relatives who expire at regular intervals through the night, victims of a malevolent force."[17] Not considered important enough for an Academy Award nomination, the film was nevertheless crucial to Toch's standing in Hollywood, marking him, in the eyes of producers, as a specialist in "spooky" music. "Paramount . . . seems to have been proud [of him]," says John Russell Taylor in *Strangers in Paradise,* for "he was generally credited, grandly, as 'Dr. Ernst Toch,' "[18] an honor hitherto accorded only to MGM's staff composer Dr. William Axt.

Having typecast him, Paramount next offered Toch *Dr. Cyclops* (1939), a minor science fiction classic about a mad scientist (Albert Dekker) in the Amazonian jungle, who uses a group of travelers as guinea pigs for his miniaturization experiments. Because the director was Ernest B. Schoedsack, who had been codirector of *King Kong,* there are excellent special effects and Technicolor too. The rather slow narrative is bolstered by almost nonstop music, a demanding project that necessitated Toch having the assistance of two collaborating composers, Carbonara and Albert Hay Malotte, the latter a protégé of Victor Herbert best remembered for his popular setting of The Lord's Prayer.

At RKO-Radio, Toch arranged the *Hallelujah* for chorus and orchestra featured in the finale of *The Hunchback of Notre Dame* (1939), for the film's composer Alfred Newman. It was even rumored that Toch had actually composed the *Hallelujah,* which Newman, as was his practice, incorporated into other scores, for *The Song of Bernadette* (1943) and *The Robe* (1953). It can also be heard at the conclusion of RKO's *It's a Wonderful Life* (1947), which has a score by Dimitri Tiomkin. *The Hunchback of Notre Dame* itself, directed by William Dieterle and starring Charles Laughton as Quasimodo, is the best-realized and best-loved version of the Victor Hugo story, a picture that has gained in stature over the years.

Toch's only other film in 1940 was *The Ghost Breakers,* Paramount's follow-up to *The Cat and the Canary,* again teaming Bob Hope and Paulette Goddard, in which the heroine, heiress to a mansion in Cuba, is involved in a plot replete with ghosts, zombies, and buried treasure. Toch's music is exemplary throughout, heightening the action and reinforcing the "creepy" atmosphere.

In 1941, Toch began an association with Columbia Pictures. His first assignment was *Ladies in Retirement,* from the successful play by Reginald Denham, in which a housekeeper (Ida Lupino) tries to cover up a murder committed to protect two insane sisters. Although tame by today's standards of cinema horror, and by comparison with its remake, *The Mad Room* (1969), it seemed shocking at the time and was considered a suitable subject for a composer who had the power to represent the grotesque and the ghoulish in music. Toch's evocative score brought him his second Academy Award nomination.

Columbia next assigned Toch to provide heroic martial themes in a trio of wartime dramas, beginning with *First Comes Courage* (1943), about a Norwegian girl (Merle Oberon) who fraternizes with the Nazis in order to gather secret information. One critic dismissed it as having "little to commend it except as propaganda."[19]

His second wartime effort was *Address Unknown* (1944), in which Paul Lukas plays a naturalized German-American incriminated by letters from his past. The film was rather low on production values, but Toch's somber music was thought worthy of receiving an Academy Award nomination, his third and final one. The prolific Italian émigré composer Mario Castelnuovo-Tedesco also contributed one sequence to the score.

The third of the wartime trio was *None Shall Escape* (1944), the story of a war criminal told in flashback, a "taut drama that retains quite a punch."[20]

From his four Columbia films, the studio made subsequent use of Toch's cues in about forty other (mainly low budget) productions, among which were *The Adventures of Martin Eden* (1942), *Sullivan's Travels* (1942), *They Live in Fear* (1944), *U-Boat Prisoner* (1944), *Okinawa* (1952), *A Yank in Indo-China* (1952), *The Big Heat* (1953), and *El Alamein* (1953).

Toch's ten years as a film composer, which began at Paramount with the romantic fantasy, *Peter Ibbetson,* ended at Paramount with another picture on a supernatural theme, *The Unseen* (1945), which was an attempt to duplicate the success of *The Uninvited,* produced a year earlier. Both films starred Gail Russell, and both were directed by Lewis Allen.

In *The Unseen,* Russell plays a governess who comes to believe that a foul deed has been committed in the house next door. Strong on atmosphere but weak on plot, in spite of the facts that Raymond Chandler collaborated on the screenplay with Hagar Wilde and that the film borrows elements from *Gaslight* (1943), not even Toch's expert *misteriosos* could make it a great commercial success.

The Uninvited has a memorable main theme by Victor Young rendered into a popular song, "Stella by Starlight." No song hits came from the scores Toch composed; he had not that kind of musical gift. Nor have there been any as yet commercial recordings of his film music. Suites from *Peter Ibbetson, The Cat and the Canary, Ladies in Retirement, Address Unknown,* and other pictures would make fine additions to the catalog of rediscovered "classic" film scores of the past.

Toch himself came to despise the film industry, believing that composing exclusively for films was a "prostitution of [his] talents." He soon discovered, too, that the opinion of musical America at the university or concert hall level, seemed to be "once a film composer, always a film composer." To Toch, as to Karol Rathaus and Schönberg, the big business system of Hollywood was synonymous with artistic sellout, and some of the film composers may have felt that they would never again be able to compose "serious" music.[21]

Moreover, the émigré film composers had other reasons to be critical of Hollywood. Accustomed to being treated with dignity in Europe, they were sometimes insulted by their studio employers. Their assignments, too, sometimes lacked proper directions or underutilized their talents, and their salaries were often inequitable, considering the enormous contribution they made to American filmmaking. The film scores that Toch composed between 1935 and 1945 constitute an important and distinctive part of that contribution to an artistic medium which for too long has been insufficiently appreciated.

▬ Southern California, 1936–1949

Toch's daughter Franzi recalls what it was like to grow up in a distinguished though displaced household, viewing Hollywood from the outside and still wondering at all the fuss over her father, who, although employed there, seemed to loathe it, intent upon protecting himself from the outside world.

> "Confusing" is an adjective that comes to mind. Entering my first school in California at the age of eight, I was the only foreigner there. Pacific Palisades was . . . far from the melting pot image of America, but close enough to Hollywood to be imbued with its mystique. Beautiful little Elizabeth Taylor, immaculate in a crisp new outfit every day, was delivered and fetched by a uniformed chauffeur in a big shiny car. . . . Darryl Zanuck's children had a Halloween party at their house on the beach to which the classes were invited, featuring elephant rides and other attractions from the Barnum and Bailey Brothers Circus. I did not go. . . . I was far too shy, but mother never would have allowed it. I was arduously shielded from becoming tainted by Hollywood's glitz. . . . Back at my house there was also much commotion and fuss made over

my father, but there were no elephant rides in my backyard, and I frankly never did understand what the fuss over HIM was all about.[22]

In his article "German Émigrés in Southern California in the 1930s and 1940s," Jarrell Jackman discusses the confrontation of different cultures. "What resulted was an interaction between the émigrés who represented an Old World culture, and Southern California; a New-World future-oriented region . . . [On] the surface . . . these two forces were irreconcilable. . . . But, in actuality, the threads connecting them became strong, and an actual synthesis took place."[23]

Certainly the Southern California way of life contrasted sharply with what the émigrés had known in Europe!

First of all, there was the physical beauty, the supposed "paradise" to which the Europeans had been exiled. The Tochs' custom-built home in Santa Monica to this day remains a symbol of the dichotomy of a displaced, though superbly placed, European-in-American culture. "The view from the terrace of the Santa Monica mountains, still almost uninhabited at the time, the oak and eucalyptus studded greens of the Brentwood golf course in the foreground, a formal border of towering palms swaying in the breeze along its edge, nothing but the song of birds breaking the silence, our hill was our private Elysium."[24]

Secondly, there was the lack of central meeting places, especially coffeehouses, where the émigrés could congregate. Even though they tended to be clustered together in Pacific Palisades, Hollywood, Santa Monica, or Brentwood, the Europeans, accustomed to shorter distances and public transportation, often felt isolated. And so, the inner circles gathered in their friends' homes, for prearranged rather than spontaneous, socializing. These circles helped to keep the high culture of prewar Berlin and other European cities alive, but they could not take the place of the coffeehouses, where young and old, new and familiar personalities had congregated.

During the 1940s, the Tochs enjoyed the company of a few close émigré friends, among whom Thomas Mann, Bertolt Brecht, and Alma Mahler could be counted among their dinner guests. Describing the intimate though elaborate dinner parties at their Santa Monica home, Toch's daughter recalls that

> the menu at these parties was always carefully planned and my father kept a diary of what was served to whom and when. . . . Mother was known as a great people-mixer and she was also an excellent cook.

. . . Usually (her) helpers were victims of the Holocaust. . . . I used to help serve the seated guests. Once, when I was about twelve, Alma Mahler was there for dinner, and I saw her chauffeur sitting in the car in the driveway the entire evening. I felt sorry for him and went out to talk to him and bring him a plate of food. Mother was shocked and said sternly, "Das tut man nicht" . . . I must not do that again, it wasn't proper. Though a kind and generous woman, mother still held on to vestiges of her own upbringing.[25]

Reminiscing about these exclusive gatherings, Gertrude Zeisl, the wife of the composer Eric Zeisl, describes the New Year's Eve party where they first met the Tochs:

It was at the home of (the author) Emil Ludwig, and Emil was a fabulous host. He had a very beautiful home in the Pacific Palisades . . . and he pointed to the home of Thomas Mann, who was just opposite, in a kind of valley. . . . His hospitality was sumptuous—wonderful cooking, and the most exquisite dishes. And he also provided all this entertainment. . . . Eric and Ernst Toch, without talking about it, sat down at the piano and began to play four hands, in a kind of funny way, and went through the waltzes of Vienna . . . and it was very funny. . . . I remember (also) an evening where (Hanns) Eisler and Eric and Paul Dessau were all invited to Toch's. There was a funny controversy between Dessau and Eric, and Toch mediated.[26]

The distinguished émigrés Mann, Schönberg, Theodor Adorno, Franz Kafka, Darius Milhaud, Alexander Tansman, among many others, sought out each other for many reasons, the pleasures of intellectual company and stimulating conversation being high on the list.

But relations among them were not always cordial. For instance, when Mann's novel *Doctor Faustus* was published (1947; English translation, 1949), Schönberg chose to see its main character, a devious and tyrannical composer by the name of Adrian Leverkuhn, as a caricature of himself. He accused Mann of misrepresenting his moral character, especially because Leverkuhn had supposedly signed a pact with the devil. In that Mann did not find it necessary to justify his innocent portrayal, the relationship between Schönberg and Mann began to deteriorate. In fact, the émigré community began to take sides, and Toch found himself unwittingly involved in the ensuing feud. He intervened, calling upon their mutual friend Alma Mahler, pillar of the émigré community, to pacify both sides, which she did successfully. What is telling, however, is that Mann dedicated a copy of *Doctor Faustus* to Toch with the following inscription: "To Ernst Toch who does not need the devil."[27]

Apart from the private gatherings in fellow émigrés' homes, in film studios, or in the universities and colleges, the transplanted composers and performers had a very important central forum: the Monday concert series, "Evenings on the Roof," established by Peter Yates. And if the Los Angeles Philharmonic under Alfred Wallenstein, its conductor from 1943 to 1956, chose virtually to ignore Schönberg, Stravinsky, and Toch during the 1940s, at least some of their works were brought to a sympathetic audience through this series.

The friends Toch made in Hollywood, the students, teachers, and conductors at the universities and colleges, and the colleagues who offered encouragement through the Monday evening concerts became Toch's most consistent support system in Los Angeles. Among the Los Angeles performers who played his works, and whose friendship he enjoyed, were Jascha Heifetz, Jakob Gimpel, Rudolf Kolisch, Feri Roth, the members of their string quartets, Louis and Annette Kaufman, Gregor Piatigorsky, Julian Brodetsky, and Emanuel Feuermann. In addition, the Tochs enjoyed the friendship of such composers as Ingolf Dahl, Paul Pisk, Miklós Rózsa, Alexander Tansman, Peter Yates, E. W. Korngold, and Eric Zeisl. Conductor-friends in Los Angeles included Otto Klemperer (conductor of the Los Angeles Philharmonic from 1933 to 1939), Carl Bamberger, Hanns Poppey, Hugo Strelitzer, and Heinrich Jalowetz.

As for Toch's relationship with his neighbor Schönberg, it was, at best, stormy. It seems that as Toch became less enchanted with Schönberg's music, not to mention his egotism and temper, that he, like many others, kept his distance. Nevertheless, the two composers' families stayed in touch. Franzi Weschler relates the following story about Schönberg and his daughter:

> Once when we (Franzi, age nineteen, her fiance, Irving Weschler, and his friend) decided to go to the opera, I suggested we invite Nuria Schönberg to come with us. She had just turned sixteen, and negotiating for her parents' consent was no easy matter. . . . When we arrived at the Schönbergs to pick Nuria up, all turned out in our evening finery, Arnold himself handed his lovely daughter over to us at the door. As we turned to leave, Arnold queried hesitatingly, "What time will you bring her home?" to which we replied that it was a long opera, and we might stop for a snack on the way back. Arnold paled then brightened up as an idea came to his mind: "Oh, must it be so late? . . . Couldn't I just give her a sardine sandwich to take along?"[28]

The vocal chamber piece *Poems to Martha* is Toch's only work composed during the war years. It was commissioned by a friend, Joseph Haft, and is dedicated to the memory of his wife, Martha. From a group of simple, heartfelt poems written by Mr. Haft for his wife, Toch chose four and built his composition around them. The following excerpt from the second song, "In the Train," shows a simplified, rhythmically uncomplicated, vocal line, with the accompanying strings providing a faint reminder of Toch the master composer of string quartets. (Musical Example 4.3.)

During the war years, the Tochs were also engulfed in such practical matters as soliciting performances from conductors. Besides Koussevitsky and Klemperer, Toch's chief promoters were William Steinberg, Erich Leinsdorf, and Antal Dorati. However, other prominent conductors, such as Eugene Ormandy and Herbert von Karajan, to whom he sent copies of his scores, answered with a polite, but disheartening, "Thank you. . . . We may consider."

During these years, Toch seemed to be a spent creative talent, disillusioned by world events as well as by the apparent lack of interest in his music. Two letters written to Mrs. Coolidge, one in 1943, the second two years later, reflect his despair:

> For quite some time I am not in a very happy frame of mind. Disappointments and sorrows render me frustrated and lonesome. I become somehow reluctant to go on writing if my work remains more or less paper in desks and on shelves.[29]

and

> The reason for (my) delay is that I always waited and hoped for a better frame of mind in which to write you. . . . It is my work that keeps me in not too happy a mood. . . . This is not a good state for writing to friends. But it is a wonderful state for receiving a dear letter. Love is, as you know, always greedy for love. . . . This every new assertion is a new heavenly gift, doubly blessed when received at low ebb.[30]

After the war, in 1946, as if he dared to hope again, Toch returned to serious composition and to the genres with which he had started his career—piano pieces (*Profiles,* Op. 68, and *Ideas,* Op.69) and, after a twenty-year hiatus, another string quartet (Op. 70).

The four short pieces in *Ideas* are similar in style to Toch's piano collections of the mid-twenties, *Burlesken,* Op. 31, *Drei Klavierstücke,*

Musical Example 4.3. *Poems to Martha* — Quintet for strings and medium voice. Score by Ernst Toch. © Copyright 1943 by MCA Music Publishing, a division of MCA Inc., New York, NY 10019. Copyright renewed. Used by permission. All rights reserved.

Op. 32, and *Fünf Capricetti*, Op. 36. Had the composer, after the world's catastrophic events, consciously decided to take up where he felt he had left off, on his rise to fame in Germany? The medium-difficult pieces in *Ideas* remain mini examples of twentieth-century piano technique, in their melodic and harmonic emphasis on fourths and sevenths. (Musical Example 4.4.)

III

Toch's slow return to inspired composing is perhaps best described in the motto he attached to his String Quartet, Op. 70: "I do not know what it is I mourn for—it is unknown sorrow; only through my tears can I see the beloved light of the sun" (from Eduard Mörike's poem *Verborgenheit*—meaning concealment or secrecy). This quartet, though similar in melodic and harmonic vocabulary to his German ones, is markedly more subdued, as indicated by the performance direction in the first movement, "calmly and evenly flowing, with utmost tenderness and intimacy." (Musical Example 4.5.)

In the fall of 1948 Toch suffered a heart attack, undoubtedly brought on by the accumulated stresses of the war years, the frustrations with publishers and conductors, and the burdens of his selfless dedication to teaching. But recuperating from the attack, he realized what a blessing it was to have time to compose again. Toch's regeneration of creativity began a new phase of frenzied composition in which he found his final voice—predominantly a symphonic one.

The Symphonic Voice, 1949–1964

At the age of sixty-two, Toch began a new career as a symphonic composer, producing seven symphonies in the last fifteen years of his life.

While recovering from his heart attack, Toch wrote to Mrs. Coolidge that he was thinking about writing a third book, to be called "The Undemonstrable Aspects of Music Composition." Although the book never materialized, Toch continued to write articles, essays, and speeches up to the last decade of his life. These writings, as well as the music itself and the philosophical inscriptions to his first three symphonies, represent a composer increasingly inspired by an almost religious or spiritual source.

Toward the end of 1948, Toch was invited by the Columbia Broadcasting Company to play his First Piano Concerto in New York. Fully recovered from his illness, he resumed practicing the piano. Early in 1949, his performance, along with a recorded interview, was broadcast on CBS, and the success of the interview resulted in an invitation to speak on Radio-Free-Europe.

Determined to find a locale where Toch could work without inter-

STRING QUARTET

I

ERNST TOCH, Op. 70

Musical Example 4.5. String Quartet, Op. 70, mt. 1, mm. 1–16 — miniature score by Ernst Toch. © Copyright 1947 by MCA Music Publishing, a division of MCA Inc., New York, NY 10019. Copyright renewed. Used by permission. All rights reserved.

ruptions, the Tochs returned to Europe, eventually to Switzerland, but first taking up residence near Innsbruck, and then settling in the outskirts of Vienna. It was here, in the city of his birth, that Toch composed his First Symphony, Op. 72, in the spring of 1949.

The summer was occupied with European concert tours. Toch was invited by his former student in Berlin, the Danish composer Vagn Holmboe, to perform his First Piano Concerto in Copenhagen, and by Erich Leinsdorf, who came to Holland to conduct, to perform the same work on a radio broadcast there.

While living in Zurich, the Tochs had become friends with the cellist Frédéric Mottier, who later performed and recorded Toch's Cello Concerto, Op. 35, and his String Quartet No. 12, Op. 70. Seeking absolute quiet and solitude, Toch was able to secure, through Mottier, a secluded apartment in Zurich, where he completed, with great speed, his Second Symphony, Op. 73.

In 1951, Toch wrote to Mrs. Coolidge: "I finished my Second Symphony and I am very happy with it, for I know for sure that it is the best work I ever wrote. Having written these two symphonies, I have for the moment—my fill of the kind of music which calls for a big orchestra. It was an obsession which had me in its grasp, but I am willing retrospectively to grant it all the power it had over my life."[31]

While Toch was in Switzerland composing, Mrs. Toch enrolled as a student of psychology at the Jung Institute in Zurich. Her student days did not last long, for she soon had to resume what she calls her fateful task of managing her husband's correspondence with publishers, in an effort to unfreeze royalties from European performances of the past twenty years.

Although Toch had given up formal teaching after his heart attack, he was invited to deliver occasional lectures in Switzerland, and in the United States, too, in the early 1950s.

But in 1950 and 1951, Toch's thoughts were far from teaching. The Second Symphony evolved out of a deep respect for and a hero worship of Albert Schweitzer, to whom it was dedicated. For Toch, he was a kindred soul, a physician-musician who disclaimed fame and fortune, ministering to the neediest of humanity. Toch sent the score, with an explanatory letter, to Schweitzer, whose reply indicates the closeness that developed between them.

> I was deeply moved that a creative composer felt urged to express my thoughts or better, the impression that my thoughts left, in a symphony.

. . . I repeatedly read your thoughts about "I won't let you be." How strange the coincidence: Even in my youth those words made a great impression on me, and in difficult situations I have often had recourse to them. . . . I don't know how to express to you what I feel towards you and about the symphony. If I had to say it in [a few words], I would say it meant great encouragement for me to be understood by you, a creative and deeply sensitive person. . . . And your music helps to prepare the way for the idea of respect for life and man. This is something entirely overwhelming for me.[32]

The first three symphonies can be considered a triptych, with mottoes taken from religious or spiritual sources. The First Symphony was prefaced with a motto from Martin Luther: "Although the world with devils filled should threaten to undo us, we will not fear, for God has willed his truth to triumph through us." The Second Symphony's motto was taken from the Old Testament (Gen. 32), the story of Jacob wrestling with the angel: "I will not let thee go except thou bless me." And the Third Symphony's motto was from Goethe's *The Sorrows of Young Werther:* "Indeed I am a wanderer, a pilgrim on earth—but are you anything more?" This last motto had special relevance to Toch himself, a "wanderer" and an émigré composer, and more broadly, to a whole generation of refugees from catastrophic world events.

The Third Symphony contains novel instrumentation that recalls Toch's earlier German experiments with mechanical instruments; as such, it is representative of the twentieth century's preoccupation with unusual tone colors. The orchestration of the Third Symphony calls for four temple blocks of differing pitches, a Hammond organ, a pipe organ, a glass harmonica, tuned glass bells to be struck by a soft mallet, and two sound-effect "instruments" to be placed backstage: the "hisser," a tank of carbon dioxide that hissed through a valve, and "cranks," which consisted of a wooden box in which croquet balls were set in motion by a rotating crank. The composer intended this battery of new percussion instruments to be introduced in the orchestra, not as an experiment, but as means of genuine artistic expression.

In its profusion of linear counterpoint and in its frequent shifting of meters and tonal centers, the Third Symphony contains many elements characteristic of the earlier concertos. However, this Pulitzer Prize winning symphony truly synthesizes the old and the new. Melodies built on fourths, sevenths, and ninths are prominent, but so are those that outline triadic harmony. What sometimes sounds like bitonality sometimes develops into almost functional harmony. Tone clusters abound, but so do open fifths and octaves. Romantic chromaticism coexists with linear counterpoint. Cross-rhythms and displaced accents are present in the same movement with folk-dance rhythms. Perhaps here, more than in any other work, the modern-sounding symphonist exists side by side with the postromantic tradition of Erich Korngold, Alexander von Zemlinsky, and Franz Schreker, complete with motto theme at the beginning.

The first three symphonies were given many performances in both Europe and the United States in the 1950s. The First Symphony, Op. 72, had its premiere with Herbert Haefner in Vienna in 1950, and then it was performed by the Concertgebouw Orchestra in Amsterdam under Otto Klemperer, the Cologne Radio Orchestra under Joseph Kielberth, and the Pittsburgh Symphony under William Steinberg. The Second Symphony, premiered at the Frankfurt International Music Festival, was later performed in Zurich by the Tonhalle Orchestra under Erich Schmid, the Boston Symphony under Charles Munch, the Northwest German Radio Orchestra, and the Los Angeles Philharmonic under Alfred Wallenstein in 1953. The Third Symphony, premiered by Steinberg, was also performed by the Royal Liverpool Philharmonic under John Pritchard and the Vienna Symphony under Massimo Freccia.

Between 1950 and 1955, the Tochs spent their time in Switzerland, Vienna, New York, and Los Angeles. They also made stops in the Chicago suburb of Glenview, Salt Lake City, the University of Utah at Provo, and the University of Oregon, where Toch served as Composer-in-Residence for one term.

However, Toch's frustrations with publishers and conductors continued, and this was not limited to America. During his first trip back to Europe, Toch had taken the score of his First Symphony to his former publisher, B. Schott, had shown it to their vice-president, Ludwig Strecker, and had received this response: "Aber Lieber Toch, jetzt müssen Sie etwas frescher schreiben." Roughly translated, what Mr. Strecker was telling Mr. Toch was:

> Now, dear Toch, now you have to write something with real nerve, you know, something with an affront to it.[33]

It is small wonder that Toch felt abandoned and understandably depressed, when he penned the following note to Schott: "I am now in my sixty-fourth year. I would like very much to live to see something from my life's work, and to experience the effect of my music around me."[34]

However, there was respite from such concerns, especially in Toch's most beloved temporary home, in Peterborough, New Hampshire, at the MacDowell Colony. In 1953, Marian MacDowell, aged ninety-seven, invited Toch to spend a summer at the colony. After his first week there, he proclaimed it the true paradise on earth. In his letters to his wife during his first summer there, he repeatedly expressed his profound gratitude for the colony as well as his amazement that such a perfect setting could be created and endowed for people like himself who needed solitude, with no practical demands made on them.

In 1953, Toch returned to Los Angeles and, at the invitation of the composer John Vincent, spent much of his composing time at the Huntington Hartford Foundation in Pacific Palisades in the hope of finding surroundings like those at the MacDowell Colony. However, the demands of family and friends on his creative energies made Toch restless. He longed for a more distant, quiet retreat—Switzerland, perhaps, or, if it could be arranged, the MacDowell Colony during the winters.

In the spring of 1954, the Tochs returned to Europe only for a short while, because an invitation from Aaron Copland for Toch to teach at the Berkshire Festival in Tanglewood called them back in August. In the fall, Toch became Visiting Lecturer at the University of Minnesota in Minneapolis, where Antal Dorati performed his First and Second Symphonies.

Continuing their gypsy life, the Tochs shuttled between the guest lectureships at American universities and colleges, Europe, returning home via New York City, Chicago, or Pittsburgh to visit friends or to negotiate with publishers.

Other than the three symphonies, the works composed during the early 1950s were the short chamber work for mezzo-soprano and four instruments *There is a Season for Everything,* commissioned by the Rothschild Foundation for Arts and Sciences in 1953; the cantatalike *Vanity of Vanities,* Op. 79, commissioned the same year by the University of Judaism, Los Angeles; the String Quartet No. 13, Op. 74, Toch's only excursion into quasi-twelve-tone composition, commissioned in 1953 by the Coleman Chamber Music Association of Pasadena; the *Circus Overture,* 1953, performed by André Kostelanetz in New York; the orchestral work *Notturno,* Op. 77, commissioned by the Louisville Symphony Orchestra and later recorded for their contemporary music series; and *Peter Pan,* Op. 76, subtitled "A Fairy Tale for Orchestra," commissioned by the Koussevitsky Foundation and premiered in Seattle, 1956, by Milton Katims.

The Tochs returned to Europe in February 1956. From Venice, where they visited Schönberg's daughter Nuria, to the Swiss Alps, from Zurich to Vienna, the Tochs searched for the perfect balance of seclusion and social contacts with friends. In Vienna on 8 May 1956, a telephone call informed them that the Third Symphony had been awarded the Pulitzer Prize!

Soon after the Pulitzer award was announced, the Third Symphony was performed in Vienna and was attended by Theodor Heuss, former president of the Federal Republic of Germany, Toch's friend and neighbor from the prewar days in Berlin. In Amsterdam, where the Third Symphony was also performed, Toch composed the piano pieces *Diversions,* Op. 78a, and Sonatinetta, Op. 78b, which were published by Leeds Music of New York. In London, the Tochs had several business meetings with representatives from Mills Music, negotiating for publishing advances and arranging for the English translation of *The Geographical Fugue.*

Back in Berlin, the Tochs began the long process of filing for the monetary reparations due them calculated on their Berlin house, the loss of a publisher, and the livelihood based on their pre-Hitler status in Germany. Reunion with friends in Zurich was the usual pattern of their European visits before they returned to New York. Having spent that winter at the MacDowell Colony, Toch went back to Los Angeles in the spring, again seeking refuge at the Huntington Hartford Foundation.

In the late 1950s, the Tochs settled down again in Santa Monica. Among their friends were the composer Mario Castelnuovo-Tedesco, Toch's former student Peter Jonas Korn, the musicologist Gerald Strang, the music lexicographer Nicolas Slonimsky, and the violinist Eudice Shapiro. Still remaining in the Los Angeles émigré community were Marta Feuchtwanger and Alma Mahler Werfel, whose daughter, Anna Mahler, sculpted a portrait bust of Toch in honor of his seventy-fifth birthday. Marta Feuchtwanger gave Toch a book by her husband Lion Feuchtwanger, containing a version of the Biblical story of Jephthah, thus inspiring Toch to compose *Jeptha — Rhapsodic Poem,* subtitled Symphony No. 5, Op. 89 (1959–1960).

One Los Angeles musician, Lester König, was significant in Toch's career in that he masterminded a recording project of modern composers for his new company, Contemporary Records.

In 1958, new recordings of Toch's works began.[35] The Contemporary series was of the string quartets, the Cello Concerto, the Piano Concerto No. 1, and the Quintet for Piano and Strings. Capitol Records released the Third Symphony, with the Pittsburgh Symphony under William Steinberg. Both the Louisville Series and Columbia expressed interest in future recordings. In 1958, too, Toch was elected as a member of the National Institute of Arts and Letters.

It may have been the stimulus of the recordings that brought Toch, in the summer of 1958, to Cologne to learn more about electronic music. Ever since the late-1920s and the Donaueschingen Festival on music for mechanical instruments, he had been fascinated by the possibilities of electronically produced tone colors. As early as 1932, during his *Pro Musica* tour in America, Toch had been interviewed on the subject of tone color as the art of the future:

> A new type of music consisting entirely of the interplay of varied tone colors is contemplated by Ernst Toch. With the aim of expanding the resources of the modern orchestra in the direction of timbre, Herr Toch has investigated the possibilities of various substances as materials for the construction of new instruments. . . . Pushing the idea to the extremes, it is conceivable that a work might be written in which both melody and harmony are totally absent. . . . The composer will have, in the field of timbre alone, sufficient material for all the elements of unity and contrast, which are necessary in the work of art.[36]

Curious about electronic music because he wanted to use it in the new opera he was then contemplating, Toch enrolled in a course in the electronic music laboratory at Columbia University in 1960. He did not, however, pursue beyond a few weeks the technical language and skills necessary to become proficient at composing electronic music.

Wishing to compose another opera, after a thirty-year hiatus, Toch began searching for a suitable libretto. His reputation as a composer of one-act operas was based on the success of *The Princess and the Pea,* Op. 43. His other one-act opera, *Egon und Emilie,* Op. 46, had been published in an English translation by Associated Music Publishers and had enjoyed occasional American performances. His third opera, *The Fan,* a three-act opera-capriccio incorporating jazz elements, had been performed only once, at the Deutsches Tonkünstlerfest in Königsburg, 1930, before the Nazi brownshirts interrupted Steinberg's rehearsal of it in Cologne in 1935.

In the spring of 1960, through his friend Feri Roth, Toch received a copy of a libretto to *Scheherazade,* which was an English translation of the Hungarian original by Melchior Lengyel. Despite the facts that the story was cumbersomely handled and that other readers were not satisfied with it, Toch was determined to use the libretto for his opera *The Last Tale,* Op. 88 (1962). Published by Mills Music and translated into German, this one-act opera, over ninety minutes in length, has yet to be performed. Aside from its sheer length, the reasons for its neglect may lie in its difficulty. Some unwieldy vocal leaps, pitted against competing dissonances in the orchestra (winds, brass, strings, percussion, harp, and celesta), are shown in this score with piano reduction.

Begun in April 1960, *The Last Tale* was not completed until August 1962. In that same period, Toch also composed short works for the piano: *Three Little Dances,* Op. 85; *Reflections,* Op. 86; and a Sonata for Four Hands, Op. 87; as well as two new chamber works: Five Pieces for Wind Instruments and Percussion, Op. 83, and Sonatinetta, Op. 84, for flute, clarinet, and a bassoon, which had its premiere in Los Angeles by Ingolf Dahl in the Monday Evening Concert Series. During this time Toch also completed the a cappella work for mixed chorus, *Song of Myself,* "I think I could turn and live with animals," from Walt Whitman's *Leaves of Grass.* The implied harmony is not overtly dissonant, as seen in the rehearsal-only piano part; the vocal parts, with the exception of the soloists, do not make excessive demands upon the performers; and the result is a quiet, reflective, almost self-portrait. (Musical Example 4.6.)

Toch was working on his opera when, in April of 1962, he received word that his son-in-law, Irving Weschler, had been killed in a car accident. The loss for Franzi and her four young children was profound, and this personal tragedy was not without adverse effects on Toch's health.

Other personal losses were the deaths of the violinist Julian Brodetsky, and of Toch's lifelong friend and physician, Hans Schiff. In the fall of 1962, Toch entered the hospital for a prostate operation, recovering just in time to accept his seventy-fifth birthday tributes in Los Angeles and New York.

On the committee for the University of Southern California cele-

Musical Example 4.6. *Song of Myself* (1961), mm. 1–5. Source: Original manuscript, Toch Archive.

bration were such notables as Jack Benny, Ingolf Dahl, Martha Feucht-wanger, Jascha Heifetz, Peter Jonas Korn, Gregor Piatigorsky, and Eudice Shapiro. Dahl, conducting the university orchestra, performed Toch's Fourth Symphony, and Heifetz and William Primrose performed the Divertimento for Violin and Viola, Op. 37, No. 2 (1926). Among other tributes, Toch received a Citation of Honor from the City of Los Angeles.

That same season, the Los Angeles Philharmonic, under a visiting conductor, performed Toch's *Comedy for Orchestra,* Op. 42 (1927), *Big Ben Variations,* Op. 62 (1932), and the Music for Orchestra and Baritone, Op. 60 (1931).

In New York, the birthday celebration took place at the Austrian Institute, arranged by friends Alvin Johnson, the Paul Klemperers, the Gustav Stolpers, and Lester Cowan and his wife, the composer Anne Rinnel.

In Zurich, the Cello Concerto, Op. 35 (1925), was recorded and programmed on Radio Zurich, as was the Fourth Symphony. In Vienna, Toch was decorated with the Austrian Cross of Honor for Art and Science, his second such European tribute, the other being the Grand Cross of the Order of Merit, which had been given to him by the Federal Republic of Germany in 1958.

Perhaps the most important event of his seventy-fifth year was the publication of the Toch Catalog of Works, a joint effort of Mills Music in New York and Berlin, MCA Music (Leeds) in New York, Associated Music Publishers in New York, and B. Schott Söhne, in Mainz, London, and New York.

In the last two years of his life, Toch composed to the exclusion of almost every other activity. His Fifth Symphony, *Jephta,* was awaiting its premiere by Leinsdorf in Boston (March 1964), when Toch was already at work on his Sixth Symphony.

Three other compositions were published in 1963, around the time he completed the Sixth Symphony, Op. 93. These were the Three Impromptus, Op. 90, for violin, viola, and cello solo, written for Gregor Piatigorsky's sixtieth birthday; the *Capriccio for Orchestra,* Op. 91, and the *Three Pantomimes for Orchestra,* Op. 92, written for Toch's friend Herbert Zipper, who had conducted performances of *The Princess and the Pea* in the Philippines. The third piece of that group, entitled "The Enamored Harlequin," published separately as Op. 94, by Mills Music, was completed in November 1963.

Returning to Zurich in the winter of 1964, Toch began work on his Seventh Symphony, Op. 95, which he finished in March of that year. In spite of serious health problems and a misdiagnosis in a Zurich hospital, Toch continued to work relentlessly. Oblivious to his physical discomforts, but perhaps realizing that his time was short, Toch completed the *Sinfonietta for String Orchestra,* Op. 96, in May, and the *Sinfonietta for Wind Orchestra,* Op. 97, shortly afterwards.

Back in Los Angeles, Toch completed what was to be his final work—a quartet, this time not for strings alone, but for Oboe, Clarinet, Bassoon, and Viola, Op. 98. It was as if he consciously chose to end his composing career as he had begun it, with a quartet.

In September, after he had fainted following his morning walk, Toch was admitted to a Los Angeles hospital. Still unaware that his digestive problems were in reality terminal stomach cancer, Toch continued to compose. In retrospect, Lilly Toch was grateful that the misdiagnosis in Zurich had allowed her husband the extra peace of mind in which to work as he did.

In his last few days, now relieved of the compulsion to compete against time, Toch again showed his tenderness toward his wife. Asking her to forgive his single-minded devotion to his art and any hardships it might have caused her, he wrote to her:

> Ich treibe nicht, ich werde getrieben.
> Ich schreibe nicht, ich werde geschrieben.
>
> I do not push, I am being pushed.
> I do not write, I am being written.[37]

And, having composed almost to the last moment of his life, Ernst Toch died on 1 October 1964, leaving next to his bed the unfinished sketch for his most beloved genre, a string quartet.

≡ 5

Toch the Teacher

≡≡≡ Tributes, Former Students, the Composer Speaks

Toch's reputation as a teacher did not begin with his work at the University of Southern California. On his teaching reputation in Germany, Paul Pisk observed that "his ever-growing success as a creative artist made it possible for him to move to Berlin in 1929, where he was active until 1932 as a composer, concert artist, and teacher of composition. Many students from ever so many countries came to Berlin to study with him, drawn by his reputation, which had spread abroad in Europe and America."[1]

Similarly, the Danish composer Vagn Holmboe (b. 1909), who had studied with Toch in Berlin, wrote the following tribute to his teacher:

> It is now two years since I was in Berlin and worked under you, but this short time is unforgettable to me—also it was a turning point for me. Since that time I have begun to look more deeply into things, and I realize that what went on then was not so much my own work, but also the humane and artistic personality of you, Dr. Toch. And I know also that not only did you mean so much to me, but also to all the others who came in contact with you. . . . I know that one can never thank a person such as you, but I wanted so much to thank you.[2]

In his review of the performance of Toch's Piano Concerto No. 1 with the Boston Symphony, the author-critic David Ewen paid further tribute to Toch the teacher in Europe: "As a teacher his importance can not be overestimated. A theoretician of prime scholarship, he has succeeded in clarifying the existing problems for the younger men who have turned to him for guidance. He has strengthened their artistic touch in pointing the way upon which they are to travel.[3]

The Russian born composer Nikolai Lopatnikoff (1903–1976) studied composition with Toch in Mannheim, 1921, and again in Berlin, between 1929–1933. A lifetime friend of Toch's, Lopatnikoff eulogized his teacher and mentor, saying that "ever since I became his pupil at the age of seventeen, my admiration for Toch the composer, the teacher and the man has grown continually. The world of music has lost one of its truly great creative spirits."[4]

Two other students of composition during Toch's German years should be mentioned, although their musical careers were not in the field of composing. Miss Suse Loeb and Mrs. Liesel Lehmann-Hamburger, both of whom were accomplished pianists, continued their friendship and correspondence with the Tochs after they had all come to America. About Miss Suse Loeb, who studied with Toch in both Mannheim and Berlin, Mrs. Toch wrote, "A very good pianist, musician, and devoted friend, she was one of the few who ever got also a few piano lessons."[5]

The fact that Toch was an esteemed and dedicated teacher before he came to America is of central importance to this study. Like that of his contemporaries Schönberg and Hindemith, Toch's European experience, as a teacher and author of a German textbook, gives substance and credence to his writings about teaching composition in America. More importantly, it was in part due to his European reputation as a teacher that Toch was invited by Alvin Johnson to teach at the New School for Social Research, thereby assuring him of employment, i.e., the coveted visa, for emigration in the fall of 1934.

Among the students that Toch taught at the New School or, privately, in his New York apartment, two have achieved considerable recognition: the composer-teacher Jeanne Behrend (b. 1911) and the film composer Alex North (b.1910). When Toch went to Hollywood, he encouraged North to send his compositions to him, which he did. North was full of praise for his long-distance teacher: "He was a beautiful man. He would comment on my music, correct things and send them back. It was a great help."[6]

The most impressive rostrum of former students comes from Toch's teaching years in California, where he was sought out by established composers, including composers for the films, by aspiring popular and classic composers, and by students at the University of Southern California. Among the established composers who sought his help were Douglas Moore (1893–1969), who studied with Toch in 1940 while both were writing for the films and who remarked of his teacher that "he was the only European composer who treated me on equal footing"; Mel Powell (b. 1923), who studied with Toch in the mid-1940s; and George Gershwin.[7]

In the fall of 1936 Gershwin wrote to his friend, the composer and music theorist Joseph Schillinger, "I've been considering doing some studying with either Schönberg or Toch." To which Schillinger replied that if "I were you, I would study with Schönberg AND with Toch. . . . I think it would be a good idea to work with Schönberg on four-part fugues and to let Toch supervise your symphonic compositions."[8]

Another illustrious Toch student is the composer-pianist-conductor André Previn (b. Berlin, 1929) who, as a youth in Los Angeles, studied with Toch and Mario Castelnuovo-Tedesco. Previn's family, after immigrating to America, had settled in California where his great uncle, Charles Previn, was the music director for Universal Studios in Hollywood. The young Previn sought Toch's help when he, himself, became an orchestrator for MGM studios. It is interesting to note that Previn's early musical career as a composer for the films began shortly after Toch decided to call it quits in Hollywood.

Several other distinguished composers, teachers, or performers studied with Toch in Los Angeles: Peter Jonas Korn (b. Berlin, 1922), who studied with Schönberg at UCLA in 1941, and with Toch and Hanns Eisler at USC in 1946–1947, and is currently professor of composition at the Richard Strauss Conservatory in Munich; Gerald Strang (b. 1908), who had been an assistant to Schönberg at UCLA and studied with Toch in the mid-forties, while completing his doctorate degree at USC, and was chairman of the music department at California State in Long Beach; Aurelia de la Vega (b.1925), who had also been a student of Schönberg before becoming a private student of Toch's in 1947–1948; Matthew Doran, who studied with Toch at USC from 1946–1948, and who is currently Professor of Music Theory and Composition at Mount Saint Mary's College, Los Angeles; and the late John Scott Trotter, former music director for "The Kraft Music Hall," who was a private student of Toch's during the late 1940s and early 1950s.

Among other composition students who worked with Toch in

California and who subsequently became well-known in the field of musicology, were Pauline Aldermann and Mantle Hood. Other former students include Larry Adler (b.1914), George Bassman (b. 1916), Jay Chernis (b. 1907), Robert Emmett Dolan (1906–1972), Hugo Friedhofer (1902–1981), Marlin Skiles (b. 1906), and Harry Sosnik (b. 1906).

What was it like to study with a famous teacher whose late-in-life conclusion seemed to be that "the teaching of music composition is futile?" As if anticipating such queries, former student Dr. Mantle Hood wrote the following tribute to his teacher:

> For about five years, beginning in late 1945, I had the privilege of studying with Ernst Toch. On occasion, when I was introduced as Toch's pupil to one or other professional composer or performer, the reaction was predictably one of admiration, great respect, sometimes even a hint of mystery and awe about this composer who quietly insisted that composition could not be taught. . . . Frequently I was asked what system he used, what techniques he espoused, what took place in the course of the lessons with a composer who maintained that composition could not be taught. . . . It was conceded that his style was highly individual. . . . What SYSTEM OF COMPOSITION? . . . I am not sure how many of my questioners were convinced when I tried to explain that these were not appropriate questions applied to the genius of a composer like Ernst Toch. . . . As a neophyte I used to ponder his occasional reminder, "Either you are a composer or you are not. All I can help evoke is what is already within you."[9]

In the fall of 1945 when Hood, a young jazz and popular performer-composer inquired of Toch, "Is it possible to study with you?" Toch quipped, "No." Hood pressed on, "Is there any possibility we can discuss it?" To which Toch replied, "No, I already have too many students now." A few hours later the phone rang and Lilly Toch said to Hood, "Bring whatever you wrote," and from that time on, Hood worked with Toch on a variety of serious or popular compositions, in sessions that sometimes lasted "the whole day."[10]

Hood recalls that Toch's "presence put [him] at ease at once." In the first lesson Toch inquired, "Who is your favorite composer?" and "How do you like Beethoven?" The first five lessons were in counterpoint and harmony, before progressing to orchestration, when Hood's assignment was to orchestrate the first movement of a Mozart piano sonata. When, on the sixth lesson, Hood showed the orchestration to Toch, the teacher's devastating reply was, "Too bad you can't hear how bad it is." At that point Toch announced, "So much for the academy," and from then on teacher and student tackled whatever Hood was working on at the time. Hood, lavish in his praise for his teacher, was also quick to point out that studying with Toch was "very humbling . . . he was always very honest, never offering great praise." When the Tochs announced to Hood, in 1949, that they were returning to Europe, Hood inquired of his teacher, "Will you think of someone with whom I can study?" to which Toch answered, "The man you must study with is YOU."[11]

Hood, like several other former students interviewed, believes that Toch's teaching was a major influence in his life; furthermore, he echoes the sentiment that *The Shaping Forces in Music* should be required reading for students who want to learn about musical composition.

Professor Matt Doran described Toch's teaching in this way:

Toch's greatness as a teacher stemmed from his unique ability and willingness to see everything that his students produced, from their point of view. Never forcing his own creative insights on the students who were expected to develop their own style and personality of writing, Toch permitted and encouraged his students, of greatly diverse background abilities, to write in a wide variety of idioms and tonal languages. Since the composition classes were always small, with never more than four or five students per hour, usually lasting two hours, however, Toch was able to supervise the development of each individual, whether he was writing a twelve-tone composition or a simple waltz. According to Toch, "it [was] better to write a good march than a bad symphony."[12]

According to Doran, Toch never pencilled any annotations or corrections on the students' scores. All criticisms were verbal, Toch usually asking such questions as, "Does this make sense? Where is everything going?" A composition was never analyzed without relating the specific details to the whole work.

The students were required to study the scores of Mozart, Bach, Beethoven, Brahms, Schubert, and Wagner, in particular. One semester, about 85 percent of Toch's illustrations came from Mozart's string quartets, operas, and symphonies, notably the *Jupiter,* the *Prague,* and the G Minor No. 40; another 10 percent of them were devoted to works by Brahms; and the remaining 5 percent came from early twentieth-century music, namely Stravinsky's *L'Histoire du Soldat* and Debussy's *Prélude à l'après-midi d'un faune.* Toch was convinced that a composer could learn everything he had to know from the study of Mozart and of Bach's *Well-Tempered Clavier.*

Doran recalls that Toch was an impressive pianist. In the classroom, he played his own piano renditions of excerpts from operas, his favorites being *Die Meistersinger* and *Così fan Tutte,* and he also performed Beethoven's piano sonatas with remarkable facility. As for his own compositions, Doran recalls he never played any in class, and he certainly "never even mentioned his films."[13]

John Scott Trotter, arranger and later conductor for the radio and TV show the "Kraft Music Hall," began his study with Toch after having considered both Schönberg and Mario Castelnuovo-Tedesco as possible teachers. Trotter decided on Toch, who at the time was writing film music. He felt that because "the other two (Schönberg and Castelnuovo-Tedesco) hated it" (teaching), he would try Toch, about whom he "never had that feeling."[14]

Although Trotter had no formal academic background in music, he found that Toch was the perfect teacher for him. Suggesting that Trotter expand his harmonic and melodic vocabulary beyond that of popular ballads, Toch showed him how to do so by composing three popular "Songs without Words." Both the freedom of harmonic movement and the unexpected changes in melodic direction in these pieces were remarkably similar to those in Toch's early piano works, such as the three *Burlesken,* Op. 31. Trotter claims that, with Toch's encouragement, he was able to develop a freedom he had never known before in his composing and arranging. And Trotter showed his appreciation to his teacher on the Kraft Music Hall programs when he conducted several of Toch's works, of which "The Marionette Dance" from *Die Bunte Suite* were favorites.

Trotter particularly respected Toch's ability to communicate with students whose ambitions and talents lay in popular music. One of Toch's favorite students, Trotter was a weekly dinner guest in the Toch home in Santa Monica for nearly ten years. Speculating on why he showed such a personal interest in Trotter, Lawrence Weschler, Toch's grandson, suggests that perhaps it was his ingratiating sense of humor and his extraordinary optimism, which Toch desperately needed at that time in his life.

When asked if Toch ever conveyed to Trotter his feeling of disillusionment with teaching, Trotter replied, "Absolutely not. I came to the conclusion, myself, that 'the teaching of music composition is futile,' but I was reluctant to give up the sessions — every Monday night."[15]

The composer Mel Powell — in Hollywood in 1947 to write for the films — studied with Toch before returning to the East Coast. His recollections about Toch the teacher, and, particularly, Toch the contemporary of Paul Hindemith, are of special interest:

> In 1948 I became a student of Hindemith, for which Ernst, among other things, had prepared me quite, quite beautifully. He had a lot to talk about Hindemith. . . . He was not possessive in that sense. We talked at length about Hindemith, and I can remember how his brow furrowed and said, "Well, you know, Hindemith is (and he didn't want to use the word) . . . he's a genius."[16]

Although not specifically referring to Toch's teaching, Powell told the story of Hindemith's respect for Toch. When his Yale class questioned him "Who, now, is a great composer?" Hindemith stunned the class with his reply, directed at Powell, "Well, your fellow Ernst Toch." Powell goes on to set the record straight that "Hindemith expressed great esteem for Toch as a composer."[17]

Pressed to compare his two teachers, Toch and Hindemith, Powell concluded that

> Ernst was, in short, a very warm and kind of concerned teacher, quite different . . . if you want to separate the technical and the aesthetic, he was more interested in the aesthetic. His whole personality and his whole mode of dealing with music and people was therefore extremely removed from Hindemith's posture.[18]

Discussing the presumed advantage of studying with two famous though very different teachers, Powell recalled how Peter Korn studied with both Schönberg and Toch. Upon suggesting to Schönberg that they proceed to more advanced studies, Korn got the following response: "I can't teach you unless you've had five years of counterpoint." Korn reported this to Toch whose immediate reply was, "I'm afraid I can not share Schönberg's opinion, and I know I never had five years of counterpoint, and I can assure you, he never had five years of counterpoint."[19]

Powell's observation about Toch's concern for his students correlates with other students' accounts of how their teacher gave so much of himself to his students. "A teacher who is more concerned with his students would be more drained by teaching, and perhaps that's why teaching became such a burden for him, and he just quit teaching in 1948."[20]

The Cuban-born composer Aurelia de la Vega described a similar commitment from his teacher. "Sometimes the lessons would last all day. I would arrive at the house at 10:00 A.M., work till noon, and proceed again from 2:00 to 5:00 P.M. . . . twice a month. He would never write in a solution, but ask, 'Where is this going?'"[21]

De la Vega recalls some of the scores he studied with Toch: string quartets and piano music of Max Reger, Berg's *Wozzeck* and his *Lyric Suite,* and chamber music of Hindemith, among others.

Composer Gerald Strang, a student of Toch's in 1948, commented upon Toch's major emphasis in teaching, saying that "compared to Schönberg, Toch had a greater articulateness and was willing to explain things many times. . . . But his concern was with general concepts and attitudes, and matters of aesthetics and philosophy."[22]

As regards Toch's later comments that "he quit teaching out of despair," Strang clarified that Toch's pessimistic proclamation, following his heart attack in 1948, was "not so much a reaction against teaching as an affirmative commitment to drop out of teaching."[23]

Toch really did go all out for his students. Perhaps no better testimony to this fact came from the composer-teacher himself: "Later on I was a fanatic teacher. Half of my students were very poor and did not pay me anything, and I gave them lessons although I never had lessons myself, but through my knowledge I expanded and expanded, and I loved to teach music."[24]

In that no examination of Toch the teacher is complete without consideration of his article "The Teaching of Music Composition is Futile" (*Musical Courier,* March 1954), Strang's statement is of crucial importance. In view of what the former students have confirmed here, one can only conclude that Toch did indeed care so much about teaching, or his students, that he gave tremendously of his time and of himself. There had to be a stopping place, sometime, and it is in this light that Toch's pronouncements and subsequent self-defense should be considered.

The original article had been the result of an interview by music critic Albert Goldberg for the *Los Angeles Times.* In the interview, Toch observed that Beethoven, who sought instruction from Haydn and Albrechtsberger, would have become a great composer regardless of what any teacher might have taught him. "He who is destined to be a composer will be one in spite of what he is taught. Bartók never gave a lesson in composition—only piano."[25]

The particular discussion then developed into a philosophical generalization:

> The only teacher to study composition with, if you have everything else, is life. Of course every musician has to know his language, just as a poet must know grammar. A musician must study elementary theory, but composition is something different. . . . When I was in Europe every interview started with, "With whom did you study?" Would anyone think to ask with whom a poet studied? . . . I tell them I had the good fortune to study with Mozart. . . . Once the parents of a student came to me and asked, "How long will he have to study?" And I replied, "How do I know how long he will live?"[26]

In June 1954, the *Musical Courier* published Toch's clarifications of what he had meant in the article:

> My striving as a teacher was passionate and sincere. I had a number of passionate, sincere, and gifted students; some of them may have felt that I helped them along, some of them were grateful. But in the end I came to see that you cannot make a composer out of somebody who would not be a composer without you. Or, as Schönberg put it, *"Lernen kann man nur was man schon kann"* (You can learn only what you already know).[27]

In an unpublished article, "Finale," Toch elaborated more positively on his attitudes toward teaching composition. "One of my colleagues referred to Hindemith as having said all composers should teach—I go even further: only composers should teach—if this were at all possible. At least this method might lead us closer to the aspired goal of educating not virtuosos but musicians."[28]

In another unpublished article, "About the Teaching of Music Theory," Toch questioned the university's traditional practice of separating the discipline of music theory from its closely related subjects, arguing that

> knowledge of what we call "Theory of Music" belongs indispensably to all kinds of musical practice, be it singing, playing any instrument, conducting, etc. It should therefore be taught together with any "practical" music instruction, from the very beginning and not only later; and should be considered an integral part of any music tuition, not a subsidiary branch of it. . . . Training of fingers or throat without parallel tuition in so-called "musical theory" equals training of the tongue alone in a

foreign language without minding at all the meanings of its words and sentences. I say "so called" because I object to the term "theory" which in reality stands for the very core and essence of music and musical knowledge.[29]

In an unpublished article entitled "Blueprint for a Demonstration Method of Teaching Instrumentation," Toch took issue with the traditional textbook approach, and proceeded to outline his own subheadings: "The Parade of Instruments, the Society of Instruments, 'Feathers Make Birds,' and 'The Fluoroscope.' " In essence, his point of departure from traditional teaching was that

> you cannot describe colors — red, white, blue — you can only SHOW them. Likewise you cannot describe tone-colors to a music student, you have to let him HEAR them. Books on instrumentation try to describe tone colors by all kinds of insufficient comparisons, then they give quotations of master scores . . . but they never can show the results themselves, namely the actual sound. . . . A book on tone painting (instrumentation) should contain the tone-color prints . . . with gramophone records . . . the records would be a resource of information and reference in matters of instrumental sound, like a dictionary in matters of language.[30]

The Two Textbooks

Perhaps more important than these remarks from the composer and his former students in understanding Toch the teacher are his two books, *The Shaping Forces in Music* and *Die Melodielehre*. Both books seek to clarify for the composer and student the forces at work in music composition. Because the emphasis in this study is on Toch's contribution as a teacher of, and a writer for, American students, his American textbook will be considered before his earlier German one.

In his article "America's Influence on Émigré Composers," Ernst Krenek discussed the problems that confronted the exiled composers as they tried to establish careers in the United States.

> For men like Hindemith and Schönberg, there was nothing new about this experience [teaching], but for many others, a teaching position meant a way of living that was still untried. In general, the teaching composer was left to determine his aesthetic principles. . . . Yet more often than not, he was made to realize that his pedagogical effectiveness was viewed with distrust if the teaching was overly progressive.[31]

Although not mentioning Toch specifically in the category of veteran teachers, Krenek's observations describe the kind of situation under which *The Shaping Forces in Music* (1948) was created. The remarkable thing is that Toch, left to determine his aesthetic principles, succeeded in writing a book that is accessible to all music lovers.

As to how and why the book came to be written, the composer himself talks about its genesis in a letter to Mrs. Coolidge.

> It is my work that keeps me in not too happy a mood. I started a book, in fact long ago. Alongside the widespread interest for music goes so much misconception in matters of music. It is brought home to me every day and reluctantly as I teach, because it wears me out and completely saps my energy, I feel that what those tormentous procedures with my students accumulate in me, should not be lost and should at least benefit others.[32]

In Toch's *The Shaping Forces in Music* and in *Die Melodielehre,* there is a quality of timelessness, not unlike that which Hindemith and Schönberg embrace in their textbooks, seeking to merge the traditional with the new. As different as he was from Hindemith and Schönberg in musical composition, Toch, in his pedagogical principles, was remarkably similar to his more renowned colleagues. In general, the textbooks of Toch, Hindemith, and Schönberg exhibit two distinct themes, each having two distinct parts:

> 1. Homage to Tradition (backward looking) vs. New Modes of Musical Expression (forward looking)

> 2. Philosophical/Abstract Thought (Old World) vs. Practical Solutions (New World pragmatism or "how to")

In *The Cultural Migration* (1953), Franz Neumann explained how such integration of thought came about.

> The German intellectual exile, bred in the veneration of theory and history, and contempt for empiricism and pragmatism, entered a diametrically opposed intellectual climate: optimistic, empirically oriented, a historical, but also self-righteous. . . . In Germany, the universities considered themselves to be training ground for an elite. . . . The American universities were examples of a democratic educational principle — participation of the largest possible number of its citizens. . . . The impact of these differences can have the following effects: (1) the exiled scholar may abandon his previous intellectual position, and accept the new orientation, (2) he retains his old pattern, then withdraws with dis-

dain and contempt into his own island, and (3) he may attempt to integrate the new experience with the old tradition—the most difficult, but most rewarding choice.[33]

Most of the exiled composers exhibit the third choice in their teachings and writings. Although Hindemith's and Schönberg's books are well-known and still in use today, Toch's two books also present a compelling synthesis of the old and the new, representing a remarkable contribution to the teaching of music.

Toch directs his American book, *The Shaping Forces in Music,* to both students and appreciators of music.

> This book contains a compilation of observations and ideas which have accumulated through years of experience as a composer and teacher. It attempts to bring out and emphasize the timeless and permanent features of music, as against the time-bound, transient ones. In so doing, it attempts to reconcile the at-times "classical" with the at-times "modern" . . . it is intended for those who may have gone through a certain amount of elementary music theory, say fundamentals of traditional harmony as they are commonly taught, and may find themselves at odds with prevailing traits of that music which does not correspond to this knowledge. . . . It concentrates on material not incorporated in the current textbooks. . . . It is also intended for music lovers who desire to attain an "appreciation of music," at large . . . and for practical musicians and amateurs who are aware of the incompleteness of their musical upbringing, when confronted with a more progressive type of music.[34]

It is possible to enjoy Toch's book, like Hindemith's *A Composer's World,* with minimal knowledge of music. Toch repeatedly asserts that he is not an analyzer, but an observer and a generalist. While paying homage to tradition, he also reaches toward twentieth-century forms of expression.

Perhaps the most poignant of all the reviews of *The Shaping Forces in Music* came from Thomas Mann, a close friend of the composer, when he wrote:

> Beyond any question *The Shaping Forces* is the most lovable presentation of musical phenomena that ever came to my knowledge . . . not chatting about the problems from the outside, but elucidating them from within; it is refreshing indeed, simplifying, and at the same time stimulating—productive as I rarely, or never, saw a theoretical work, because what it gives is basically no theory, but the encouragingly practical findings of a creative artist.[35]

Divided into four main sections devoted to Harmony, Melody, Counterpoint, and Form, the book consists of twelve chapters in which Toch develops his ideas on these concepts, with a final chapter called "Beginning and Ending."

The Harmony section opens with the famous quotation from the Greek philosopher Heraclitus: "Everything is in flux." Toch is concerned with the "function" of the chord, observing that "the functional significance of the chord recedes in the same measure as composition withdraws from the key-bound tone-center, until, in completely atonal music, the chord-function practically vanishes to zero as compared with the harmony function."[36]

Related to chord function is the concept of melodic or harmonic motion, and Toch discusses the interrelationships of the elements of harmony and melody:

> It is not enough to know that in the course of musical progression each tone asserts its membership in the harmony in which it is embedded as well as in the melodic line of which it is part. The truth is that the melodic impulse is primary, and always preponderates over the harmonic; that is, the melodic or linear impulse is the force out of which germinates not only harmony but also counterpoint and form. For the linear impulse is activated by motion, and motion means life, creation, propagation, and formation.[37]

The other key word that Toch used in his discussions of harmony is "streams." Citing examples from late nineteenth and early twentieth century music (Strauss's *Der Rosenkavalier,* Stravinsky's *The Firebird,* and Prokofieff's *Sarcasmes*), he clarifies his use of the term writing that

> it would obviously be absurd to relate what goes on in moving chords of the upper register to the harmonies sustained in the lower register. The latter form a sound-community united by one idea, or one harmonic will; the chord group fleetingly drifting above it another community, united by another idea or harmonic will. . . . In actual composition independent streams may partly or wholly be reduced to lines. In other words, harmonies may combine with harmonies, or harmonies may combine with lines, or lines may combine with lines.[38]

According to Toch, the terms *streams* and *motion* should replace the too technical and restrictive language of textbooks that attempt to label each nonharmonic tone. His admonition, "Beware of restraining the harmony phenomenon in a prison of mathematical symbols," may be applied not only to harmony but to all elements of music. He concludes the Harmony section with this statement: "We must never lose sight of the more important fact that harmony itself is but the casual, incidental image of arrested motion, of ever-fluctuating situation, ever-changing meaning and effect."[39]

Many of the ideas in the section on Melody are taken from Toch's earlier book, *Die Melodielehre* (1923). In the late 1940s, however, his treatment of melody appears increasingly concerned with the role of inspiration.

> Would an attempt to treat melody in a technical way be a presumption? Melody—the very essence of divine inspiration, bestowed upon chosen master-minds by the grace of God. . . . Certainly melody is a matter of inspiration. But so, no more or less, is harmony . . . nor is counterpoint, nor is form, nor is any artistic skill in any artistic field detachable from inspiration.[40]

In relating the concept of counterpoint to the element of form, Toch suggested that the latter is dependent upon the former because

> at the bottom of this feature lies the principle that any quality is apt to weaken and to lose its effect after a while; and the best preventive for that is an off-setting and reanimating intermission. This observation touches upon the basic "tension-relaxation" principle of form. . . . However, this is not the only point which links counterpoint with form, in fact makes counterpoint a powerful functional agent of form.[41]

For him, the link of counterpoint to form presupposes the recognition of two different kinds of counterpoint: the imitative and the fermentative. Distinguishing between the two, Toch writes that

> the first type is principally based on close thematic or motivic unity of the opposing voices, while the other type does not keep to such unity but either slackens it or drops it altogether. The first kind . . . covering the epoch of polyphonic writing which climaxes in canon and fugue . . . has predominantly ornamental function; ornamental in a broad sense, as an architectural designation. . . . The other type . . . favors a function which we may describe as "stirring."

> Fermentative counterpoint escapes the danger of pedantry to a great extent by being based on continuous free inventive creation, which shields the composer from the traps of technicalities. . . . The real originator and great professor of fermentative counterpoint is Richard Wagner.[42]

The last section, on Form, bears this quotation from Jack London's novel *The Sea Wolf,* which echoes the earlier epigraph from Heraclitus: "The very essence of life is movement."

For Toch, form in music is comparable to architecture in the visual arts, the difference being that architecture unfolds in the medium of space, and music in the medium of time. Form, or musical architecture, has two basic properties that do not exist independently: time and the periodic alternation of contrast.

In the chapter "The Art of Joining," Toch defines musical transitions as joints: "The smooth operation of the transition is threefoldly ensured. In the perfection of the joint we feel the skill of the joiner. . . . In putting together the proper parts in a proper way, he becomes the composer."[43]

In his final observations on form, Toch defends his use of the terminology he has coined, which might be considered inappropriate for a textbook dealing with music theory:

> The formative principles shown at work are not bound to any particular style of epoch or idiom. Even where tonality and key have a bearing, for instance in the relation of tension and attraction between secondary steps and tonic, it is the unchangeable effect which is aimed at, not the changeable and constantly changing means.[44]

Describing musical climax as an inevitable function of form, completely under the composer's control, Toch concludes the book with these remarks:

> In any narrative — epic, dramatic or musical — every word or tone should be like a soldier marching towards the one common, final goal: The conquest of the material. The way the artist makes every phrase of his story such a soldier, serving to unfold it, to support its structure and development, to build plot and counterplot, to distribute light and shade, to point incessantly and lead up gradually to the climax, in short the way every fragment is impregnated with its mission towards the whole, makes up this delicate and so essential objective which we call form.[45]

An interesting feature of the book is the wide range of composers whom Toch cites, representing virtually every period and style in music history, from Albéniz to Vaughan Williams and Tcherepnin, and including, in addition to such masters as Bach, Mozart, Beethoven, and Brahms, a considerable number of less familiar figures from all eras, among whom are Cannabich, Hassler, Krebs, and Kuhnau.

Equally impressive in the scope of its musical examples, and re-flecting Toch's eclecticism, is the list of composers' names appearing in his first book, *Die Melodielehre:* Busoni, Dittersdorf, Korngold, Pfitzner, Cyril Scott, and Wagner, among many others, testifying to Toch's lifelong preoccupation with a variety of styles and musical expression.

Toch's American textbook, like those of Schönberg and Hindemith, is the product of a large mind that not only helped to shape the musical thinking of American students and concert goers but also contributed to the process of synthesis in American musical life. For what Toch's writings have conveyed is a sense of timelessness that does not fluctuate with the public's musical taste.

■■■ *Die Melodielehre*

Although there are many music theory books containing chapters on melody and melodic development, as well as classic texts dealing with modern harmony, there exists, to my knowledge, no other book written in the first quarter of the twentieth century exclusively on the phenomenon of melody, not even in the publications of Schenker. The material for *Die Melodielehre* stems from his first experience as a teacher, in 1913, at the Musik Hochschule in Mannheim.

In the Preface, Toch gives his reasons for undertaking a comprehensive study of melody from earliest times up to and including the early twentieth century:

> Riemann, Bussler, Jadassohn, Leichtentritt, and others have battled with the question of studying melody, by assigning it its own particular modest place in the all inclusive treatises on form. But Riemann himself states in his *Musiklexikon* that he regrets the lack of a systematic treatise on the subject of melody. The book which, in the meantime, has appeared, by the Bern musicologist Ernst Kurth *(Grundlagen des linearen Kontrapunkts)* concerns itself in fruitful ways with the examination of linear tone phenomena, but only scratches the surface in these areas, as his book is mainly a style-critic of Bach's works. Also, this little work cannot fill the missing link, but may and will try to inspire a further examination of melody and harmony.[46]

The contents are arranged in eight chapters on melody. In the Introduction, Toch describes basic acoustic principles and the relative differences among the five senses, the highest in importance being sight and hearing; and characteristics of hearing are interpreted musically through intervallic relationships.

> First there is the simplest form of visual impression, the line. It is the simplest because it is an expression of a one-dimensional expansion. Anything other than a one-dimensional expansion offers the eye an impression of area and solidness. The line impression is differentiated from area and solids by the bare eye. Actually, the picture our eye receives is not a line, but an area. It is only possible for us to differentiate areas and solids by automatically connecting practical experience with touch. Without this habit of connecting [things], it would not be possible for us to realize that we are in a two-dimensional mirror, three-dimensional thing, a body. It has repeatedly been observed that persons born blind and later healed through an operation needed a long time to differentiate between a circle and a ball, since they had to learn the combination of touch and vision. In addition to the line and area impression, is the color impression. The equality of the "face impression" is extremely different; it is not connected with any expansion-terms.[47]

Concluding the Introduction, Toch restates his conviction that twentieth-century musicians must develop a more direct sensitivity to linear counterpoint, that is, melody. Much has been written on harmony, he says, on how melody, or the horizontal, and harmony, the vertical, are intertwined. Perhaps the reason no one has written on the subject of the linear is that it is so flexible, but so "natural." Yet it really is not difficult to write about.

> Up to now, the investigation of acoustic phenomena of harmony has taken up the largest space in the theoretical disciplines of music. Instrumentation deals with the color phenomena, while the subject of counterpoint is the mutual penetration of line and plane, the linear motion of sound under the always alert control of harmony. Only the nature of the truly linear sound phenomena (i.e., of pure melody) has not yet received a comprehensive description, although it will seem to me that this subject, by its nature, quite readily lends itself to such a description.[48]

The list of musical examples in 1923 reflects the transitional nature of the era—away from blatant nineteenth-century romanticism to twentieth-century styles, by way of postromantic composers, who were then very much in vogue, such as Bruckner, Busoni, Hindemith, Iwan Knorr, Korngold, Mahler, Pfitzner, Reger, Schönberg, and Richard Strauss.

After World War I, there was renewed emphasis on linear counterpoint and sheer melodic events. That Toch foresaw these trends when
he first wrote *Die Melodielehre* in 1913, just two years after Schönberg's
Harmonielehre and four years before Ernst Kurth's *Grundlagen des linearen Kontrapunkts,* is remarkable.[49]

Comparing Toch's two books, one notes that in the second work,
subtitled *An Inquiry into the Nature of Harmony, Melody, Counterpoint, and Form,* the subject of rhythm receives no special attention,
while in the earlier work, rhythm merits its own separate chapter. It
could be that in the intervening twenty-five years Toch came to regard
rhythm as inseparable from melody and harmony.

In general, Toch's method of inquiry and discussion in *Die Melodielehre* is to start with the larger concept and then move to the smaller
proof, whereas *The Shaping Forces in Music* proceeds from the smaller
ideas to the larger conclusions. Although both books are dependent
upon the musical examples, the 1923 volume has a greater profusion of
them, perhaps on the assumption that the German reader is more of an
expert in music. On the other hand, perhaps indicative of the new
American readership and the less sophisticated students for which the
second book was written, *The Shaping Forces in Music* can be understood by amateurs, but *Die Melodielehre* cannot.

In his book *Musical Form,* Hugo Leichtentritt referred to *Die
Melodielehre* in considering textbooks dealing with specific musical elements:

> A useful help in the study of melodic structure may be found in a little
> book by Ernst Toch, *Die Melodielehre.* . . . All good melodies, whether
> antique, medieval, or modern in origin, whether . . . Italian or German
> obey the same laws of logical structure. Their form, proportions, sub-
> division, melodic outline, accents, rhythm, etc., are subject to a few
> rather simple axioms formulated in these basic theories of melody.[50]

It was with considerable disillusionment that I discovered a letter
in the Toch Archives, from the New York publisher W. W. Norton & Co.,
refusing to accept *Die Melodielehre* for translation and publication:
"The view of our advisors is that the translation for appearance say in
1945 of a book written in 1922, unless it is an absolute classic in the field,
is not good publishing for our house at this time."[51]

Norton's mistake was in not recognizing *Die Melodielehre* as an absolute classic in its field. This mistake was more regrettable because in 1945 there were, to my knowledge, no books in English in the United States dealing exclusively with melodic phenomena.

Toch, in *Die Melodielehre,* has made a unique contribution to music theory as well as aesthetics in general. As such, it is an invaluable source of musical thought in the first quarter of this century, besides providing insights into Toch's early convictions as composer, teacher, and aesthetician. To this day, this book remains untranslated, to the detriment of all.

=6
Musical Aesthetics and Life

Two years after his death, Toch's essay "Some Thoughts out of Season" was published in the journal of the Music Library Association. At the bottom of the first page, in the smallest of print, was this revealing postscript: "This essay was found among the literary papers left by the composer who was celebrated for his speculative thinking."[1]

The kinds of literary papers that were left by the composer and the type of speculative thinking they represent are varied and complicated, like the man himself. However, the published and unpublished articles, essays, and speeches to which this postscript refers, and which are considered in this chapter, can be divided into three general categories: (1) the practical, offering advice or opinions on specific music topics, such as "The Situation of the Composer in the United States Today"; (2) the musical aesthetic, defending or taking to task "modern music," defining *his* position, "The Credo of a Composer" in the maze of twentieth-century "ism's"; and (3) the timeless, the philosophical, relating music to times past and present, "A Link in the Chain," and/or proclaiming a spiritual genesis behind creation and inspiration.

The writings in the first category are typical of any twentieth-century composer struggling for recognition in America. However, Toch, in characteristic *bei uns* fashion, cannot help comparing the American situation with the idealistic situation in the Germany he had left. The writings in the second group could be viewed as a defending of one's turf, as mid-twentieth-century composers struggled to define their art, their goals, and to wrestle with the questions of communication—to which audiences, for which purposes? The writings in the third category represent the man who, throughout his life, was preoccupied with philosophy and great literature. As has been observed, several of his symphonies bear philosophical, even biblical, inscriptions, and much of his vocal music is set to texts from revered poets and philosophers or to religious texts. These are largely representative of the composer-philosopher in his later years.

Whatever their subject matter, Toch's essays and articles represent a significant contribution to twentieth-century musical aesthetics. Nevertheless, a study of Toch's writings is not without its difficulties, and, as such, has never really been addressed.[2] It is precisely because Toch is *not* generally known for his speculative thinking (with the exception of his American textbook) that these brief summaries are included here.

One of the problems of interpreting Toch's writings is his often old-fashioned mode of expression. He had studied Schiller, Goethe, Kant, and Nietzsche, among others, before entering medical school, where he learned to reason systematically about natural phenomena. The result of this combination of influences is a writing style often as eloquent as that of any German writer of the postromantic period.

Because this study focuses on Toch's contribution to, and influence on, musical America, his American writings are considered first and his German ones second. This placing is not, however, meant to minimize the German writings' overall importance. They are representative of that remarkable decade in European twentieth-century music, when new music did have its day, and when experiments in electronic music, music for the stage, radio, or films made the headlines. Articles such as "The Transitional Character of the Present Music," or "Music for the Stage" may indeed be worthy documentaries, but they are difficult to translate. Furthermore, the long, drawn-out sentences, complete with analogies and references to art and life, often appear more abstract than his American writings. Because of their complexity, Toch's German articles are summarized in the form of short commentaries at the conclusion of this chapter.[3]

Although his American writings are more accessible than his German ones, Toch's exact and deliberate choice of verb, noun, adjective, metaphor, or simile produces a style of writing as distinctive as his style of musical composition. His careful writing becomes apparent when the original drafts and copies of his articles, essays, and speeches are examined. To enlarge and improve his vocabulary, from 1933 to the year of his death, Toch compiled hundreds of pages of dictionaries in which he entered every new English word he learned with appropriate German synonyms!

In the first category of practical writings are two articles written in the 1950s, a time when Toch was becoming increasingly disillusioned with the publication and performance of his music. The later essay, which remains unpublished, is entitled "Comparative Points in European and American Music Development." Here he not only voices his discontent with the practical side of being a composer but also laments the status of twentieth-century music in general. Toch noted how "the tradition" developed and spread in premechanized Europe.

> Music in Europe developed and spread at a time when there was very negligible concert life, when there was no radio, no gramophone, no music machinery whatsoever. Whoever was attracted to music had to go into music making himself, into singing, playing, chamber music playing, group music making of all kinds. This brought about a wide and active participation in music by non-professionals obsessed with the passion for music. The great works that were loved were approached, tackled by amateurs who in so doing, gained by hearing music twenty-four hours a day.[4]

America, however, regardless of its top caliber professional orchestras and music institutions, had been denied, according to Toch, the phase of "playful, serious, ardent music making" that Europe had enjoyed for centuries. Naive, and revealing a *bei uns* attitude, his arguments betray an apparent ignorance of American music history and of the existence of the many amateur performance groups that were active in the past and in his own time. His appreciation of high school and college orchestras and ensembles is limited to discussing their low qualities of performance, as compared with more accomplished amateur chamber groups in Europe. Predictably, Toch also deplored the use of tape recorders and recorded music used as substitute for participation in live musicmaking.

Regarding the role of government in supporting or encouraging the art of music, Toch described the situation as it existed in Germany, where there were state-owned radio stations and departments of art education.

This concept (music as public domain) has far-reaching implications. It was already in existence when broadcasting started and the European states took over the administration of the radio stations, making standards for music an essential part of the daily program. They give a chance to the young composers and performers of their countries and do not confine themselves to the music available on commercial recordings.[5]

Suggesting that the United States lacked an official consciousness in fostering the arts and in helping the composer, Toch continued, writing that

most European governments have departments of education in matters pertaining to art. These departments are entrusted with the organization of universities, schools, and conservatories. Subventions to orchestras and operas are traditionally granted on a large scale. All this accomplishes a certain unity of direction and purpose, a naturally organizing set of standards. . . . You may like it better or like it less. It is not only in music that America has gone a different way of evolution, regarding most of its institutions. There would be no possibility just to carry over one way or the other. We have to examine our 'Voraussetzungen' (suppositions, assumptions) and to start working from there.[6]

In answer to a letter from his friend Hermann Scherchen requesting him to elaborate on the differences between musical life in America and Europe, Toch wrote a seven-page description of other problems facing the composer in the United States.

Toch observed that in the United States few composers can earn a living from their compositions alone. A composer must also be a teacher or a critic, or practice another profession or craft; and he must accept these conditions and the problems they create. Comparing the American music public, or music consumers, to European concert-goers, Toch believed that because the music profession in America existed without dependence upon twentieth-century music or its composers, the listening public or consumers did not exert the influence they might have in fostering new music and artists.[7] Of course in the area of public acceptance of new music, regardless of nationality, the public has always kept slower pace with new developments than the creators themselves.

For Toch, the most serious challenge to the American composer was finding and keeping a publisher. In his article "The Situation of the Composer in the U.S.A.," Toch again made comparisons with Europe.

The publishing business functions very unfavorably for the composer in America. The American publisher is first of all a businessman, and as such wants to sell his goods quickly and profitably. European publishers, on the other hand, have realized in the course of their long experience that current commercial considerations are inappropriate in music publishing and should not be applied to this particular kind of merchandise. Such an understanding of the cultural mission of the publisher is generally not to be found in America.[8]

Toch, first a member of ASCAP (American Society for Composers, Authors, and Publishers) and then of BMI (Broadcast Music Incorporated), did have the majority of his American works published in the United States, but because many contracts were never renewed, a number of his scores became unavailable a few years after their publication.

In view of the above comments, Toch's later remark about being "the most forgotten composer" appears to have a more practical basis. Within this context, he probably considered himself to be a victim of the times and of what seemed to him to be America's artistic insensitivity.

In the area of debating and defining aesthetic theories and principles in twentieth-century music (category two), Toch was especially vocal. Writing in the late 1940s, the 1950s, and early 1960s, at a time when modern composers were facing a "credibility gap" with their audiences, Toch's "stating his case" frequently developed into what might appear today like full-blown romanticism within twentieth-century strictures.

Disagreeing with the thesis that art is a reflection of the times in which it is produced, Toch opposed the assumption that much of twentieth-century music is necessarily contrived because such is the spirit of our age. He argued that "good art never focuses on the vessel but on its contents. It is the contents, not the vessel, that the real artist is struggling for, suffering for. The composer of former times whose primary concern was to be adjusted to the then 'modern' style was just as unfit to create good music as the composer of today whose primary concern is to be adjusted to the now prevailing style."[9]

Toch expressed occasional dissatisfaction with much twentieth-century music written before the mid-1950s; it seemed to stress intellect over inspiration. He was dissatisfied with any kind of uninspired music, particularly twelve-tone composition, believing that "the timely music of our day places its emphasis on formalistic and structural elements. Sets of laws are developed for their operation. Argument and logical deduction are now the valid measure. Whatever, in spite of the atomic age, may have remained common fibre in man's nature — common ground between yesterday and today—is being by-passed. Influx from emotional, unconscious sources is sifted to the minimum."[10]

It might be noted that as early as 1929 Toch had voiced his discontent with the twelve-tone composers in Vienna: "I personally believe that we live in an extraordinary and terrible period of music production. Vienna will not be able to stop the things that are now going on."[11]

Writing in 1945, and expanding his views on the essentials of good music, Toch expressed his reservations about the power of much twentieth-century music to elicit emotional responses from its listeners.

> Disliked as true art may have been by the masses at the time of its creation, the passing of several decades has, so far, always been enough to make it liked and even loved generally. Have we witnessed the same process of slow but steady growth in sincere response and passionate abandon that former generations experienced with their music, though they resisted violently at first? There is no lack of esteem for contemporary music, but the signs of love, or irresistible love seem to be missing.[12]

Toch rejected the idea that the musical vocabulary of atonality was responsible for this lack of irresistible love, arguing that

> there is a prevailing inclination to blame atonality for that phenomenon. This accusation must be rejected. The development into the musical idiom of today was natural, logical, and inevitable. It means no destruction of the old, but an extension of it. Like the English, Spanish, or any other language of today, it constitutes a modern form of expression. As such it can have as little bearing on content as these languages may have on any content expressed by them. If [the] music of our century has, so far, failed to compel general devotion, as in the past, the reason for it should not be sought in technicalities. They most probably lie in the spiritual sphere.[13]

And he devoted considerable attention to the evolution of public opinion.

> To pinpoint the issue, let us concentrate solely on absolute music, which is to say music not joined by words, drama, or any form of extraneous content. . . . It can not be "tested" except by spontaneous, individual reaction. Eventually some consensus tends to form on the merits of a musical work, and in due course it is either rejected or incorporated by affirmation into the common domain. In view of the irrational nature of music, such acceptance has significant meaning.[14]

Toch also rejected the notion that familiarity with modern music develops appreciation of it. "The opinion prevails that music only has a chance to be understood after repeated hearings, and therefore we must not at once reject something that sounds ugly or beyond our grasp. Mahler once said: 'Art is what displeases.' But that does not mean that what displeases is necessarily art . . . . Puccini and Chopin appealed instantly to their audiences . . . . What is good is bound to become better. What is bad gets worse and worse."[15]

In spite of his sometimes negative judgments on much twentieth-century music, Toch believed that people should listen to more of it. As early as his *Pro Musica* tour in 1932, he was urging American audiences to open their ears to modern music.

> You must hear without always wanting to compare with the musical basis you already have . . . . You must imagine that you inherited from your ancestors different compartments, just as you have inherited any other physical or intellectual qualities. . . . When music for which you have no prepared compartments strikes your ear . . . it does not fit, you blame it on the music. But in reality you are to blame because you force the music into the compartment which it does not fit . . . . And this is only possible when you expose yourself again and again to this new music without always wanting to compare it with the old, in fact without wanting anything at all.[16]

Realizing that the general public finds the new music often difficult to understand, Toch described the complex role of listeners, who in the end decide what they do and do not like. In his radio speeches, which were frequently music appreciation lectures, Toch offered the listener a new rationale for listening.

> As with any organism, life is inseparably bound up with continuation— while continuation, in turn, is identified with progressive evolution and constant renewal. If this seems to overemphasize the matter in its function and importance, let me appeal to your imagination: Suppose that at any one time music lovers had decided that there was enough great music to enjoy, and that nothing new needed a hearing. We would have had no Wagner, no Brahms, no Tchaikovsky, no Debussy—to speak only of some great favorites. Say that the same had happened fifty years ago . . . with equally great losses![17]

Continuing his plea that the general public should not be satisfied with repeated performances of the traditional masterpieces, Toch compared the new music to new works in other arts.

> Just as literature could not exist by unceasingly repeating even its greatest masterpieces without admitting new thoughts and new modes of expression, so it is with music. Our spirit of adventure could not endure such a dead end. Though our desire to seek new experiences varies in degree with each individual, nevertheless it is universal. You certainly read many more new books than you read old ones, and you see ten modern plays for each old one. In music, however, the ratio is completely reversed.[18]

Believing that the continuing validity of a work of art lies solely in the idea that "good art will endure," Toch rejected the importance of fluctuating taste: "Indeed, what is good art? Does the fact that I like a certain piece of music or painting or poetry make it a good piece of art? And aside from individual taste, what about the known differences in taste of nations, generations, etc.? Even the same individual is apt to change his taste at different times to the same object of art. If taste is such a vague and fluctuating criterion, we must exclude it in our search for the right answer."[19]

And just as Toch argued against individual taste as a criterion for good art, he protested the tendency for some listeners to put a label on a twentieth-century composer's style.

> Beware of being charmed into the traps of stylistic considerations. This danger is all the greater today as the notion of style is so monstrously, absurdly, senselessly over-rated. All interest today seems to be concentrated on the question: In what style do you write? . . . Interesting and noteworthy as the features of style may be, they can never rise to superior importance in the work of art. Good art is, and remains, as far beyond all matters of style as beyond all matters of taste, knowledge, and technique. The real artist may even, perhaps, be unconscious of his own style, but he will never be unconscious of the inferiority of stylistic considerations, as against the essence, the substances, the message of his work.[20]

Perhaps because he, himself, was often labeled a "romantic" composer, Toch took pains to redefine such labels, to put them in a much broader context, writing that

> while romanticism in music repelled us almost to the point of nausea (Wagner), we can not deny that music in itself, the very conception of

music, is romantic. And while sentimentality has no place in true art, we must not confuse sentimentality with sentiment. Bach, Mozart, Schubert can surely not be accused of being sentimental; what makes us love their works . . . is the greatness, the lofty nobility of their sentiments. And it is this quality that makes them timeless, independent of age, of epoch.[21]

and

Refreshing as it is to get away from the over-emotional type of music at the end of the century, it is like plunging into cold water on a tropical day. But, isn't that plunge a temporal reaction, rather than the search for an element to live it? The freezing man needs warmth.[22]

Likewise, Toch was also labeled as an "atonal" composer, a label that today means very little. However, in the period of German New Music and in the decades following World War II in America, the subject of atonality was of prime interest, surfacing frequently in music journals and reviews. Toch was just one of many modern composers who offered his own definition.

My music is not atonal. It originates in tonality—a tonality which, however, appears in a floating form, and is, without exception, attracted by the gravity of a solid tonal center.[23]

and

Although I pass for a modernist, my music is in no way atonal. It is rooted in tonality, which is, however, treated in a hovering, gyrating manner, gravitating always toward a definite tone center.[24]

Interconnected with these observations on certain philosophical and stylistic aspects of twentieth-century music is Toch's preoccupation with the process by which a composer transfers his musical ideas into sounds, notated on paper. His statements about the nature of good art confirm his belief that the composing process can never be mechanical. "Good music originates in the depths of the soul, travels from there to the mill, the well-equipped refinery, of the brain, continues over the manuscript paper and arrives in the *soul* of the listener. After completion of the *Missa Solemnis* Beethoven wrote on the title page of his manuscript, 'From the heart it came, may it go to the heart' *(Vom Herzen ist es gekommen, moge es zu Herzen gehen).*"[25]

Toch, as we have seen, believed that "inspiration is everything and nothing," a statement that originally appeared in a 1926 unpublished German essay entitled "Ich habe erfahren: der Einfall ist Alles und

Nichts" (I Have Experienced: The Idea Is Everything and Nothing). Commenting upon Toch's "credo of inspiration," the composer Paul Pisk observed that

> in a roundrobin on the subject of the creative impulse, Ernst Toch said: "Inspiration is everything and nothing." Here is revealed the essence of his being. Inspiration is everything to him, because all the technical proficiency seems to be dissipated to no purpose unless it is extended upon subject matter which arouses personal reaction or is potentially expressive . . . and inspiration is nothing because the most sublime thought can take on no enduring form if the ability be lacking to formulate and present it.[26]

In many of his writings, Toch attempted to define "der Einfall," idea or inspiration, explaining its role in the process of composition:

> The passive element within the genesis of a composition (the idea), this contribution from an unconscious source—arbitrary, sovereign, decisive—is, of course, an essential element in any creative process, but because of the unique properties of music it has a more significant implication here. In every other medium of the arts, ideas fuse with the material which serves to construct the artistic creation. Although conditioned and determined by the nature of the material employed, ideas operated in conjunction with objective elements, be they words, color, stone, etc. In music, however, the idea is preserved close to its pure, original form. It first presents itself in a sequence of sounds and as such—or modified as the creator sees fit—enters into the work. Yet this idea may mean nothing—or everything. It is nothing unless it is coupled with the potential of the creative mind, its knowledge, resourcefulness, and craft.[27]

As has been seen, Toch's aesthetic theories are, more often than not, set in a philosophical context, relating musical concepts to art, history, and life in general. It is, therefore, difficult to assign certain writings to "category two," for instance, or to classify others as belonging to "category three"—the timeless, the philosophic, the spiritual. However, one concept that Toch frequently addressed certainly belongs in category three, and that is the composer's concept of "religiousness." This spiritual emphasis appears with increasing frequency during the last decade of his life: "Good art is religious. It is religious irrespective of its subject. . . . Good art has directness, immediateness, nearness to life, nearness to nature and humanity. Nearness to life, nearness to nature and humanity —Who has it? I think the one who contains in himself an irrational, unconquerable bastion, untouched, for which I have no other word but religiousness."[28]

What he believed is that music, good music, is "mysterious," naive, hence religious:

> Music is religious because it functions in the impenetrable margin of human thinking on which art lives . . . . The greatest men in history, scientists as well as artists, were very religious, because of their failure to believe that science will eventually be able to explain everything. . . . Religion is (therefore) a mystery that lives in our soul . . . it has little to do with anything taught in any church. It means SUBMISSION to life, in its fullest extent.[29]

Toch emphasized the timelessness of good art—that is, art which is not contrived or novel for the sake of being novel. Valid art cannot be the product of the intellect alone. Art is communication. Ever-fluctuating public taste does not matter either because good art—good music—endures.

Continuing on the universality of good art, Toch affirmed that

> art supposedly reflects the essential spiritual content of its period. . . . Man has not changed . . . human life has circled in times past and will circle in the future [around] love, death, suffering, struggle, hope, despair, and the urge and search for God. These are the things around which human life really revolves, independent of epochs and localities of races and languages, habits and fashions, in short all changeable aspects of any given epoch. And these are the things which great art of all ages and races has encompassed.[30]

Perhaps nowhere are these spiritual references more pronounced than in the composer's commentary on the forces behind the creation of specific works. When his "idea" is intertwined with a literary reference, quotation, or text, Toch describes the importance to him of that particular source. For instance, what starts out as a fairly mundane description of the inspiration behind his *Cantata of the Bitter Herbs* (1938) quickly evolves into a spiritual statement. The work is based on the Jewish Haggadah story of the Exodus of the Jews from Egypt, traditionally read at the family table during Passover:

> Obviously it was implicitly assumed that I would turn to the store of existing traditionally established music in the Passover services, and integrate some of it into mine. Strangely enough, that thought had never occurred to me. My conception of the tale told in the *Haggadah* was quite different, was non-denominational and broadly universal. It is the formula of a fate that men have inflicted on men time and time again. Whenever it happens, it causes sufferings told and untold, and calls up

powers of resistance told and untold. It happened to the Jews and it happened to others. . . . It is the privilege of all intrinsically religious men to submit to, to accept, to reconcile the unfathomable with the assurance, the flooding, the ringing happiness of a faith.[31]

Reflecting upon the creation of his Fifth Symphony, entitled *Jeptha: Rhapsodic Poem,* Toch wrote that

as biological, psychological beings we are unchanged, untouched. We are functioning as we ever did, breathing; our hearts still so made that their beat is subject to our emotions, halting from joy and horror, recording all the antimonies of human existence, love and hate, jubilation and despair, struggles, winning and losing; with senses so made as to carry images to the store of our memories, to take delight and enchantment from what we name beauty. . . . With a mind so made as to reflect on what happens in ourselves, to gather up and grasp and express what it perceives from the outside and from within, forging it all into one, in the white heat of a human universe.[32]

Paying tribute to Albert Schweitzer as the inspiration for his Second Symphony, Toch described the meaning, for him, of the symphony's motto:

As my work proceeded, this sentence assumed even richer and more varied connotations. The very life of Schweitzer appeared to me as a symbolic representation of it, climaxed by his return at the age of seventy-seven from Europe to Lambarene, the place of his sacrifice and consecration. Furthermore, the sentence spoke to me (in my own silent and deferential relationship to Schweitzer) through all these years. Finally, as may be experienced by many a creative artist, it became the ever so imperious summons of the work itself, from the first nebulous conception up to the last stroke of the pen: "I will not let thee go except thou bless me."[33]

One composition in particular is almost a biographical illustration of Toch as an astute observer of life. In his cantata *Das Wasser* (The Water), Op. 53 (1930), he contrasted two types of mankind. The first, the rationalist or scientist (tenor), seeks to discover the chemical formula of water; his music is often grotesque and humorous, suggesting Toch's distrust of composers who write according to formula. The second, the humanist (baritone), who is more interested in metaphysics than physics, seeks to find meaning and beauty in the world's creation; his music is in a more natural style, with no attempts at humor or satire. The finale, decrying the unsatisfactory description of water as mere H_2O, proclaims the ultimate victory of the metaphysician who extols the wonders and limitless capabilities of God's creation, *Das Wasser.*

In conclusion, Toch the philosopher understood that his place in music history, regardless of favorable or unfavorable circumstances, was that of "A Link in the Chain." Writing about the creation of his First Symphony, he reflected: "I believe that we can only be the product of a long line of ancestors, and that each creating artist, involuntarily, is placed as a link in this chain. He cooperates on the continuity to the degree in which the timeless is more important to him than the time-bound."[34]

And so, despite his frustrations as a composer in America, Toch could still see himself in historical perspective. Deeply concerned about the world around him and about the place of music in it, he put his concerns into the larger framework of the timelessness of good art and of the continuum of life itself, which he saw as the inspiration for self-expression and artistic creation.

Summaries of Selected Writings in German

Out of the many articles that Toch published in German from 1922 to 1932, consideration of nine of them will shed some light on his thoughts, opinions, and attitudes relating to musical ideas and events during this important period of his life.

The sample of German writings presented here reflects Toch the emerging modernist composer, whose musical ideas were in keeping with the times, but whose mode of expression recalls an earlier, romantic, written tradition. These brief summaries are taken from the author's translation of the following German essays and articles:

1. "Kontrapunkt" (Counterpoint) — article from *Mannheimer General-Anzeiger,* 1922.
2. "Musik für Mechanische Instrumente" (Music for Mechanical Instruments) — article from *Frankfurter Zeitung,* 21 July 1926.
3. "Der Uebergangscharakter der Gegenwartsmusik" (The Transitional Character of the Present Music) — unpublished essay, c. 1926–1928.
4. "Beethoven in der Gegenwart" (Beethoven in the Present) — article from *Die Neue Leipziger Zeitung,* 3 March 1927.

5. "Ich habe erfahren: der Einfall ist Alles" (I Have Experienced)—unpublished essay, c. 1927.
6. "Klavier als Instrumentalkörper" (Piano as an Instrumental Body)—article from *Das Klavierbuch,* November 1927.
7. "Schauspielmusik" (Music for the Stage)— article from *Bühnenblätter,* 1928 or 1929.
8. "Die Musikalischen Ausdrucksformen im Wandel der Zeiten" (The Forms of Musical Expression in the Course of Changing Times)—unpublished essay, c.1930.
9. "Arnold Schönberg"—article from *Neue Badische Landeszeitung,* 8 March 1932.

In the earliest article of this selection, "Kontrapunkt" (Counterpoint), 1922, Toch defines the term as "battle" and goes on to declare that it is counterpoint which makes a work of art alive and interesting.

The role of rhythm in this battle is complex, because two or more competing voices never perform the same rhythmical movement, one resting while the other moves. Other sources of contrast are contrary motion, dynamics, and tone color.

A battle of another kind, that between man and the machine, is revealed in Toch's article on "Music for Mechanical Instruments," which he wrote for the summer music festival at Donaueschingen in 1926.

He defines music for mechanical instruments as music for such instruments as the piano, influenced by the essence of the instrument, and points to the fact that this music is deprived of its soul.

The only type of music free of the battle of the machine is singing; after the singer, Toch places the violinist, then the wind instrumentalist, and, finally, the keyboard players.

On the other hand, he claims that the Welte-Mignon factory's reproduction of Mozart's original composition for organ roll (*Fantasy,* K. 608) sounds as good as, or even better than, a live performance.

He also refers to what he calls a certain coolness in the music produced by the drawn organ roll, and although this coolness in mechanical music does not eliminate the warmth of the usual music, it is something special nevertheless. Just as Alois Hába says of quarter-tone music, "it is not a destruction of half-tone music, but an enlargement of the territory," so does mechanical music enlarge the territory.

The enlargement of the territory in music in general is a concern in Toch's article on "The Transitional Character of the Present Music," c. 1926–1928.

Identifying the crisis of transition in the New Music, Toch asserts that he and other composers are living through a time very similar to the Mannheim School of the mid–eighteenth century, when the Mannheimers instinctively turned away from the overrefined polyphonic style of Bach.

Likewise, he contends, Richard Strauss's music represents a great talent of a bygone era that the young artists of Toch's time cannot understand, just as Mozart would not have understood Bach.

Toch is also interested in the necessity of teaching modern music, especially to young school pupils, who are unprepared for it and confused by it. He recommends the active, systematic and well-planned inclusion of New Music into the curriculum, from the lowest grades, conditioning students to the practicing and understanding of live and genuine art of all types.

Instructors should view the New Music much as Hába viewed quarter-tone music, or, as Toch puts it, not as a destruction of the old, but of its enrichment, through filling the new in with the old. And the New Music will require a new way of teaching.

Beethoven held a unique position in Toch's pantheon of composers, as is clear from his article "Beethoven in the Present," 1927. Beethoven's work stands beyond approval or rejection, he says, and his appearance belongs more to the history of mankind than to the history of music.

It is his humanity, Toch believes, that gives Beethoven's works their power of intensity and popularity. With a small rearrangement of his inner makeup, Beethoven could have been a great revolutionary or a philosopher.

The *Pathétique* and the *Appassionata* piano sonatas are prayers of thanks, as by one who has experienced the deity. In comparison, the titles of Haydn's or Mozart's works, such as the *Lerchenquartet* or the *Jupiter Symphony,* are simple means of distinction.

At present, composers and musicians are in a general mental process endeavoring to dissolve the synthesis from the nineteenth century, Toch concludes prophetically. This has made us long for a cleaning up, for a separating again into transparent elements. People have returned to making music for the sake of music.

Because of this process of dissolution, as far as Beethoven is concerned, time-related attitudes will bring him closer to other epochs than to the present one.

Toch turned to consider his own experience as a composer in "I

Have Experienced," 1927, in which he explains how all masterful works unite both intuition and skill.

Like unexpected lightning, the idea is independent of the condition of the soul, mood, or occupation. "I have almost never changed anything about the intuition," he says; "its origin is an absolute secret to me."

And the idea, when it comes unexpectedly, brings with it everything it needs — its designation (such as sonata), its instrumentation, its length.

Besides these reflections on the nature of a musical idea, Toch also considered, in 1927, more practical musical questions, as in "The Piano as an Instrumental Body."

In the New Music, Toch maintains, the piano has lost one of its former functions, that of being a projection apparatus for chamber and orchestral music. Furthermore, the harmonic building principle has been replaced by sound-color and linear counterpoint.

Toch notices, however, that music written especially for the piano has been newly introduced, although what is missing is the composer of the time who lives in the spirit of the instrument and creates for it as did Chopin and Liszt. Toch ends his article with this urgent appeal: we need a composer who can be both a piano player and a thinker.

Another aspect of the practical work of composition that Toch considers is "Music for the Stage," 1928. Again he returns to the metaphor of a battle, this time in the relationship between the music and the drama, which he sees as a battle for dominance.

Composing music for, say, *A Midsummer Night's Dream* or Goethe's *Egmont* would have been unbearable if the music were to play throughout either of these dramas. But both Mendelssohn and Beethoven left the poetic ideas untouched, thus keeping their musical ideas pure. Opera composing, he believes, is easier.

Comparing incidental music to the chorus of ancient tragedy, Toch feels that music can support a poetic work by preparing for events, connecting ideas or themes, and intensifying the action. He regrets that this form of dramatic music, which was formerly much cultivated, is rare today.

A subject of abiding interest to Toch is discussed in "The Forms of Musical Expression in the Course of Changing Times," c. 1930. First, he distinguishes between form and forms. Form, he says, is an aesthetic, psychological entity that embraces what is common to all artists and all art epochs. Forms, however, change with the times, such as the dance, the lied, the gavotte, or the shimmy. They are more theoretical or style-critical, and grow out of the epoch.

What is needed is the development of a common expression of form or forms, recognizing the contributions of a common intellectual and expressive will. That common expressive form would be, naturally, the sum of the expression of individuals. As long as a work of art is conscious only to the artist, and not yet communicable to others, it is chaotic. Only when the work of art has passed from the artist has it taken form.

As an experiment, Toch divides human beings into three types and relates them to three art types. Type one people are completely noble, good and intelligent, but they cannot project these qualities because they are too inhibited.

They demand too much of others, and with their inhibited ethos, they are rather burdensome. In art, type one is the work of art in which the good substance has not found adequate form. It is the content without the form, in a true masterpiece, although this type of art is relatively rare.

Type two people are those who show forth their qualities in their correct form, and thus are the most valuable. In art, this type person wrestles with the form of expression, and, as it belongs to him, he overcomes it. Such was the case with Beethoven and Brahms, whose strong feeling for form drove them to do the hard work until the form adequate to the substance had been found. This is the fulfilled demand of the ideal: the fulfilled masterpiece.

Type three people are those whose inner quality certainly does not have to be bad, but is still pale. They blame their parents that they never had a course in Form and Analysis.

Mozart inherited music forms from Haydn and the Mannheimers. Mastering the sonata form, he used it as a scaffolding of his unending wealth of ideas. On the other hand, in Beethoven's thirty-two piano sonatas, the so-called sonata form is nothing but exceptions.

Summarizing his ideas, Toch states that form itself is an artistic experience. In order that form can originate, the artist needs, first, the building materials and, second, the building reasoning or will power, along with the technique to organize and put the material together.

Lastly in this selection of articles, Toch discusses two of his contemporaries in "Arnold Schönberg," 1932, the other composer being

Hans Pfitzner. These two minds, though seeming to be opposites, are united by a wondrous bond of interior law. What separates them is merely their ideologies; what unites them is their combativeness.

Like the Spartans in the time of Leonidas, Pfitzner defends his vigorous individuality in his own type of romanticism. Schönberg, however, aims at conquest; his war has opened the gates of a new land, for a wider group of settlers and followers.

Toch speculates on why acceptance of Schönberg's works has been difficult, concluding that it is because the composer is always filled with an immense sense of responsibility for each note, with an overpowering concentration. He is, therefore, quite different from Stravinsky, who embodies the most elementary, the most vital musicianship, which is often brutally released.

This brief survey of nine of Toch's German articles, published between 1922 and 1932, makes clear his personal and intellectual commitment to music, in general, and the New Music, in particular. Whether in appraisals of two composers, Beethoven and Schönberg, whom he revered, or in comments on the more theoretical and practical aspects of music making, the European Toch was a serious, substantial thinker and writer about music.

—7

The Émigré Contribution to Musical America

Ernst Toch and his generation of émigré composers contributed substantially to musical life in twentieth-century America. In evaluating their creativity, one must consider the émigrés' productivity not only in musical composition, but also in their chief means of employment, namely teaching, writing, and/or composing for the films. Each composer combined one or several of these creative endeavors in a significant contribution to American music; these must be enumerated if one is to place the creative output of Ernst Toch into perspective.

Several of the composers who became naturalized American citizens had gained enough prominence to be included in the 1945 edition of *Who's Who in America*. Among them were Paul Hindemith, Erich Wolfgang Korngold, Darius Milhaud, Arnold Schönberg, Igor Stravinsky, Ernst Toch, and Kurt Weill, most of whom made some accommodations to their new American environment.

Regardless of the degree to which the European composers adapted to American idioms or changed to a simpler musical style, somehow they often felt like they were selling out.

The composers may have been in danger of (1) compromising too much, or (2) of taking what Artur Schnabel called "the line of most resistance," that is, not wanting to compromise at all. Although such émigrés as Weill, Eisler, and Dessau had made abundant use of popular idioms in their German compositions, once in America, they found that a few of their compatriots were critical of their accommodations to American taste. Defending the émigrés' Americanization, Ernst Krenek observed that

> Composers whose American works point up new characteristics unknown to their earlier works should not for that reason be automatically accused of having struck an unethical compromise. That is, they ought not be reproached for having taken great pains, against their better judgment, to cultivate modes of writing conditioned by their surroundings. . . . [Regarding Kurt Weill], as he himself told me, he did what seemed necessary to comply with the natural, invincible urge to communicate via the musical theater: he adapted this communication to the only vehicle at his disposal, namely, the Broadway stage.[1]

The following summaries of the careers of the more successful émigrés illustrate to what extent each composer adapted to his American environment. With the exception of this century's greats, Igor Stravinsky and Béla Bartók, who are not included in these summaries, parallels can be drawn in almost every case with the varied contributions of Ernst Toch.

During the decade before emigration, Arnold Schönberg (1874–1951) composed mostly in the twelve-tone idiom. But his first American work was his *Suite for Strings,* a tonal work, with extensive chromaticism and polyphony. In 1936, when he accepted a professorship at UCLA, he also acquired a new American publisher, G. Schirmer, whose president became a close personal friend.

Schönberg's American career offers some interesting contrasts. In his *Suite for Strings* the five movements were entitled Overture in G Major, Adagio in E Minor, Minuet in G Major, Gavotte in B-flat Major, and Gigue in G Major. This was the first time he had used a key signature since 1908! Thus, in the Americanization of Schönberg, tonal works coexisted with his twelve-tone style.

In the category of tonal works composed in America, in addition to his *Suite for Strings,* which was intended for use by students, Schönberg composed a *Kol Nidre,* Op. 39, for speaker, chorus, and orchestra (1939); *Variations on a Recitative for Organ,* Op. 40 (1940); *Theme and Variations for Orchestra in G Minor,* Op. 43B, a reorchestration of a student work for band; *Ode to Napoleon* (1944); and *A Survivor from Warsaw* (1948), on an English text by Schönberg, to commemorate the Jews who perished in Nazi Germany.

On the whole, however, Schönberg the composer tried to remain true to himself. Even with his American excursions into tonality with works that may have been more accessible, Schönberg did not achieve the type of audience appeal that some of his contemporaries were able to accomplish. One difficulty in his attaining performances in this country was that conductors such as Furtwängler, Walter, Kleiber, and Klemperer, all of whom worked in Berlin when Schönberg was there, did not champion his objective, orderly approach to composition. Despite his excursions into tonality, Schönberg's intellectual demands on both listeners and performers were considered risky to program.

But Schönberg was, all his life, a dedicated teacher. In Vienna, his renowned disciples were Alban Berg and Anton Webern; in Berlin, Hanns Eisler and Josef Rufer; and in Los Angeles, among others, Leonard Stein and Dika Newlin, who later chronicled her teacher's dual career as teacher and composer.

Schönberg mastered the English language to be able to speak and write with remarkable proficiency. His books *Style and Idea, The Structural Functions of Harmony,* and *Fundamentals of Musical Composition,* are still in use today, attesting to their universal appeal.

In contrast to many other émigrés, Schönberg never composed for the films, although he was asked to do so.

Since the time of his death, Schönberg's importance as a musical innovator has been widely recognized. His explorations into and devotion to a set theory of predescribed and ordered musical elements have had profound repercussions on modern composition.

During the 1920s, Darius Milhaud (1892–1974) had appeared in the United States as conductor and performer of his works. As a lecturer on modern music, he had given seminars at Harvard, Princeton, and Columbia Universities. His music was popular with American audiences, especially in that Milhaud, fascinated with American jazz, had used that idiom in many of his compositions. He had also incorporated South American rhythms in his works, and compositions such as *La Création du Monde* and *Scaramouche* held considerable appeal for American audiences.

When Milhaud came to this country in 1937 at the age of forty-five to teach at Mills College in California, he was commissioned to write a string quartet by Mrs. Coolidge; it was first performed at the Library of Congress in October 1940. During the next seven years, before returning to Europe, he composed music for American school bands and orchestras—songs and choral music for colleges, a suite entitled *Kentuckiana,* a marimba concerto for the St. Louis Symphony, and one film score for Hollywood.

Milhaud was very successful in America, having his works premiered by major performing groups all over the country. Two of his symphonies were commissioned by the Chicago and Boston Symphonies. The Columbia Broadcasting Orchestra invited him repeatedly to conduct his music, and the League of Composers in New York arranged many programs of his works.

As a professor of composition, Milhaud enjoyed his teaching assignments at the small liberal arts college and was very complimentary about his students. Although he left America in 1947 to live in Paris, he returned every second year to teach at Mills College and the Aspen Summer Institute and to guest conduct his works throughout the United States.

His book *Notes Without Music* was first published in Paris in 1949 and in English translation in 1952.

His musical genres run the gamut, from modernistic music dramas, full length operas, electronic experiments, ballets, symphonies, orchestral pieces, string quartets, and chamber music, to popular arrangements, and even the Mills College theme song! One of the most prolific of twentieth-century composers, Milhaud wrote well over three hundred works. His style is distinct in its lyrical melodies, rhythmic versatility, and polytonality. Its universal appeal is in its directness, its noncerebral orientation. Believing that melody was the prime element of composition, Milhaud retained a melodic and rhythmic clarity even in his polyphonic textures.

Of course Milhaud made concessions to American popular taste, in the works cited from 1940–1947. But, with a lifetime output so vast and varied, it is difficult to assess what impact emigration actually had on his creative psyche. Milhaud's "Americana" was evident before he came here to live. The renewed interest in his work in Europe following the war can be attributed to a wartorn continent's desire to restore a cultural heritage, but more than likely his European and American popularity was genuinely based upon his agreeable modern style. So lyrical as to please even the most skeptical critics of modern music and so American in its incorporation of jazz idioms, Milhaud's music was readily accepted in America.

Like Milhaud, Viennese-born Ernst Krenek (1900) had adopted

American jazz rhythms in the 1920s and achieved success with his jazz opera *Jonny spielt auf* (Leipzig, 1927).

In the late 1920s, Krenek's style had been essentially one of atonality, whose organizing force was in rhythmic vitality. When the jazz opera was first performed, it brought immediate recognition, including translation into eighteen languages and performances in more than a hundred opera houses!

A neoclassic style, which had preceded the atonal and jazz phase, eventually gave way to an adoption of the twelve-tone system. His opera *Karl V* (1933) was in the serial technique, but the work was banned by the Third Reich, and Krenek, a Catholic, was labeled a *Kulturbolshevist*.

His emigration to America in 1937, at the age of thirty-seven, and his subsequent teaching posts at Vassar College and Hamline University in Minnesota, led him into an academic career that produced many essays and articles on the history of music and modern music in general. His books include *Music Here and Now* (1939), *Johannes Ockeghem* (1953), *Exploring Music,* a compilation of essays and articles spanning the years 1929–1956, and his autobiographical *Horizons Circled—Reflections on My Music.*

Krenek settled in Hollywood in 1947 to compose for the films, although he never achieved particular acclaim as a Hollywood composer.

Despite the fact that the Los Angeles Philharmonic waited until 1971 to program a Krenek composition, Krenek is recognized as a prolific composer as well as an esteemed scholar. Among his one hundred-plus works are eleven operas, three ballets, incidental music for plays, many choral pieces, five symphonies, six piano sonatas, four piano concertos, and eight string quartets.

Although most of his works since 1930 are in the twelve-tone idiom, often earning him the reputation of a cerebral composer, many of his American compositions are very accessible. One of his first American works was his *Lamentation of the Prophet Jeremiah* (1942) for unaccompanied chorus. Another concession to Americanism is *The Santa Fe Time Table* (1947), in which a chorus intones the names of stations on the Santa Fe Railroad from Albuquerque to Los Angeles.

His fame is perhaps greater in Europe, where he has appeared on numerous television and radio broadcasts. But as a teacher, author, and writer in twentieth-century musical America, his influence has been substantial.

Hanns Eisler (1898–1962) had already carved a niche for himself in Berlin when he became an advocate of music for the people, or political music; having joined the Communist party in 1926, he had publicly denounced the New Music, including the twelve-tone compositions of his former teacher Arnold Schönberg. His European compositions took the form of solo songs, choral works, marching songs, incidental music for stage dramas, and film scores, expressing his socialist philosophies. In the early 1930s he began a lifelong friendship and collaboration with Bertolt Brecht.

From 1933 to his emigration in 1940, Eisler's career was extremely varied: three visits to the United States, including a one-year appointment at the New School for Social Research; composition of several film scores in Europe; Professor of Composition at the Mexico Conservatory; and in 1940, the awarding of a Rockefeller Grant to research the function of film music. The results included not only numerous film scores but also a book written with Theodor Adorno, *Composing for the Films*.

His teaching career at the University of Southern California was not especially distinguished. But in Hollywood he had enormous success, becoming the musical assistant to Charlie Chaplin, resulting in the composition of more than forty film scores in eight years.

Deported back to Germany in 1948 during the period when Hollywood personnel were interrogated by the Committee on Un-American Activities, Eisler settled again in Germany, accepting a teaching post at the Berlin Hochschule für Musik. His main contributions to America were in composing for and writing about the new era of Hollywood films.

Paul Hindemith (1895-1963), as we have seen, was one of the leading exponents of the New Music during the 1920s and early 1930s in Germany. During his tenure at the Berlin Hochschule für Musik (1927–1937), his music was widely performed at the New Music festivals and throughout Germany. During this time, Hindemith was also active as a violist and chamber music performer. At the same time, his enthusiasm for educating young listeners and performers led him to compose in a *Gebrauchsmusik* style, and, like Toch, Hindemith experimented with music for mechanical instruments. He also composed for German films.

Upon emigration in 1940 to the United States from Ankara, Turkey, at the age of forty-five, Hindemith continued his teaching career at Cornell University, at the Berkshire Music Festival, and later as professor at Yale University, where he remained until 1953. At that time, he returned to Switzerland, assuming a teaching post at the University of Zurich.

Like Milhaud and Stravinsky, Hindemith composed a large quantity of music that enjoyed considerable success and popularity in this country. Chamber music occupies a substantial amount of his output, and his vocal works range from solo songs to cantatas and oratorios. His more renowned American works include the revised version of *Das Marienleben,* the Cello Concerto (1941), Symphony in E-flat Major (1941), Sonata for Two Pianos (1942), *Ludus Tonalis* for solo piano (1943), and the Clarinet Concerto (1950).

The majority of Hindemith's works were composed prior to his emigration. Regardless of whether the music was composed here or in Germany, certain stylistic traits remained consistent throughout his composing career. First and foremost is an unswerving devotion to tonal and formal unity. Whether through linear counterpoint or simpler homophonic settings, melody is of prime importance in its gravitation toward a central tonality. Although divided between *Gebrauchsmusik* simplicity and twentieth-century linear counterpoint, Hindemith's appeal was in its sense of spontaneity. His music contained a definite rhythmic vivacity, though not of the complexity of Stravinsky or Bartok. The only instances of excursion into twelve-tone composition were the Tuba Sonata of 1955 and the *Pittsburgh Symphony* of 1958.

Like Krenek, Hindemith established himself in this country as a scholar and pedagogue, in addition to achieving considerable recognition as a composer. His influence as a composer for amateurs helped young American instrumentalists become familiar with twentieth-century musical vocabulary. His influence on American composition students led to a serious study of older forms and a renewed interest in Early Music.

Extolling solid craftsmanship, Hindemith's books include *The Craft of Musical Composition* (1941), *Elementary Training for Musicians* (1946), and *A Composer's World* (1952). Although he had held a professorship in Berlin, it is possible to assume that the American students, receptive but less sophisticated, inspired him to write the above texts.

Unfortunately, Hindemith's first few years in this country did not provide him with the opportunities for practical music-making he had enjoyed in Europe. The series of early music concerts that he prepared for the Yale Collegium Musicum were about the only outlets for his performing abilities in this country.

To assess the impact of emigration on his American compositions is speculative, at best, in that Hindemith was a lifelong composer of a large variety of instrumental media and genres. But as a teacher, Hindemith upheld the highest standards. During his twelve-year tenure at Yale, only twelve degrees in composition were awarded. Among his American students were Lukas Foss, Norman Dello Joio, Ulysses Kay, and other composer-teachers who currently hold faculty positions throughout this country. Regarding curricula, Hindemith believed that composers should be taught to play several instruments as well as to handle choruses and/or orchestras, and they should be required to take courses in voice in addition to musical form. All his composition students had to participate in performing groups.

Although adaptation is hardly an issue when considering his musical style, his influence in America as a serious composer and teacher greatly facilitated both amateur and professional musicians alike to become familiar with the musical vocabulary of post–World War I. He spent the last decade of his life traveling all over the world as conductor and exponent of both old (Early Music) and New Music.

A prolific composer, Hindemith's catalog of works contains examples from almost every medium and genre, for a great variety of instruments and chamber combinations.

The case of Kurt Weill (1900–1950) is especially interesting in that up until recently Weill was known in America as a successful contributor to the history of American Musical Theatre. None of his European works were performed professionally in this country during his fifteen years here.

The rediscovery of his German works indicates that Weill was, indeed, a composer to be taken seriously. His early compositions, some written while studying with Busoni, include string quartets, solo sonatas, one chamber symphony, and a ballet.

Not dissimilar to Hindemith's, the early works of Kurt Weill represent much of the stylistic versatility that typified the musical life of Berlin in the late 1920s and early 1930s.

Weill's setting of Bertolt Brecht's version of *The Threepenny Opera* in 1928 brought him immediate success all over Europe and, subsequently, in America. As the more progressive opera houses and theatres in Germany performed his works, Weill emerged as one of the most successful composers for the stage in the Weimar Republic.

After the success of *The Threepenny Opera,* Weill began composing radio cantatas. In 1928 and 1929 he turned his attention to reaching the nonmusical elite, but still within a contemporary idiom of composition. Realizing that jazz and the American popular song style were the big hits in Europe, Weill sought to incorporate these with his own type of modern lyricism into dramatic writing.

In 1935 when he came to New York, he collaborated with the New York Theatre Group in the staging of his antiwar musical play *Johnny Johnson.* A few weeks later he attended the Broadway premiere of his *The Eternal Road.* Even though these works were somewhat modernistic for American taste, Weill's connections with the writers Maxwell Anderson and Moss Hart and composers Marc Blitzstein and George Gershwin helped him to make a place for himself on Broadway. This was, after all, the only avenue for a dramatic composer such as Weill in the United States, aside from Hollywood or commercial radio.

From the time of his emigration in 1935 to his early death in 1950, Weill devoted himself exclusively to musical theatre and to some film composing. His success on Broadway during the war years was rather phenomenal.

While the preemigration composer had been part of the modern movement in Germany, the post-1940 Kurt Weill appeared fully Americanized—almost as if he had never thought of himself as a German composer.

In America, Weill never sought or was offered a university teaching position. Furthermore, as there were no forthcoming commissions for concert music, he was left without an alternative; it would have to be either Broadway or Hollywood. Therefore, one tends to be unsympathetic to the musical establishment's criticism that Weill subordinated his previous artistic criteria to purely popular ones.

The composer himself did much to substantiate his total break with the past by making public pronouncements during the 1940s implying that the European tradition of high culture music was outmoded. In fact, he even discouraged the resurrection of his former German compositions.

In evaluating his musical style, it is difficult to speculate on his creative growth or stylistic development, as there were essentially two

Kurt Weills. His gift of lyricism, whether in a modernistic German stage play or a tuneful Broadway musical, is undeniable. However, the compromises that Broadway demanded of him in the choice of subject matter, harmonic idiom, or scope of dramatic composition were real.

His absorption into the mainstream of American life was complete. Quick to realize that neither his inherited German tradition nor his modernistic settings of political satires in stage or radio plays would contribute to his American success, Kurt Weill rapidly accommodated to what American musical theatre demanded of him. His success there can be viewed as one remarkable story.

Erich Wolfgang Korngold (1897–1957), like Toch, was a well-known composer of orchestral works and operas in Europe before his emigration in 1934. As such, he was often considered one of the last great romantic composers. However, after the war his serious music suffered considerable neglect, namely because of his association with Hollywood. Max Reinhardt, with whom Korngold had collaborated on new versions of classic operettas by Johann Strauss and Jacques Offenbach, invited Korngold to Hollywood in 1934; the occasion was the Warner Brothers production of *A Midsummer Night's Dream.*

Until he retired from Warner Brothers in 1947, Korngold composed some of the most revered music ever written for film: *Anthony Adverse* and *The Adventures of Robin Hood,* both of which won him Academy Awards, *The Sea Hawk, Captain Blood, Elizabeth and Essex, The Sea Wolf, Deception,* and *King's Row*—twenty-one film scores between 1935 and 1947! Regarding his American reputation as a film composer, it is a tribute to his abilities in this field that in 1972 RCA Records released an album of his classic film scores. Ironically, the success of these recordings led to a renewed interest in his concert and operatic music.

Some of his European classics that have been revived have included the three-act opera *Die tote Stadt* (1916–1920), recorded under Erich Leinsdorf; the one-act opera *Violanta* (1914–1915), performed in Santa Fe; the one-act opera *Der Ring des Polykrates* (1913–1914), performed in New York City; and the Piano Concerto for the Left Hand (1923), performed by Gary Graffman in 1985 with the New York Philharmonic.

Unlike Toch's, Korngold's teaching career was confined to Europe, where he was awarded the title of "Professor Honoris Causae" for his teaching of opera and composition at the Vienna Staatsakademie.

Perhaps because he was never required to define his teaching ideas to American students, Korngold left no textbooks or books on film composing.

However, Korngold's career as a serious composer presents striking similarities to that of Toch. His earliest works composed in Vienna between 1906 and 1912 were piano pieces and orchestral music, with the exception of the two-act ballet-pantomine *Der Schneemann*. During the 1920s and early 1930s, he composed several neoclassic works, a piano quintet, two string quartets, and a piano sonata, in addition to the Concerto for Left Hand. Of the few concert works he was able to compose during his tenure in Hollywood, one represents a concession to American taste, the symphonic poem *Tomorrow* (1942).

Also like Toch, Korngold returned to Vienna in 1949 and composed his First Symphony, Op. 40. Unfortunately, postwar Europe at this time, with its new musical trends, was incompatible with Korngold's melodic, tonal style. Rather than finding regeneration in his new symphonic voice, as Toch had, Korngold composed only two more concert works, including his Theme and Variations of 1952.

The recent revival of the concert music of Erich Wolfgang Korngold may be indicative of the twentieth century's renewed interest in romantic music composed in this century. However, Korngold's major contribution to American music remains his film scores.

Karol Rathaus (1895–1954), like Toch, experienced considerable success with his orchestral and piano music in Europe before emigration (1938). Going from New York City to Hollywood, his brief career as a film composer was distinguished. Among the directors he worked with in Hollywood were Fedor Ozep *(The Brothers Karamazov, Amok, Dame de Pique)* and John Brahm *(Broken Blossoms, Let Us Live)*. Also like Toch, he had attempted to find work in London as a film scorer and as a composer for the BBC, where, in 1937, a job offer was rescinded because he was not a British citizen.

However, unlike Toch, when Rathaus became disenchanted with Hollywood, he moved back to New York, switching careers permanently to become a college teacher at Queens College. Even though Rathaus had always considered himself foremost a composer who enjoyed considerable success in Europe, from 1940 until the time of his death he dedicated himself to teaching the younger generation of composers. Students and faculty alike considered him a true mentor. He felt his primary job as a teacher was to expose his students to as many components of musical totality as they could handle. Like Toch, he was a formidable pianist, often performing orchestral scores at the piano for his students.

Always optimistic, Rathaus never resented the fact that teaching took him away from serious composing. At Queens College he developed an innovative curriculum for creative musicianship and served as department chairman from 1944 to 1946, while at the same time being on the advisory boards for the International Society of Contemporary Music (the American section) and for the Fulbright Award.

Nevertheless, Rathaus was able to compose a few concert works during his years of college teaching. Among these are: *Music for Strings* (1941), *Symphony No. 3* (1942–1943), two symphonic poems (1945 and 1949), a sinfonia concertante (1950–1951), several educational pieces, songs, and two works for chorus. Too busy teaching, serving on boards, and in his spare time trying to compose, Rathaus never formulated his teaching ideas in the form of a book.

As a tribute to Rathaus the teacher, Queens College still offers a Karol Rathaus prize every year to a promising student of composition. Although Rathaus the composer was known, admired, and performed in prewar Europe, he consciously chose to devote himself to university teaching in America, where the generation of students he taught has produced a substantial legacy.

Like his contemporaries Schönberg, Hindemith, and Krenek, Toch made early concessions to American taste, but after a decade in this country he went his own way, composing two more string quartets, seven symphonies, his smaller works for woodwind ensembles, and another one-act opera, among the thirty-plus compositions he wrote during the last fifteen years of his life. Certainly, these compositions are major contributions to twentieth-century music in America.

Toch's former student, the composer Nicolai Lopatnikoff, has evaluated Toch's stature as a mature composer in America. "Toch was by nature an individualist, a loner who stayed aloof from artistic trends . . . and went quietly on his own way. This was his strength and this also partly accounts for the undeserved neglect of his music in the postwar period – a time when his creativity worked at a high pitch and when some of his most significant music was written."[2]

As discussed in Chapter 2, some of Toch's lighter works, whether written in America or Europe, have proven to be consistently popular, and rightly so. The one-act opera *The Princess and the Pea,* the work for spoken chorus *The Geographical Fugue,* the piano piece *The Juggler,* the orchestral pieces *Big Ben Variations, Pinocchio,* the *Circus Overture,* and *Peter Pan* could all be considered programmatic, and therefore of considerable appeal to listeners today. But the chamber pieces for woodwinds, *Five Pieces for Winds and Percussion* and *Sonatinetta for Flute, Clarinet and Bassoon,* are not programmatic—and they have remained staples of the literature.

What has happened/will happen to the symphonies, the concertos, the string quartets, the last opera, to name just a few of Toch's very significant "forgotten" compositions? Why have American audiences not, since the banner Pulitzer Prize-winning year, been more receptive to symphonies that might seem too "German" in their neoromantic proportions?

In evaluating the purely musical contributions of émigré composers such as Toch, one cannot avoid looking at the seeming love-hate relationship that twentieth-century musical America has had with compositions perceived as German neoromantic. To understand this on-again, off-again fluctuation of public taste, one might briefly review certain trends in the history of American music from the early twentieth century up to the present.

At the turn of the century, Germanic music still dominated musical life in America. After all, there had been a continuing flow of German instrumentalists, conductors, singers, and teachers who were particularly influential in performing organizations and music schools. More often than not, composers and performers-to-be considered the German style and aesthetic the epitome of high culture, and German music was programmed far more than anything written by an American. At the turn of the century, up until World War I, the Americans who went to Europe to study composition tended to view composing in American idioms as a step backward.

All of that changed, however, when the United States went to war with Germany. But, once the war was over, the criss crossing of the Atlantic began again, as discussed in Chapter 1.

The composer who put American music on the map, so to speak, was George Gershwin, whose *Rhapsody in Blue* (1924) won new recognition for American music, both in the United States and abroad. His premature death in 1937 coincided with the rise of a new breed of American composers, among them Aaron Copland, Roy Harris, Virgil Thompson, and Roger Sessions. Like MacDowell, they were at first uncertain about how much to yield to American idioms, but, unlike

MacDowell, they had already composed in styles notably different from the Germanic tradition.

Coming back to the United States from Paris, Aaron Copland typified American composers in the late 1920s who felt the influence of European modern music, as he explained: "I was an adolescent during the first world war, when Germany and German music were very unpopular. The new thing in music was Debussy and Ravel—also Scriabin. Germany seemed like that old-fashioned place where composers used to study music. . . . All the new things seemed to be coming from Paris—even before I knew the name Stravinsky."[3]

If musical America in the 1920s was still searching for a kind of music to call its own, the Great Depression changed the direction of this search toward a new domestic market. In Copland's words: "In all the arts, the depression had aroused a wave of sympathy for . . . the plight of the common man. . . . Now, suddenly, functional music was in demand as never before. Motion picture and ballet companies discovered us. The music had to be simpler and more direct. There was a market especially for music evocative of the American scene."[4]

American composers returning home in the 1930s were unsure whether to write in American idioms or to assimilate the new styles they had studied in Europe. Roy Harris and Virgil Thompson were hailed as true American composers, with performances of theirs and other American composers' works, bringing composers and performers together with audiences and critics in a common cause. This was hardly the right time for an influx of European, especially German, composers!

But Roger Sessions, who had been trained in Italy and Germany, had misgivings about America's reaction to the émigré composers. In the late 1930s he wrote that

> there are those who believe that the presence of so many new Americans of so great distinction will in some way impair the integrity of our native culture . . . that some specially American quality is threatened by the influx of so-called foreign ideas. We are told, for instance, that a budding musical culture stands in the gravest danger from the encroachment of so-called "European tradition." There can be only one conclusion—America's finding itself means nothing more nor less than the discovery that . . . Americanism is by its very definition inclusive, all-inclusive, not in the smallest degree exclusive, and that loyalty to America means nothing less than a consistent devotion to the human principle in that inclusive sense.[5]

On America's seeming preference, at that time, for composing in an "American style," the émigré musicologist Alfred Einstein said that

the greatest foe of freedom, independence and truth in art — and science — is Nationalism. . . . Monteverdi never worried about writing Italian music, Bach about good German music. I do not mean to underestimate the feeling for a more intimate musical home . . . but blood and soil do not form the creative spirit. The whole future of America's music will stand or fall by this truth. I do not know if there is as yet an American music; if there is, I should be grateful to have its identifying characteristics defined. What I do know is that once a few great musicians in America have composed great music, without worrying about American traits, there will be an American music.[6]

In 1939, aware of the conflict that existed between American and foreign composers, and imploring the Americans to be more accepting of the émigrés' influence, Einstein wrote that

the fear of internationalism . . . is a definite sign of weakness in individuals and nations. The courage to accept a foreign influence has always rewarded strong creators and peoples. . . . How could a German opera like *Fidelio* develop without French opera-comique? What would the Russian Stravinsky have done without France? . . . Courage is needed to look beyond the boundaries. . . . America's position is at once fortunate and difficult. It is the only country really on the sidelines. The hospitality which it has offered so many musicians from old Europe has its complications; the invasion must be "digested." But America will soon find out which of the new arrivals it can utilize and which not. America has an opportunity, a splendid duty, not only to produce good music, but to foster good music no matter where it may originate. It has the opportunity and duty of tolerance . . . and tolerance in matters of art has always borne lasting fruit.[7]

It was not until after World War II, however, when the émigrés had become accepted in the United States, that American composers sincerely attempted to achieve an international style, perhaps in collective response to Stravinsky's damning pronouncement that "most of our homespun American style is fatuous in expression and in technique the vilest cliché. . . . In the phrase 'American music,' 'America' not only robs emphasis from 'music,' but it asks for lower standards."[8]

Fifteen years after World War II began, the international assimilation was gaining greater acceptance. American composers, many of whom had been students of European composers now in the United

States, retreated to their university positions, determined that they could no longer compose in a provincial style. By 1956, when the new internationalism was firmly established as the prevailing musical mode, the Pulitzer Prize in Music was awarded to an Austrian-German émigré, a naturalized American citizen, Ernst Toch, for a symphony written in the grand European tradition!

But, in almost predictable on-off fashion, between the late 1950s and early 1960s, the music of all but the most famous émigré composers went out of style again. Some of the transplanted composers were very old, and some had died, either in the United States or in Europe, where a number of them had gone in a kind of reverse musical migration after the war.

At any rate, musical America in the 1960s and 1970s was not particularly interested in listening to what could be perceived as more of the heavy Germanic tradition. Why should they? After all, American-trained composers clamored to be heard—many of whom had been students of Hindemith, Schönberg, Toch, Rathaus, or Krenek, on this side of the Atlantic. At a time when the so-called crisis in twentieth century music limited the amount of modern music included on concert programs, should not the American composers, whose styles, by this time, could be considered international, be encouraged?

With this background of German vs. American vs. internationalism in a fluctuating public taste, it seems difficult, at best, to assess the impact of the musical migration on America by simply considering the frequency of performance of the émigrés' works. With competition from former students and younger American composers for newly commissioned works, the contributions of Ernst Toch and his generation of émigré composers, as emphasized at the beginning of this chapter, must therefore extend beyond their concert work, to include their teaching, their writing, and their film scoring.

What a pity that Toch seemed unable to accept the fact that his contributions to America might involve more than just being a composer—that his dry spell in serious composition between 1938 and 1946 appeared to him singularly unproductive! It almost seems as if the impact of his teaching, writings, and film scoring did not count—to him. For regardless of what Toch himself may have preferred to be doing (composing more string quartets?), his impact on American musical life, along with those of his fellow émigrés, was very real. As the American musicologist Charles Hamm has noted:

At one point—the second half of the 1940s—four of the most celebrated European composers of the twentieth-century—Stravinsky, Bartok, Schönberg, and Hindemith—were in the United States. And there were many others of only slightly lesser talent and accomplishments, including Ernst Toch, Bohuslav Martinu, Erich Korngold, Mario Castelnuovo-Tedesco, Milhaud, and Rachmaninoff. . . . Perhaps most important, many of them—Hindemith, Milhaud, Schönberg, Martinu—were active and dedicated teachers of theory and composition, willing and eager to pass on to younger Americans their knowledge of the techniques and aesthetics of European classical music.[9]

That the above statement comes from a textbook devoted to the history of American music substantiates the fact that the musical migration, which includes those composers mentioned above, represents an extremely important era in this country's musical history. The reference to the émigré composers as teachers is significant in its recognition that the distinguished émigrés contributed more to America than just musical compositions.

Like Hindemith, Schönberg, Krenek, and Milhaud, whose American textbooks are still in print today, Toch belonged to that generation of remarkable émigré teachers and writers, whose writings aimed at synthesizing the old and the new. Although he did not write the type of practical "how to" texts as did Schönberg and Hindemith, some of his more philosophic articles and certainly his *Shaping Forces in Music,* written by a self-taught composer, seem timeless in their appeal to music lovers.

Ironically, the way that Toch preferred not to be remembered, as a film composer in Hollywood, remains one of the chief ways his name is known in America today. Although he never achieved the fame and recognition of his contemporaries Korngold, Eisler, and Miklos Rózsa, his being nominated for three academy awards is indicative of his important contribution to that medium. No hit songs emerged from the film scores Toch composed, and there have been no commercial recordings of his film scores. But excerpts from *Peter Ibbetson, The Cat and the Canary, The Ghost Breakers, Ladies in Retirement,* and *Address Unknown* would make a valuable contribution to the recordings and cataloging of rediscovered film music from the late 1930s and early 1940s. Certainly his gift as a film composer was recognized within the industry, because excerpts from many of Toch's Hollywood scores were reused in other films from 1936 to 1955.[10] As discussed in Chapter 4, several successful films neglected to credit Toch as the composer. Only later research by film music scholars has rightly restored Toch's name to those scores.

Fortunately, the musical establishment of today, including scholars, critics, and composers themselves, is coming to recognize the achievements and musical imagination of film composers such as Toch. The names of Korngold, Eisler, Waxman, Steiner, and Rózsa are recognized today as major film composers of the 1930s and 1940s, but their concert music, with the exception of the recent Korngold revival, has been all but ignored. Perhaps a revival of interest in Toch — the composer of seven symphonies — will come as a result of renewed interest in film composers. And would that not be ironic?

But it would make sense. Just as he became known in Hollywood as the master of an eerie, mysterious musical style, including his famous chase scenes, Toch could become famous for those same elements as they appear in such nonmovie compositions as *Phantastische Nachtmusik, Komödie für Orchester, Hyperion,* subtitled "A Dramatic Prelude for Orchestra" or the *Circus Overture,* among others.

One area of frustration, however, remains for evaluating the musical contributions of émigré composers such as Toch, and that is the shrinking availability of published scores and recordings. Toch, like many composers today, was never able to obtain a single publisher for his works, a process that lasted twenty years. As his scores went from Delkas to Leeds to Mills Music, a not unfamiliar situation with other émigré composers, the performance of his music, Toch felt, was greatly hindered. In that he had enjoyed the benefits of having one publishing firm, B. Schott, for ten years in Germany, Toch must have felt some resentment that his compatriots, Schönberg and Hindemith, retained one publisher during their years in America.

Certain aspects of Toch's personality may have contributed to his partial eclipse as a serious composer in America. Because he was, by nature, shy, introverted, and, by choice, unsociable except among close friends, it is difficult to speculate on how much the experience of transplantation contributed to his later withdrawal in America. For many of the creative talents who came to America, "emigration had trained [the refugees] in the arts of concealment . . . the émigré style has rendered its exponents peculiarly opaque."[11]

Toch's self-reference to "the forgotten composer of the twentieth century" is representative of a disillusioned émigré psyche. Certainly his lament is significant when one considers the American careers of Kurt

Weill, Karol Rathaus, or E. W. Korngold, among others, who, during their lifetimes, knew virtually no recognition of their prewar contributions to twentieth-century concert music. Only sometime after their deaths did scholars start to investigate "the European Kurt Weill," for instance.

But, unlike other émigré composers, at age sixty-two, Toch began a new career for himself as a composer of not one, but seven symphonies. Considering this remarkable creativity, Toch rightly felt more recognition was due him. After all, he composed more than thirty-five concert works during his stay in America. Thus, he outdid his émigré contemporaries, with the exception of the renowned Stravinsky and the popular Paul Hindemith. At the time of this writing, Toch's extant compositions total one hundred forty-five, forty-nine of which remain unpublished.

Two of his most significant contributions, which were certainly unique at the time they were written, are now out of print. These are his textbook on melody, *Die Melodielehre,* and his collection of piano etudes, utilizing the new twentieth century techniques in graded difficulty, *Five Times Ten Etudes,* which, in functional value, can be compared to Bartok's six volumes of the *Mikrokosmos.* A man of his times, yes, but also a thinker and composer ahead of his time.

Taking a cue from the recent Korngold and Zemlinsky revivals and from the Toch Centennial celebrations in Europe and America, one might cautiously predict a more sustained interest in the music of Ernst Toch and his fellow émigré composers. After all, the decade of the 1980s, marking the fiftieth anniversary of the forced exodus from Europe, has evidenced more than passing interest in the lives and times of Thomas Mann, Bertolt Brecht, Walter Gropius, Mies van der Rohe, Albert Einstein, Hannah Arendt, Herbert Marcuse, and Enrico Fermi. As for the exiled composers, in addition to the biographies cited in Chapter 1, the internationally celebrated Centennial of Igor Stravinsky, in 1982, prompted heightened awareness of the personalities and forces that shaped this century's musical history. Quite rightly, the focus of these documentaries and celebrations shifted to the country that took in the gifted émigrés. What is the obvious conclusion?

That "Hitler's loss was our gain," is the usual response, or, as H. Stuart Hughes concluded a decade ago, "The migration to the United States of European intellectuals fleeing fascist tyranny has finally become visible as the most important cultural event, or series of events, of the second quarter of the twentieth century."[12]

Certainly the life, works, and times of Ernst Toch are representative of the generation of composers forced to flee Hitler, who helped to bring about that momentous cultural transference from Europe to America.

The result is that America became the music capital of the world. The postwar generation of foreign students came here to study their art; the postwar generation of American musicians, concert-goers, and music consumers integrated twentieth-century music into their musical experiences; Hollywood thrived; universities developed graduate music departments; publishing houses capitalized on the successes; and the children of the distinguished émigrés melted into the pot, though frequently unaware of what their parents had really accomplished.

Those accomplishments have been individually and collectively summarized. However, the very essence of the émigré composers' contribution to musical America, aside from in the concert halls, the film studios, the classrooms, and the publishing houses, could be summed up in two simple words: "their presence." Quite remarkably, an American writing about American music, fifty years after Hitler's purge, has said it all:

> The presence of these men had a considerable impact on musical life of the country . . . they were celebrities who were interviewed, photographed, quoted, and talked about. . . . Their compositions were more often played and their mere presence prompted a greater interest in contemporary music.[13]

May the musical migration, with its distinguished cast of characters, find its rightful place in more histories of American and twentieth-century music.

A

Migration of German-Austrian Composers

Composer born died	Emigration to USA			Occupation
	Year	Age	Came to USA	
Jean Berger b. Hamm, 1909	1941	32	via Rio de Janeiro	Teaching job at Middlebury College, Vermont; Univ. of Illinois; and Univ. of Colorado.
Max Brand b. Lwow, 1896	1940	44	via Brazil	Composed electronic music and numerous pieces for modern plays. Returned to Austria 1975.
Ingolf Dahl b. Hamburg, 1912 d. Berne, 1970	1938	26	via Switzerland, 1933–38	Hollywood films studios; teacher of composition, Univ. of Southern Calif.; conductor and pianist; collaborator with Stravinsky; lecturer on twentieth-century music; instigator with Peter Yates, of the Monday Evening "Concerts on the Roof," introducing the West Coast to new music.
Paul Dessau b. Hamburg, 1894 d. E. Berlin, 1979	1939	44	via Paris, 1933–38	Hollywood: collaboration with B. Brecht; film composer. Returned to E. Berlin, 1948. Further collaboration with Brecht; 1952–68: Professor at the Deutsche Akademie der Künste.

APPENDIX A (*Continued*)

Composer born died	Emigration to USA			Occupation
	Year	Age	Came to USA	
Hanns Eisler b. Leipzig, 1898 d. E. Berlin, 1962	1940	42	after lecturing at the New School for Social Research 1935–38 – via Mexico	Hollywood: film composer; collaborator with Brecht, and coauthor with T. Adorno, *Composing for the Films*. Returned to Europe, 1948– extradited by the House Un-American Activities Committee; 1950–62: Professor at the E. Berlin Hochschule für Musik.
Lukas Foss b. "Fuchs" Berlin, 1922	1937	15	via Paris	Philadelphia: studied at the Curtis Institute; Boston: pianist with Boston Symphony; Los Angeles: Professor at UCLA; Tanglewood, Mass.: summer appointments; Buffalo, N.Y.: Conductor of Philharmonic; prolific composer in America.
Bernard Heiden b. Frankfurt, 1910	1935	25	after studying with Hindemith at the Berlin Hochschule für Musik	Detroit: teacher at the Art Center Music School and conductor of the Detroit Chamber Orchestra, 1929–33; assistant bandmaster in U.S. Army during the war; further studies at Bloomington, Ind.: Professor and Chairman of the Composition Dept., Indiana Univ., 1947–retirement.
Paul Hindemith b. Frankfurt, 1895 d. Frankfurt, 1963	1940	45	via Switzerland and Turkey	Not officially expelled from Germany, he made several concert tours abroad during his tenure at the Berlin Hochschule. Professor of Composition at Yale, 1940–53; founder and conductor of the Yale Collegium Musicum; lecturer on twentieth-century music throughout U.S. Returned to Switzerland, 1951, dividing his time between the Univ. of Zurich and Yale; 1953: permanently

APPENDIX A (Continued)

Composer born died	Emigration to USA			Occupation
	Year	Age	Came to USA	
Friederich Holländer b. London, 1896 d. Munich, 1976	1934	38	from Berlin	Hollywood: film composer (as Frederick Hollander). Returned to Germany in late 1950s.
Erich Itor Kahn b. Rimbach, Gr., 1905 d. N.Y., 1956	1941	36	via France and N. Africa	New York: pianist, organized the Albeneri Trio (Alexander Schneider, Benar Heifetz, and Erich Kahn). Composed his most important works after settling in America.
Ernst Kanitz b. Vienna, 1894 d. Menlo Park, 1978	1938	44		South Carolina; teacher at Winthrop College and Erskine College; L.A.: taught at Univ. of Southern Calif., 1945–59; also at Marymount College.
Erich Wolfgang Korngold b. Brünn, Austria, 1897 d. Hollywood, 1957	1934	37		Hollywood: film composer, 1934–35; composer of absolute music following the war.
Ernst Krenek b. Vienna, 1900	1938	37	after a visit in 1937	Poughkeepsie, N.Y.: Professor of Composition, Vassar College, 1939–42; St. Paul, Minn.: Dean of Hamline Univ.; L.A., 1947–66: composer, conductor, author, guest lecturer.
Kurt Mannschinger b. Austria, 1902 d. N.Y., 1968	1940	38	via London	Changed his name to Vernon Ashley and continued to compose. New York: earned his living as a calligraphist for music publishing firms.

APPENDIX A (Continued)

Composer born died	Emigration to USA			Occupation
	Year	Age	Came to USA	
Paul Pisk b. Vienna, 1893	1936	43		Redlands, Calif.: Professor of the Music Dept. the Univ. of Redlands, 1937–51, Chairman, 1948; Austin: Professor, Univ. of Texas, 1951–63; St. Louis: Professor at Washington Univ., 1963–72; L.A.: teacher, composer, lecturer, and writer.
Karol Rathaus b. Tarnpool, Poland, 1895 d. N.Y., 1954	1938	43	via Paris and London	Hollywood: film composer, 1939–40, which he continued even after settling in New York; Professor of Composition at Queens College, 1940–54.
Arnold Schönberg b. Vienna, 1874 d. L.A., 1951	1933	59	from Berlin via Paris	Boston: teacher, Joseph Malkin Conservatory, 1933–34; Hollywood: private teaching, composition; Univ. of Calif., L.A., 1936–44.
Ernst Toch b. Vienna, 1887 d. L.A., 1964	1934	47	from Berlin via Paris and London	New York: teacher at the New School for Social Research; L.A.: film composer, 1939–45; Professor of Composition at the Univ. of Southern Calif., 1936–48; composer, author, guest lecturer; annual returns to Europe to perform his work, 1949–64.
Frank Waxman b. Königshütte, 1906 d. L.A. 1967	1934	28	via Paris	Hollywood: film and TV composer.

APPENDIX A (Continued)

Composer born died	Emigration to USA			Occupation
	Year	Age	Came to USA	
Kurt Weill b. Dessau, 1900 d. N.Y., 1950	1936	36	via Paris, 1933–36	New York: collaborator with Max Reinhardt and Maxwell Anderson in the composition of Broadway musicals.
Karl Weigl b. Vienna, 1881 d. N. Y., 1949	1938	57	from Vienna	Connecticut: Hartt School of Music, 1940–42; New York: Brooklyn College, 1943–45; Boston: New England Conservatory, 1945–48.
Stefan Wolpe b. Berlin, 1902 d. N.Y., 1972	1938	36	via Palestine, 1933–38	Philadelphia: Settlement Music School and Philadelphia Musical Academy, 1946–52; North Carolina: Black Mountain College, 1952–56; Chairman of the Music Dept. at C. W. Post College, Long Island Univ., 1957–68.
Eric Zeisl b. Vienna, 1905 d. L.A., 1959	1939	34	via Paris, 1938–39	Hollywood: film composer and teacher and City College.
Alexander Zemlinsky b. Vienna, 1871 d. Larchmont, N.Y., 1942	1938	67		Died four years after coming to America – no American compositions.

163

▬ B

Toch Worklist
Compiled by Alyson McLamore

▬▬▬ Ernst Toch's music has been published by many different firms, some of which have in the course of time become defunct or merged with other firms. Among Toch's earliest publishers, P. Pabst has ceased publication, but Josef Weinberger is still in existence, while Tischer and Jagenberg has been bought by Leuckart. When Toch came to the United States, some of his music was published by small American firms: Delkas, Leeds, MCA Music, and Affiliated Musicians Inc. All of these have been bought by Belwin-Mills. For current availability, please contact the publishers cited at the end of the Worklist.

▬▬▬ Orchestral Music

Big Ben: Variation-Fantasy on the Westminster Chimes, Op. 62. Orchestra. Composed 1934. Published 1935. AMP/G. Schirmer.
Bunte Suite (Motley Suite), Op. 48. Orchestra. Composed 1928. Published 1929. B. Schott.
Circus: An Overture. Orchestra. Composed 1953. Published 1954. Belwin-Mills.
Concerto for Piano and Orchestra, Op. 38. Composed 1926. Published 1926. B. Schott. Two-piano score published 1926.
Concerto for Violoncello and Chamber Orchestra, Op. 35. Composed 1924. Published 1925. B. Schott.
The Covenant. (Sixth movement from the *Genesis Suite.*) Orchestra and narrator. Composed c. 1945. Unpublished. Score lost; see Discography.
The Enamoured Harlequin, Op. 94. Orchestra. Composed 1963. Unpublished.
Epilogue. Orchestra. Composed 1959. Published 1964. Belwin-Mills.

Fanal (Beacon) for Organ and Orchestra, Op. 45. Composed 1928. Published 1928. B. Schott.

Five Pieces for Chamber Orchestra, Op. 33. Composed 1924. Published 1924. B. Schott.

Hyperion: A Dramatic Prelude for Orchestra, Op. 71. Composed 1947. Published 1950. Belwin-Mills.

"The Idle Stroller" Suite. Orchestra. Composed 1938. Unpublished. First movement, reorchestrated, became *Epilogue.*

Intermezzo. Orchestra. Composed 1959. Published 1962. Belwin-Mills.

Jeptha, Rhapsodic Poem, Op. 89. (Symphony No. 5.) Orchestra. Composed 1963. Published 1965. Belwin-Mills.

Kleine Ouvertüre zu der Fächer (Little Overture to the Fan), Op. 51. Orchestra. Composed 1929. Published 1929. B. Schott.

Kleine Theater-Suite (Little Theater Suite), Op. 54. Orchestra. Composed 1930. Published 1931. B. Schott.

Komödie für Orchester in Einem Satz (Comedy for Orchestra in One Movement), Op. 42. Composed 1927. Published 1927. B. Schott.

Notturno, Op. 77. Orchestra. Composed 1953. Published 1957. Belwin-Mills.

Peter Pan, Op. 76. Orchestra. Composed 1956. Published 1956. B. Schott.

Phantastishche Nachtmusik (Fantastic Serenade), Op. 27. Orchestra. Composed 1920. Published c. 1921. Leuckart.

Pinocchio: A Merry Overture for Orchestra. Composed 1935. Published 1937. AMP/G. Schirmer.

Scherzo in B Minor, Op. 11. Orchestral version. Composed 1904. Published c. 1905. P. Pabst.

Short Story. Orchestra. Composed 1961. Unpublished.

Sinfonietta for String Orchestra, Op. 96. Composed 1964. Published 1965. Belwin-Mills.

Spiel für Blasorchester (Divertimento for Wind Orchestra), Op. 39. Composed 1926. Published 1926. B. Schott.

Symphony No. 1, Op. 72. Composed 1950. Published 1951. B. Schott.

Symphony No. 2, Op. 73. Composed 1951. Published 1953. AMP/G. Schirmer.

Symphony No. 3, Op. 75. Composed 1955. Published 1957. Belwin-Mills.

Symphony No. 4, Op. 80. Orchestra and speaker. Composed 1957. Published 1960. Belwin-Mills.

Symphony No. 5, see *Jeptha.*

Symphony No. 6, Op. 93. Composed 1963. Published 1966. Belwin-Mills.

Symphony No. 7, Op. 95. Composed 1964. Published 1968. Belwin-Mills.

Symphony for Piano and Orchestra, Op. 61. Composed 1933. Published 1933. B. Schott.

Variations on the Swabian Folk Song "Muss i denn zum Städle hinaus." Orchestra. Composed 1964. Unpublished.

Vorspiel zu einem Märchen (Prelude to a Fairy Tale), Op. 43a. Orchestra. Composed 1927. Published 1927. B. Schott. Concert version of overture of *Princess and the Pea.*

Operas

Egon und Emilie (Edgar and Emily), Op. 46. Chamber opera in one act. Composed c. 1928. Published 1938. B. Schott (full score and piano-vocal score). AMP/G. Schirmer (English version).

Der Fächer (The Fan), Op. 51. Opera in three acts. Composed 1929 or 1930. Published 1930. B. Schott (full score and piano-vocal score).

Scheherazade: The Last Tale (Das letzte Märchen), Op. 88. Opera in one act. Composed 1962. Published 1965. Belwin-Mills (English and German piano-vocal score).

Die Prinzessin auf der Erbse (The Princess and the Pea), Op. 43. Opera in one act. Composed 1927. Published 1927. B. Schott (full score, piano-vocal score, and libretto). AMP/G. Schirmer (English piano-vocal score).

Chamber Music

Adagio Elegiaco. Clarinet and piano. Composed 1950. Published 1987. Theodore Presser.

Chamber Symphony in F Major. Flute, oboe, clarinet, bassoon, horn, two violins, viola, cello, bass. Composed 1906. Unpublished.

Dedication. Two violins, viola, and cello; or string orchestra. Composed 1948. Published 1957. Belwin-Mills.

Duos for Two Violins, Op. 17. Composed 1909. Published c. 1910. Josef Weinberger. U.S. publisher: Belwin-Mills.

Five Pieces for Wind Instruments and Percussion, Op. 83. Flute, oboe, clarinet, bassoon, two horns, and percussion. Composed 1959. Published 1961 (I–III); 1963 (IV–V). Belwin-Mills.

Miniatur Ouvertüre. Two flutes, oboe, clarinet, bass clarinet, two trumpets, trombone, and percussion. Composed 1932. Published 1932. B. Schott.

Quartet for Oboe, Clarinet, Bassoon, and Viola, Op. 98. Composed 1964. Published 1967. Belwin-Mills.

Quintet for Piano, 2 Violins, Viola, and Cello, Op. 64. Composed 1938. Published 1947. Belwin-Mills.

Romanze. Violin and piano. Composed c. 1910. Published 1911. P. Pabst.

Serenade for Three Violins, Op. 20. Composed 1911. Published 1912. Josef Weinberger. U.S. publisher: Belwin-Mills.

Serenade (*Spitzweg*) for 2 Violins and Viola, Op. 25. Composed 1916. Published 1921. Leuckart. U.S. publisher: Belwin-Mills.

Sinfonietta for Wind Instruments and Percussion, Op. 97. Two flutes, two oboes, two clarinets, two bassoons, two horns, two trumpets, and percussion. Composed 1964. Published 1967. Belwin-Mills.

Sonata for Violin and Piano, Op. 21. Composed 1912. Unpublished.
Sonata for Violin and Piano, Op. 44. Composed 1928. Published 1928. B. Schott.
Sonata for Violoncello and Piano, Op. 50. Composed 1929. Published 1929. B. Schott.
Sonatinetta, Op. 84. Flute, clarinet, bassoon. Composed 1959. Published 1961. Belwin-Mills.
String Quartet in A Minor, Op. 12. Composed c. 1904–1905. Unpublished.
String Quartet in G Major, Op. 15. Composed c. 1908. Unpublished.
String Quartet in D-flat Major. Op. 18. Composed c. 1910. Published 1911. Josef Weinberger.
String Quartet in C Major, Op. 26. Composed 1919. Published c. 1920. Leuckart.
String Quartet on the Name "Bass," Op. 28. Composed 1920. Published c. 1923. Leuckart.
String Quartet, Op. 34. Composed 1924. Published 1924. B. Schott.
String Quartet, Op. 70. Composed 1946. Published 1949. Belwin-Mills.
String Quartet, Op. 74. Composed 1953–1954. Published 1961. Belwin-Mills.
String Trio, Op 63. Violin, viola, and cello. Composed 1936. Published 1955. AMP/G. Schirmer.
Tanz-Suite (Dance Suite), Op. 30. Flute, clarinet, violin, viola, bass, percussion. Additional strings optional. Composed 1923. Published 1924. B. Schott.
Three Impromptus for Unaccompanied String Instruments, Op. 90a, b, c. a: violin; b: viola; c: cello. Composed 1963. Published 1965. Belwin-Mills.
Two Divertimentos for String Duet, Op. 37. No. 1: violin and cello; No. 2: violin and viola. Composed 1925. Published 1926. B. Schott.
Two Etudes for Violoncello Solo. Composed. 1930. Published 1931. B. Schott.
Vom sterbenden Rokoko (From the Dying Rococo), Op. 16. Violin and piano. Composed 1909. Published 1910. P. Pabst.

Keyboard Music

Begegnung (Meeting), Composed c. 1908. Unpublished.
Burlesken, Op. 31. Composed 1923. Published 1924. B. Schott.
Canon *(Aus Dem "Tagebuch").* Composed c. 1914. Published 1915. Carl Grüninger.
Capriccetti, Op. 36. Composed 1925. Published 1925. B. Schott.
Diversions, Op. 78a. Composed 1956. Published 1958. Belwin-Mills.
5 × 10 Etudes, Op. 55–59. Composed 1931. Published 1931. B. Schott.
Ideas, Op. 69. Composed 1946. Published 1947. Belwin-Mills.
Kleinstadtbilder (From a small town), Op. 49. Composed 1929. Published, 1929. B. Schott.
Melodische Skizzen (Melodic Sketches), Op. 9. Composed 1903. Published, no date. P. Pabst. Published as individual pieces c. 1905.

Profiles, Op. 68. Composed 1946. Published 1948. AMP/G. Schirmer.
Reflections, Op. 86. Composed 1962. Published 1962. Belwin-Mills.
Reminiszenzen (Reminiscences), Op. 14. Composed 1909. Published 1909. P. Pabst.
Scherzo in B minor, Op. 11. Composed 1904. Published c. 1905. P. Pabst.
Sonata for Piano, Op. 47. Composed 1928. Published 1928. B. Schott.
Sonata for Piano Four-Hands, Op. 87. Composed 1962. Published 1963. Belwin-Mills.
Sonatinetta, Op. 78b. Composed 1956. Published 1958. Belwin-Mills.
Stammbuchverse (Album Verses), Op. 13. Composed 1905. Published 1905. P. Pabst.
Studie, Mechanical Organ. Composed 1927. Unpublished.
Tanz-und Spielstücke (Pieces for Dancing and Playing), Op. 40. Composed c. 1926. Published 1927. B. Schott.
Three Little Dances, Op. 85. Composed 1961. Published 1962. Belwin-Mills.
Three Original Pieces for the Electric Welte-Mignon Piano. Composed 1926. Unpublished.
Three Piano Pieces, Op. 32. Composed 1924. Published 1925. B. Schott.
Three Preludes, Op. 10. Composed c. 1903. Published, no date. P. Pabst.
[Untitled Canon.] Composed 1959. Unpublished.

═══ Vocal Music

An mein Vaterland (To My Fatherland), Op. 23. Large orchestra, organ, solo soprano, mixed chorus, boys' chorus. Composed 1913. Unpublished.
Cantata of the Bitter Herbs, Op. 65. Solo SATB, narrator, chorus, orchestra. Composed 1938. Rental, Belwin-Mills.
Chansons sans paroles. Voice and piano. Composed c. 1940. Unpublished.
Die Chinesische Flöte (The Chinese Flute), Op. 29. Soprano, two flutes, clarinet, bass clarinet, percussion, celesta, strings. Composed 1922. Published 1923. B. Schott (full score). AMP/G. Schirmer (English version).
Geographical Fugue. Speaking chorus. Composed 1930. Published 1950. Belwin-Mills.
Gesprochene Musik (Spoken Music). Speaking chorus. Composed 1930. No. 1: see *Geographical Fugue*, No. 2, 3: unpublished.
Ich wollt, ich wär ein fisch (I wish I were a fish). High voice and piano. Composed 1920. Unpublished.
The Inner Circle, Op. 67. Mixed chorus. Composed 1945. Revised c. 1953. Published 1953. Belwin-Mills.
Lange schon haben meine Freunde versucht (My friends have long tried). Soprano and baritone. Composed 1958. Unpublished.
Music for Orchestra and Baritone, Op. 60. Composed 1931. Published 1932. B. Schott.

Nine Songs for Soprano and Piano, Op. 41. Composed 1926. Published 1928. B. Schott (full score). AMP/G. Schirmer (English version).

Phantoms, Op. 81. Male and female speakers, women's speaking chorus, flute, clarinet, vibraphone, xylophone, timpani, percussion. Composed 1957. Rental, Belwin-Mills.

Poems to Martha, Op. 66. Medium voice, two violins, viola, cello. Composed 1942. Published 1943. Belwin-Mills.

Song of Myself. Mixed chorus. Composed 1961. Published 1961. Belwin-Mills.

There is a Season for Everything. Mezzo-soprano, flute, clarinet, violin, cello. Composed c. 1953. Published 1953. Belwin-Mills.

Der Tierkreis (The Zodiac), Op. 52. Women's chorus. Composed 1930. Nos. 1, 2: published in *Das neue Chorbuch,* vol. 7, 1930. B. Schott. No. 3: unpublished.

Valse (Waltz). Speaking chorus and optional percussion. Composed 1961. Published 1962. Belwin-Mills.

Vanity of Vanities, All is Vanity, Op. 79. Soprano, tenor, flute, clarinet, violin, viola, cello. Composed 1954. Rental, Belwin-Mills.

Das Wasser (The Water): Cantata after a Text by A. Döblin, Op. 53. Tenor, baritone, narrator, chorus, flute, trumpet, percussion, strings. Composed 1930. Published 1930. B. Schott.

■■■ Incidental Music

Anabasis. Radio play by Wolfgang Weyrauch, based on Xenophon. Flute, clarinet, two trumpets, trombone, tuba, percussion, chorus. Composed 1931. Unpublished.

The Gates of Carven Jade (also called *The Garden of Jade).* Radio play by C. M. Franzero. Flute, clarinet, banjo, guitar, violin, soprano solo. Composed c. 1934. Unpublished.

Die Heilige von U.S.A. (The Saint of the U.S.A.). Stage play by Ilse Langner. Wind ensemble, percussion, piano, harmonium, alto solo, chorus. Composed 1931. Unpublished.

Im fernen Osten (In the Far East). Radio play by Gerhard Mengel. Flute, two trumpets in C, mandolin, guitar, two violins, viola, cello, percussion, chorus, male solo voice. Composed 1931. Unpublished.

Der Kinder Neujahrstraum (The Children's New Year's Dream), Op. 19. Stage play by Marie Waldeck. Solo SATB, chorus, orchestra. Composed 1910. Unpublished.

Das Kirschblütenfest (The Cherry Blossom Festival). Stage play by Klabund. tympani, percussion, harmonium, strings. Composed 1927. Published 1927. B. Schott.

König Ödipus (Oedipus Rex). Radio play by Heinz Lipmann, based on Sophocles. Two clarinets, two trumpets, two trombones, percussion, strings. Composed 1931. Unpublished.

Medea. Radio play by Heinz Lipmann, based on Euripides. Wind ensemble, percussion, speaking chorus. Composed 1931. Unpublished.

Napoleon, oder die 100 Tage (Napoleon, or the 100 Days). Radio play by Christian Dietrich Grabbe. Composed 1931 or 1932. Unpublished.

Die Räuber (The Robbers). Radio version of play by Friedrich Schiller. Two trumpets in C, bass trumpet or trombone, percussion. Composed 1931. Unpublished.

Die Rollen des Schauspielers Seami (The Roles of the Actor Seami). Radio play, author unknown. flute, clarinet, violin, banjo, guitar, percussion. Composed 1931. Unpublished.

Turandot. Radio play by Alfred Wolfenstein. Flute, clarinet, trumpet in C, cello, piano, percussion. Composed 1931. Unpublished.

Uli Wittewüpp. Stage play by Marcel Gero. Clarinet, trumpet, percussion, piano, strings. Composed 1931. Unpublished.

William Tell. Stage play by Friedrich Schiller. Flute, two clarinets, bassoon, trumpet, horn, two trombones, percussion, chorus. Composed 1939. Unpublished.

===== **Motion Picture Music**

Address Unknown. Columbia Pictures. Composed 1944.
The Cat and the Canary. Paramount Pictures. Composed 1939.
Catherine the Great. London Film Productions. Composed 1933.
Dr. Cyclops. Paramount Pictures. Composed 1940.
First Comes Courage. Columbia Pictures. Composed 1943.
The Ghost Breakers. Paramount Pictures. Composed 1940.
Ladies in Retirement. Columbia Pictures. Composed 1941.
Little Friend. Gaumont British Pictures Corporation. Composed 1934.
None Shall Escape. Columbia Pictures. Composed 1943.
On Such a Night. Paramount Pictures. Composed 1937.
Outcast. Paramount Pictures. Composed 1936.
Peter Ibbetson. Paramount Pictures. Composed 1935.
The Private Life of Don Juan. London Film Productions. Composed 1934.
The Unseen. Paramount Pictures. Composed 1945.

Arrangements

[Eleven Folk Song Settings]. Choruses, strings, piano. Composed c. 1930. Published 1930. C. F. Peters.

Prelude and Fugue (after J. S. Bach's Solo Violin Sonata No. 3 in C Major). String orchestra. Composed c. 1943. Published 1953. Belwin-Mills.

[Three Folk Dances]. Chorus and orchestra. Composed c. 1946–47. Score lost; see Discography.

[Two Folk Songs.]. Voice and piano. Composed c. 1938. Published 1939. Youth Zionist Organization of America and Hechalutz Organization of America.

Variations on Mozart's "Unser dummer Pöbel meint . . . ," K. 455. Orchestra and piano concertante. Composed c. 1933. Published 1953. Belwin-Mills.

Publishers

Associated Music Publishers/G. Schirmer
    In the United States and Canada
        AMP/G. Schirmer
        866 Third Ave.
        New York, NY 10022
        rental: 1–800–221–4755
        sales: 1–800–524–1137
    In German-speaking countries
        Bote und Bock Musikverlag
        Hardenbergstr. 9a
        D–1000 Berlin, BRD
        (030) 3 12 30 81

Belwin-Mills Publishing Corporation
    In the United States and Canada
    (Performances and rental)
        Theodore Presser Co.
        Presser Place
        Bryn Mawr, PA 19010
        (215) 525–3636
    (Sales only)
        Belwin-Mills Publishing Corp.
        15800 NW 48th Ave.
        Miami, FL 33014
        (305) 620–1500

In Europe
 Contact the Toch Centennial office or consult local music
 dealer.

F.E.C. Leuckart
 In the United States and Canada
  AMP/G. Schirmer (see above)
 In Europe
  F.E.C. Leuckart Musikverlag
  Nibelungenstr. 48
  D–8000 München 19, BRD

P. Pabst
 Contact the Toch Centennial office

Theodore Presser
 See Belwin-Mills

B. Schott Söhne
 In the United States and Canada
  European American Distributors Corp.
  P.O. Box 850
  Valley Forge, PA 19482
  (215) 648–0506
 In Europe and Israel
  B. Schott's Söhne
  Weihergarten 5 D–6500 Mainz 1, BRD
  (0131) 2460
 In Great Britain
  Schott Ltd.
  48 Great Marlborough St.
  London W1V 2BN
  England
  (01) 437–1246

Josef Weinberger
 12–14 Mortimer St.
 London W1N 8EL
 England

NOTE: As we go to press, we learn that AMP/G. Schirmer has been sold to
 Music Sales
 24 E. 22nd St.
 New York, NY 10040
 (212) 254–2100

═ C

Discography
Compiled by Alyson McLamore

▰▰▰▰ The recordings listed in the following discography are 12″–33 rpm commercial discs recorded in stereo unless otherwise noted. The year in which the album was first released, if known, is given in parentheses following the label information. Other composers who are featured on a particular album are included in parentheses, as are other works by Ernst Toch (given in italics).

Big Ben Variations, Op. 62 (1934). RAI Orchestra conducted by Rudolf Kempe. Cover title: *In Memoriam Ernst Toch (1887–1964).* Educational Media Associates EMA–101 (mono; noncommercial recording) (1975). (With *Pinocchio; Symphony No. 1.*)

Capriccetti, Op. 36 (1925). Armen Guzelimian, piano. Cover title: *Ernst Toch in Retrospect.* Crystal Stereo S502 (1975). (With *Geographical Fugue; Sonata for Violin and Piano,* Op. 21; *Three Little Dances; Valse.*)

The Chinese Flute, Op. 29 (1923). Dorothy Renzi, soprano; MGM Chamber Orchestra conducted by Carlos Surinach. MGM release E 3546 (mono). (With Marga Richter.)

The Chinese Flute, Op. 29 (1923). Alice Mock, soprano; Pacific Symphonetta conducted by Manuel Compinsky. Alco AC 203 (78 rpm; mono; noncommercial recording) and Alco ALP 1006 (mono). (Sung in English.)

Circus (1953). Philharmonic-Symphony of New York conducted by Andre Kostelanetz. Cover title: *Encore!* Columbia Records A 2035 (ZEP 35523) (45 rpm; mono). (With Rachmaninoff and Tchaikovsky.)

Circus (1953). Philharmonic-Symphony of New York conducted by Andre Kostelanetz. Cover title: *Bravo!* Columbia Records CL 758 (x "LP" 34450; mono). (With Boccherini, Khachaturian, Rachmaninoff, and Tchaikovsky.)

Concerto for Piano and Orchestra, Op. 38 (1926). Ernst Toch, piano; Vienna

═══ **175**

Symphony conducted by Herbert Haefner. Cover title: *Contemporary Composers Series.* Contemporary Records S8014 (1968). (With *Cello Concerto, Op. 35.*)

Concerto for Violoncello and Orchestra, Op. 35 (1925). Frédéric Mottier, cello; Chamber Orchestra conducted by Fred Barth. Cover title: *Contemporary Composers Series.* Contemporary Records S8014 (1968). (With *Concerto for Piano and Orchestra, Op. 38.*)

The Covenant (Sixth movement from *The Genesis Suite*) (1945). Janssen Symphony of Los Angeles conducted by Werner Janssen. Cover title: *The Genesis Suite.* MGM Artists JS 10 (78 rpm; mono). (With movements by Castelnuovo-Tedesco, Milhaud, Schöenberg, Shilkret, Stravinsky, and Tansman.)

Divertimento for Violin and Violoncello, Op. 37, No. 1 (1926). Alice Schoenfeld, violin; Eleonore Schoenfeld, cello. Cover title: *Schoenfeld Duo.* Orion ORS 7267 (1972). (With Haydn and Kodaly.)

Divertimento for Violin and Viola, Op. 37, No. 2 (1926). Arranged by Piatigorsky. Jascha Heifetz, violin; Gregor Piatigorsky, cello. Cover title: *The Heifetz-Piatigorsky Concerts.* RCA Victor LSC 3009 (1968). (With Boccherini and Brahms.)

Divertimento for Violin and Viola, Op. 37, No. 2 (1926). Charmian Gadd, violin; Yizhak Schotten, viola. Cover title: *Violin and Viola Virtuosic Duets.* Crystal Records Stereo S632 (1982). (With Handel, Martinu, and Villa-Lobos.)

Five Pieces for Winds and Percussion, Op. 83 (1959). Philadelphia Woodwind Quintet (Murray Panitz, flute; John de Lancie, oboe; Anthony Gigliotti, clarinet; Bernard Garfield, bassoon; Mason Jones, horn) with Ward O. Fearn, horn; Fred D. Hinger, and Charles E. Owen, percussion. Cover title: *A Tribute to Ernst Toch and Henry Cowell.* Columbia ML 5788 (mono) and Stereo MS 6388 (1962). (With *Sonatinetta, Op. 84*; Cowell.)

Four Palestine Horah Dances. "Al Hasela" arranged by Ernst Toch. Pacific Symphonetta and Chorus conducted by Victor Young. Alco A–21 (78 rpm; mono). (With Bernstein, Diamond, and Milhaud.)

Geographical Fugue (1930). Camerata of Los Angeles conducted by H. Vincent Mitzelfelt. Cover title: *Ernst Toch in Retrospect.* Crystal Records S502 (1975). (With *Capriccetti; Sonata for Violin, Op. 21; Three Little Dances; Valse.*)

Geographical Fugue (1930). The Abbey Singers. Cover title: *Five Centuries of Song.* Decca DL 710073 (1963). (With Billings, Brahms, Byrd, Copland-Fine, Costeley, Farmer, French, Kraehenbuehl, de Lassus, Mozart, Passereau, Read, de Rivaflecha, and Weelkes.)

Jeptha (Symphony No. 5), Op. 89 (1962). Louisville Orchestra conducted by Robert Whitney. Cover title: *Louisville Orchestra First Edition Records.* Louisville LOU 661 (mono) (1966). (With Morel and Somers.)

Jewish Holiday Dances. "Yom Tov Lanu" arranged by Ernst Toch. Orchestra and Chorus conducted by Max Goberman. VOX 192 (10″; 78 rpm; mono) and Alco ALP A–12 (10″; 78 rpm; mono). (With Bernstein, Castelnuovo-Tedesco, Diamond, Eisler, Kosakoff, Milhaud, Rittman, and Wolpe.)

Miniatur Ouvertüre (1932). Louisville Orchestra conducted by Jorge Mester. Cover title: *Louisville Orchestra First Edition Records.* Louisville LOU 702 (1970). (With Guarnieri, Ibert, Talmi, and Tosar.)

Notturno, Op. 77 (1953). Louisville Orchestra conducted by Robert Whitney. Cover title: *Louisville Orchestra First Edition Records.* Louisville LOU 545 (mono) (1955). (With Mennin and Riegger.)

Palestine Dances and Songs. "Y'Mina, Y'Mina" arranged by Ernst Toch. Orchestra and Chorus conducted by Max Goberman. VOX 191 (10", 78 rpm; mono). (With Castelnuovo-Tedesco, Diamond, Eisler, Kosakoff, and Milhaud.)

Peter Pan, Op. 76 (1956). Louisville Orchestra conducted by Robert Whitney. Cover title: *Louisville Orchestra First Edition Records.* Louisville LOU 612 (1961). (With Garcia-Morillo.)

Pinocchio (1935). Berlin Radio Orchestra conducted by Ljubomir Romanski. Cover title: *In Memoriam Ernst Toch (1887–1964).* Educational Media Associates EMA–101 (mono; noncommercial) (1975). (With *Big Ben Variations; Symphony No. 1.*)

Poems to Martha, Op. 66 (1942). Compinsky Ensemble (Manuel Compinsky, violin; Albert Steinberg, violin; Cecil Figelski, viola; Laurence Lesser, cello; James Tippey, baritone). Cover title: *The Compinsky Ensemble.* Sheffield 141, 145 (mono) (1964). (With Beethoven, Franck, Ives, and Milhaud.)

Quintet, Op. 64 (1938). American Art Quartet (Eudice Shapiro, violin; Marvin Limonick, violin; Virginia Majewski, viola; Victor Gottlieb, cello) with Ernst Toch, piano. Alco ALP 1212 (mono).

Quintet, Op. 64 (1938). American Art Quartet (Eudice Shapiro, violin; Nathan Ross, violin; Sanford Schonbach, viola; Victor Gottlieb, cello) with Andre Previn, piano. Cover title: *Contemporary Composers Series No. 4.* Contemporary Records S8011 (1962).

Quintet, Op. 64 (1938). Kaufman Quartet (Louis Kaufman, violin; Grischa Monasevitch, violin; Raymond Menhennick, viola; Joseph Kahn, cello) with Ernst Toch, piano. Columbia Masterworks M–460 (mono).

Quintet, Op. 64 (1938). Kaufman Quartet (Louis Kaufman, violin; Grischa Monasevitch, violin; Raymond Menhennick, viola; Joseph Kahn, cello) with Ernst Toch, piano. Cover title: *Masters of the Bow, Vol. 6.* Discopaedia MB 1051 (1986) (reissue). (With *Violin Sonata, Op. 44; Spitzweg Serenade, Op. 25.*)

Serenade (*In Spitzwegs Art*), Op. 25 (1917). Westwood String Trio (Louis Kaufman, violin; Joseph Stepansky, violin; Louis Kievman, viola). Cover title: *Contemporary Composers Series No. 1.* Contemporary Records C6002 (mono) and Stereo Records S7016 (1958). (With *String Quartet, Op. 18.*)

Serenade (*In Spitzwegs Art*), Op. 25 (1917). Westwood String Trio (Louis Kaufman, violin; Joseph Stepansky, violin; Louis Kievman, viola). Cover title: *Ernst Toch.* Protone Records CSPR 165 (cassette) (1985) (reissue). (With *String Quartet, Op. 18.*)

Serenade (*In Spitzwegs Art*), Op. 25 (1917). Kaufman Trio (Louis Kaufman, violin: Grischa Monasevitch, violin; Raymond Menhennick, viola). Cover title: *Masters of the Bow, Vol. 6.* Discopaedia MB 1051 (1986) (reissue). (With *Violin Sonata, Op. 44; quintet, Op. 64.*)

Serenade (*In Spitzwegs Art*), Op. 25 (1917). Louis Kaufman, violin; Grischa Monasevitch, violin; Raymond Menhennick, viola. VOX 177 (10″; 78 rpm; mono).

Sonata for Violin and Piano, Op. 21 (1912). Eudice Shapiro, violin; Ralph Berkowitz, piano. Cover title: *Ernst Toch in Retrospect.* Crystal Records Stereo S502 (1975). (With *Capriccetti; Geographical Fugue; Three Little Dances; Valse.*)

Sonata for Violin and Piano, Op. 44 (1928). Louis Kaufman, violin; Ernst Toch, piano. Cover title: *Masters of the Bow, Vol. 6.* Discopaedia MB 1051 (1986) (reissue). (With *Serenade (Spitzweg), Op. 25; Quintet, Op. 64.*)

Sonatinetta, Op. 84 (1959). Murray Panitz, flute; Anthony Gigliotti, clarinet; Bernard Garfield, bassoon. Cover title: *A Tribute to Ernst Toch and Henry Cowell.* Columbia ML 5788 (mono) and Stereo MS 6388 (1962). (With *Five Pieces for Winds and Percussion, Op. 83;* Cowell.)

String Quartet, Op. 18 (1911). Westwood String Quartet (Louis Kaufman, violin; Joseph Stepansky, violin; Louis Kievman, viola; George Neikrug, cello). Cover title: *Ernst Toch.* Protone Records CSPR 165 (cassette) (1985) (reissue). (With *Spitzweg Serenade, Op. 25.*)

String Quartet, Op. 18 (1911). Westwood String Quartet (Louis Kaufman, violin; Joseph Stepansky, violin; Louis Kievman, viola; George Neikrug, cello). Cover title: *Contemporary Composers Series No. 1.* Contemporary Records C6002 (mono) and Stereo Records S7016 (1958). (With *Spitzweg Serenade, Op. 25.*)

String Quartet, Op. 28 (1920). American Art Quartet (Eudice Shapiro, violin; Nathan Ross, violin; Sanford Schonbach, viola; Victor Gottlieb, cello). Cover title: *Contemporary Composers Series No. 3.* Contemporary Records S8008 (1961). (With *String Quartet, Op. 74.*)

String Quartet, Op. 70 (1946). New Zurich Quartet (Eduard Melkus, violin; Jürg Jenne, violin; Franz Hirschfeld, viola; Frédéric Mottier, cello). Cover title: *Contemporary Composers Series No. 2.* Contemporary Records S8005 (1959). (With *String Trio, Op. 63.*)

String Quartet, Op. 70 (1946). London String Quartet (John Pennington, violin; Laurent Halleux, violin; Cecil Bonvalot, viola; Warwick Evans, cello). Alco ALP 1213 (78 rpm; mono).

String Quartet, Op. 74 (1953). Roth Quartet (Feri Roth, violin; Thomas Marrocco, violin; Laurent Halleux, viola; Cesare Pascarella, cello). Cover title: *Contemporary Composers Series No. 3.* Contemporary Records S8008 (1961). (With *String Quartet, Op. 28.*)

String Trio, Op. 63 (1936). Vienna String Trio (Wolfgang Poduschka, violin; Helmut Weis, viola; Otto Blecha, cello). Cover title: *Contemporary*

Composers Series No. 2. Contemporary Records S8005 (1959). (With *String Quartet, Op. 70.*)

Symphony No. 1, Op. 72 (1950). Vienna Symphony Orchestra conducted by Herbert Haefner. Cover title: *In Memoriam Ernst Toch (1887–1964).* Educational Media Associates EMA–101 (mono; noncommercial) (1975). (With *Big Ben Variations; Pinocchio.*)

Symphony No. 3, Op. 75 (1955). Pittsburgh Symphony Orchestra conducted by William Steinberg. Capitol Records P–8364 (mono) (1957). (With Hindemith.)

Three Little Dances, Op. 85 (1961). Armen Guzelimian, piano. Cover title: *Ernst Toch in Retrospect.* Crystal Records S502 (1975). (With *Capriccetti; Geographical Fugue; Sonata for Violin and Piano, Op. 21; Valse.*)

Valse (1961). Camerata of Los Angeles conducted by H. Vincent Mitzelfelt. Cover title: *Ernst Toch in Retrospect.* Crystal Records S502 (1975). (With *Capriccetti; Geographical Fugue; Sonata for Violin and Piano, Op. 21; Three Little Dances.*)

⁼ D

Filmography
Compiled by Jack Docherty

▬ Germany

1. *Die Kinderfabrik* (*The Children Factory*), 1928.

An experimental project as part of the Deutsches Kammermusikfest (German Chamber Music Festival) in Baden-Baden, on the theme of "Film and Music," for which Toch, Milhaud, Hindemith, Dessau, and Antheil wrote synchronization music. Toch's score is lost.

2. *Filmstudie*. A Hans Richter film, 1928.

According to Roger Manvell and John Huntley in *The Technique of Film Music* (Focal Press, 1957), 267, this film was "first presented to music by Ernst Toch," but later recorded to a fragment of Darius Milhaud's *La Creation du Monde*. The attribution of the music to Toch may be an error, however, possibly owing to confusion of this film with Toch's *Studie* for mechanical organ, written in 1927. *Filmstudie* is not included in Charles Johnson's Checklist of Compositions by Ernst Toch, 1974.

▬ Great Britain

1. *Catherine the Great* (a.k.a. *The Rise of Catherine the Great*). London Films–United Artists, 1934. 93 mins.

Producer: Alexander Korda. Director: Paul Ozinner (and Korda, uncredited). Screenplay: Marjorie Deans, Arthur Wimperis. Dialogue: Lajos Biro, Arthur Wimperis, and Melchior Lengyel, from the play *The Czarina* by Lajos

Biro and Melchior Lengyel. Cinematography: Georges Perinal, Robert Lapresle. Art Direction: Vincent Korda. Costumes: John Armstrong. Editor: Harold Young. Sound Recording: A. W. Watkins. *Music: Ernst Toch.* Musical Direction: Muir Mathieson. Cast: Douglas Fairbanks, Jr., Elisabeth Bergner, Flora Robson, Sir Gerald du Maurier, Irene Vanbrugh, Griffith Jones, Joan Gardner, Dorothy Hale, Diana Napier.

2. *Little Friend.* Gaumont-British, 1934. 85 mins.
 Producer: Michael Balcon. Associate Producer: Robert Stevenson. Director: Berthold Viertel. Screenplay: Margaret Kennedy and Christopher Isherwood. Adaptation: Berthold Viertel, from the novel *Kleine Freundin* by Ernst Lothar. Cinematography: Gunther Krampf. Art Direction: Alfred Junge. *Music: Ernst Toch.* Musical Direction: Louis Levy. Editor: Ian Dalrymple. Costumes: Schiaparelli. Sound Recording: A. Birch. Cast: Nova Pilbeam, Matheson Lang, Fritz Kortner, Lydia Sherwood, Arthur Margetson, Jimmy Hanley, Jean Cadell, Lewis Casson, Finlay Currie, Cecil Parker.

3. *The Private Life of Don Juan.* London Films–United Artists, 1934. 90 mins.
 Producer/Director: Alexander Korda. Screenplay: Lajos Kiro, Frederick Lonsdale. Dialogue: Arthur Wimperis, from the play by Henri Bataille. Cinematography: Georges Perinal. Special Effects: Ned Mann. Art Direction: Vincent Korda. Costumes: Oliver Messel. Editor: Harold Young, Stephen Harrison. Sound Recording: A. W. Matkins. Technical Director: Marques de Portago. *Music: Ernst Toch.* Song: "Don Juan's Serenade" composed by Mischa Spoliansky; lyric by Arthur Wimperis. Musical Direction: Muir Mathieson. Cast: Douglas Fairbanks, Sr., Merle Oberon, Owen Nares, Benita Hume, Binnie Barnes, Melville Cooper, Joan Gardner, Athene Seyler, Patricia Hilliard, Clifford Heatherley, Barry MacKay, Claud Allister.

United States

1. Peter Ibbetson. Paramount Pictures, 1935. 85 mins.
 Producer: Louis D. Lighton. Director: Henry Hathaway. Screenplay: Vincent Lawrence, Waldemar Young, John Meehan, Edwin Justus Mayer. Adaptation: Constance Collier, from the novel by George du Maurier and the play by John Nathaniel Raphael. Cinematography: Charles Lang, Jr. Art Direction: Hans Drier, Robert Usher. Editor: Stuart Heisler. *Music: Ernst Toch.* Musical Direction: Irvin Talbot. Cast: Gary Cooper, Ann Harding, Douglass Dumbrille, John Halliday, Ida Lupino, Virginia Weidler, Dickie Moore, Donald Meek, Doris Lloyd, Gilbert Emery, Christian Rub, Elsa Buchanan, Leonid Kinskey.
 Academy Award Nomination, Best Score: Irvin Talbot (for *Ernst Toch*).

2. *The General Died at Dawn.* Paramount Pictures, 1936. 93 mins.
Producer: William Le Baron. Director: Lewis Milestone. Screenplay:
Clifford Odets, from the novel by Charles Booth. Cinematography: Victor
Milner. Music: Werner Janssen. *Additional Music:* Gerard Carbonara, *Ernst
Toch. Musical Adaptation:* Gerard Carbonara, Hugo Friedhofer, Heinz
Roemheld, *Ernst Toch.* Cast: Gary Cooper, Madeleine Carroll, Akim Tamiroff,
Dudley Digges, Porter Hall, William Frawley, Philip Ahn, J. M. Kerrigan.
Academy Award Nomination, Best Score: Boris Morros (for Werner
Janssen).

3. *On Such a Night.* Paramount Pictures, 1937. 71 mins.
Producer: Emanuel Cohen. Director: E. A. Dupont. Story: Morley F.
Cassidy, S. S. Field, John D. Klorer. Screenplay: Doris Malloy, William Lipman.
Editor: Ray Curtis. *Music: Ernst Toch.* Cast: Grant Richard, Roscoe Karns,
Karen Morley, Eduardo Ciannelli, Alan Mowbray, Robert McWade.

4. *Outcast.* Paramount Pictures,, 1937. 71 mins.
Producer: Emanuel Cohen. Director: Robert Florey. Story: Frank Mc-
Adams. Editor: Ray Curtis. *Music: Ernst Toch.* Cast: Warren William, Karen
Morley, Lewis Stone.

5. *Heidi.* 20th Century–Fox, 1937. 88 mins.
Producer: Raymond Griffith. Director: Allan Dwan. Screenplay: Walter
Ferris, Julien Josephson, from the novel by Johanna Spyri. Cinematography:
Arthur Miller. *Music:* Charles Maxwell, Cyril J. Mockridge, *Ernst Toch.* Musical
Direction: Louis Silvers. Cast: Shirley Temple, Jean Hersholt, Arthur Treacher,
Helen Westley, Mady Christians, Sidney Blackmer, Sig Rumann, Marcia Mae
Jones, Mary Nash.

6. *Four Men and a Prayer.* 20th Century–Fox, 1938. 85 mins.
Producer: Kenneth MacGowan. Director: John Ford. Screenplay: Rich-
ard Sherman, Sonya Levien, Walter Ferris, from the novel by David Garth.
Cinematography: Ernest Palmer. *Title Music: Ernst Toch.* Musical Direction:
Louis Silvers. Cast: Loretta Young, Richard Greene, George Sanders, David
Niven, C. Aubrey Smith, William Henry, J. Edward Bromberg, Alan Hale,
Reginald Denny, John Carradine, Barry Fitzgerald, Berton Churchill, John Sut-
ton.

7. *The Story of Alexander Graham Bell* (British title: *A Modern Miracle*). 20th
Century–Fox, 1939. 97 mins.
Producer: Kenneth MacGowan. Director: Irving Cummings. Screenplay:
Lamar Trotti. Cinematography: Leon Shamroy. *Title Music: Ernst Toch.* Music:
Cyril J. Mockridge. Musical Direction: Louis Silvers. Cast: Don Ameche,
Loretta Young, Henry Fonda, Charles Coburn, Spring Byington, Gene Lock-
hart, Polly Ann Young, Bob Watson.

8. *The Cat and the Canary.* Paramount, 1939. 72 mins.
Producer: Arthur Hornblow, Jr. Director: Elliott Nugent. Screenplay:
Walter De Leon, Lynn Starling, from the novel by John Willard. Cinematography: Charles Lang, Jr. Art Direction: Hans Dreier, Robert Usher. Editor: Archie
Marshek. *Music: Ernst Toch.* Musical Adviser: Andrea Setaro. Cast: Bob Hope,
Paulette Goddard, Gale Sondergaard, Douglass Montgomery, John Beal,
George Zucco, Nydia Westman, Elizabeth Patterson, John Wray.

9. *Dr. Cyclops.* Paramount Pictures, 1940. 76 mins.
Producer: Dale Van Every. Director: Ernest B. Schoedsack. Screenplay:
Tom Kilpatrick. Cinematography: Henry Sharp, Winton C. Hoch. Special Effects: Farciot Edouard, Gordon Jennings. In Technicolor. Music: Ernst Toch,
Gerard Carbonara, Albert Hay Marlotte. Cast: Albert Dekker, Thomas Coley,
Janice Logan, Victor Kilian, Charles Halton, Frank Yaconelli, Paul Fix.

10. *The Hunchback of Notre Dame.* RKO-Radio, 1939. 117 mins.
Producer: Pandro S. Berman. Director: William Dieterle. Screenplay:
Sonya Levien, Bruno Frank, from the novel *Notre Dame de Paris* by Victor
Hugo. Cinematography: Joseph H. August. Art Direction: Van Nest Polglase.
Music: Alfred Newman. Orchestrations: Robert Russell Bennett, Edward B.
Powell, Leonid Raab, Conrad Salinger. *"Hallelujah" arranged by Ernst Toch.*
Cast: Charles Laughton, Cedric Hardwicke, Maureen O'Hara, Edmond
O'Brien, Thomas Mitchell, Harry Davenport, Walter Hampden, Alan Marshall,
George Zucco, Katherine Alexander, Fritz Leiber, Rod La Rocque.

11. *The Ghost Breakers.* Paramount Pictures, 1940. 85 mins.
Producer: Arthur Hornblow, Jr. Director: George Marshall. Screenplay:
Walter De Leon, from the play by Paul Dickey and Charles W. Goddard. Cinematography: Charles Lang, Jr. Art Direction: Hans Dreier. *Music: Ernst Toch.*
Music Advisor: Andrea Setaro. Cast: Bob Hope, Paulette Goddard, Richard
Carlson, Paul Lukas, Anthony Quinn, Willie Best, Lloyd Corrigan, Noble Johnson, Pedro de Cordoba.

12. *Ladies in Retirement.* Columbia, 1941. 92 mins.
Director: Charles Vidor. Screenplay: Reginald Denham, Edward Percy,
Garrett Fort, from the play by Reginald Denham and Edward Percy. Cinematography: George Barnes. *Music: Ernst Toch.* Musical Director: Morris W. Stoloff.
Cast: Ida Lupino, Louis Hayward, Evelyn Keyes, Elsa Lanchester, Edith Barrett, Isobel Elsom, Emma Dunn.
Academy Award Nomination, Scoring of a Dramatic or Comedy Picture: Morris W. Stoloff, *Ernst Toch.*

13. *First Comes Courage.* Columbia, 1943. 88 mins.
Producer: Harry Joe Brown. Director: Dorothy Arzner. Screenplay:
Lewis Meltzer, Melvin Levy, from the novel *The Commandos* by Elliott Arnold.

Cinematography: Joseph Walker. *Music: Ernst Toch.* Musical Direction: Morris W. Stoloff. Cast: Merle Oberon, Brian Aherne, Carl Esmond, Fritz Leiber, Erik Rolf, Reinhold Schunzel, Isobel Elsom.

14. *Address Unknown.* Columbia, 1944. 72 mins.
Producer/Director: William Cameron Menzies. Screenplay: Kressman Taylor, Herbert Dalmass, from the novel by Kressman Taylor. Cinematography: Rudolph Maté. *Music: Ernst Toch.* Additional Music: Mario Castelnuovo-Tedesco. Musical Direction: Morris W. Stoloff. Cast: Paul Lukas, Peter Van Eyck, Mady Christians, Emory Parnell.
Academy Award Nomination, Scoring of a Dramatic or Comedy Picture: Morris W. Stoloff, *Ernst Toch.*

15. *None Shall Escape.* Columbia, 1944. 85 mins.
Producer: Sam Bischoff. Director: André De Toth. Screenplay: Lester Cole, from a story by Alfred Neumann and Joseph Thau. Cinematography: Less Garmes. *Music: Ernst Toch.* Musical Direction: Morris W. Stoloff. Cast: Marsha Hunt, Alexander Knox, Henry Travers, Richard Crane, Dorothy Morris, Trevor Bardette.

16. *The Unseen.* Paramount Pictures, 1945. 82 mins.
Producer: John Houseman. Director: Lewis Allen. Screenplay: Hagar Wilde and Raymond Chandler, from the novel *Her Heart in Her Throat* by Ethel Lina White. Cinematography: John F. Seitz. Art Direction: Hans Dreier, Earl Hedwick. *Music: Ernst Toch.* Cast: Joel McCrea, Gail Russell, Herbert Marshall, Phyllis Brooks, Isobel Elsom, Norman Lloyd. *Throat* by Ethel Lina White. Cinematography: John F. Seitz. Art Direction: Hans Dreier, Earl Hedwick. *Music: Ernst Toch.* Cast: Joel McCrea, Gail Russell, Herbert Marshall, Phyllis Brooks, Isobel Elsom, Norman Lloyd.

Excerpts from Toch's Hollywood film scores were reused in many other films, including:

1936   *Let's Make a Million; Murder with Pictures*
1937   *Daughter of Shanghai; Night Club Scandal*
1938   *Bar-20 Justice; Booloo; Pride of the West*
1939   *Everything Happens at Night; The Three Musketeers*
1941   *Fly-By-Night; The Man Who Returned to Life*
1942   *The Adventure of Martin Eden; Boston Blackie Booked on Suspicion; Henry Aldrich, Editor; Sullivan's Travels*
1943   *Murder in Times Square; Passport to Suez*
1944   *The Black Parachute; The Girl in the Case; Nine Girls; Shadows in the Night; The Soul of a Monster; They Live in Fear; U-Boat Prisoner; The Unwritten Code*
1945   *The Crime Doctor's Courage; The Crime Doctor's Warning; Escape in the Fog; A Guy, a Gal and a Pal; Rough, Tough and Ready*

1946 *The Crime Doctor's Manhunt; Night Editor; The Phantom Thief; Shadowed; The Unknown*
1947 *Blind Spot; The Crime Doctor's Gamble; The Millerson Case*
1948 *Port Said; The Wreck of the Hesperus*
1949 *The Barbary Pirate; The Devil's Henchman; Law of the Barbary Coast; The Lost Tribe; My Name is Julia Ross*
1951 *China Corsair*
1952 *Okinawa; Prince of Pirates; A Yank in Indo-China*
1953 *The Big Heat; El Alamein; The 49th Man; Savage Mutiny; Serpent of the Nile; Slaves of Babylon*
1954 *The Bamboo Prison*
1955 *Women's Prison.*

Source: *The ASCAP Index of Performed Compositions* (New York, 1978).

Notes

Preface

1. Donald Fleming and Bernard Bailyn, *The Intellectual Migration: Europe and America* (Cambridge: Harvard University Press, 1969).

Chapter 1

1. Melvin Maddocks, review of *Exiled in Paradise,* by Anthony Heilbut, and *Strangers in Paradise,* by John Russell Taylor, *Time Magazine,* 20 June 1983, 76.

2. Boris Schwarz, "The Music World in Migration," *The Muses Flee Hitler* (Washington, D.C.: Smithsonian Institute Press, 1983), 137.

3. Maurice Davie, *Refugees in America: Report on the Committee for the Study of Recent Immigration from Europe* (1947; reprint, Westport, Conn.: Greenwood Press, 1974), 350.

4. The main difficulty in trying to track down the missing names is that any musician could list his occupation as "composer," provided he could receive an affidavit of financial support by teaching music, anywhere in America.

5. This list was compiled by the author with the help from the Center for German-speaking Immigration, State University of New York, Albany. It is no doubt incomplete, and we would welcome any additional names.

6. Letter from Bruno Walter to Henry Cowell, 21 Oct. 1933.

7. Laura Fermi, *The Illustrious Immigrants: The Intellectual Migration from Europe, 1930–1941* (Chicago: University of Chicago Press, 1968), 100.

8. Dika Newlin, *Schönberg Remembered* (New York: Pendragon Press, 1980), 14.

9. Davie, *Refugees in America,* 349.

10. Ibid.

11. Erwin Panofsky, "The History of Art," in *The Cultural Migration: The Euro-*

pean Scholar in America, ed. Franz Neumann (Philadelphia: University of Pennsylvania Press, 1953), 93.

12. Anthony Heilbut, *Exiled in Paradise: German Refugee Artists and Intellectuals from 1933 to the Present* (New York: Viking Press, 1983), 77–78.

13. Henry Pachter, "On Being An Exile," *Salmagundi Magazine* (Fall-Winter 1945–46).

14. Heilbut, *Exiled in Paradise,* 34.

15. Bruno Walter, *Theme and Variations* (New York: Knopf, 1946), 338.

16. Heilbut, *Exiled in Paradise,* viii–x.

17. Davie, *Refugees in America,* 357.

18. Fermi, *The Illustrious Immigrants,* 100. This article from the *New York Times* appeared on 4 Dec. 1932.

19. Davie, *Refugees in America,* 350.

Chapter 2

1. Lilly Toch, transcribed interview with Bernard Galm, 1972, Toch Archive, UCLA. *Note:* In this chapter all quotations from Lilly Toch's interviews will be designated as simply (Mrs. Toch).

2. Nicolas Slonimsky, "Ernst Toch," *Die Neue Zeitschrift Für Musik,* 12 Dec. 1967, 499.

3. Alfred Einstein, ed., "Ernst Toch," *Riemann's Musik-Lexikon,* (Berlin: Max Hesse Verlag, 1929).

4. Letter from Toch to Coolidge, 21 Feb. 1943.

5. Letter from Toch to the MacDowell Colony, summer 1953.

6. Jakob Gimpel, *The Composer and Conductor Bulletin,* Los Angeles, November 1964.

7. Toch in a response on the occasion of his 75th birthday celebration, 25 Jan. 1963, University of Southern California, Toch Archive.

8. Lawrence Weschler, Introduction to Ernst Toch, *The Shaping Forces in Music* (New York: Dover Publications, 1977), iv.

9. Toch's lecture on "What is good music?" given at the Westside Jewish Community Center in Los Angeles, 22 May 1957.

10. Weschler, Introduction to *The Shaping Forces in Music,* xxi.

11. Ernst Toch, *The Shaping Forces in Music,* 154–55.

12. Toch, "Some Thoughts Out of Season," *Notes* (Spring 1966), 1003.

13. Letter from Toni Stolper to the author, 5 May 1982.

14. Judith Heller, personal friend of the Tochs, in a letter to the author, 9 May 1972.

15. Toch, "Musing," unpublished, c. 1960, Toch Archive.

16. Letter from Franzi Toch Weschler to the author, 11 Feb. 1988.

17. Gertrude Zeisl, Transcribed memoirs of her life with Eric Zeisl, Zeisl Archive, UCLA.

18. Marta Feuchtwanger, "Tribute to Ernst Toch," in *The Composer and Conductor Bulletin,* Los Angeles, Nov. 1964.

19. Franzi Weschler to the author, 11 Feb. 1988.

20. Handwritten letter by Toch, c. 1963, Toch Archive.
21. Letter from Toch to Mr. D. B. Brimm, 4 Mar. 1945.
22. Letter from Toch to Mrs. Coolidge, 29 Mar. 1943.
23. Walter Monfried reporting in the *Milwaukee Journal* (Summer 1949).
24. Franzi Weschler to the author, 11 Feb. 1988.
25. Ibid.

Chapter 3

1. Nicolas Slonimsky, "Ernst Toch," *Die Neue Zeitschrift für Musik,* 12 Dec. 1967, 499.
2. Carl Schorske, *Fin-de-Siècle Vienna* (New York: Random House, 1981), 6.
3. *The New Grove Dictionary,* 1980 ed., s.v. "Vienna," by Mosco Carner.
4. Lawrence Weschler, Introduction to Ernst Toch, *The Shaping Forces in Music* (New York: Dover Publications, 1977), iv.
5. B. Kellner, Letter from B. Schott Söhne to Joseph Fuchs, 3 May 1906.
6. Weschler, Introduction to *The Shaping Forces in Music,* v.
7. Cyril Scott, *Bone of Contention* (London: Aquarian Press, 1969), 64–65.
8. Colin Mason, "European Chamber Music Since 1929," *Cobbett's Cyclopedic Survey of Chamber Music,* 2d ed. (London: Oxford University Press, 1963).
9. Lilly Toch, transcribed interviews with Bernard Galm, 1972, Toch Archive, UCLA.
10. Ibid.
11. Ibid.
12. Ernst Krenek, "Essay on Mahler," in *Gustav Mahler,* ed. Bruno Walter (New York: Da Capo Press, 1970), 197–99.
13. Lilly Toch, Interviews with Bernard Galm.
14. *The New Grove Dictionary,* 1980 ed., s.v. "Expressionism."
15. Nicolai Lopatnikoff, *Proceedings of the Annual Meeting of the National Institute of Arts and Letters,* 1964, 501–03.
16. Toch's remarks "About the Work," as they appear in the score of *The Chinese Flute* (G. Schirmer, English version), 1949.
17. Alfred Einstein, review in *Berliner Tageblatt* as quoted on the album cover of Toch's Concerto for Cello, Op. 35 (Contemporary Records S8014).
18. Lilly Toch, interviews with Bernard Galm.
19. Ibid., 19.
20. Peter Gay, *Weimar Culture* (London: Penguin Books, 1974), 192.
21. Bruno Walter, *Theme and Variations* (New York: Alfred Knopf, 1964), 268–69.
22. Toni Stolper, *Ein Leben in Brennpunkten unserer Zeit: Gustav Stolper, 1888–1947* (Tübingen, 1960), 211–13.
23. Konrad Wolff, tape-recorded interview with the author, Apr. 1982.
24. Gay, *Weimar Culture,* 132.
25. Lilly Toch, interviews with Bernard Galm.
26. Ibid.
27. Lawrence Weschler, "Talks on Toch," 1974, Toch Archive.

28. Lilly Toch, interviews with Bernard Galm.
29. Ibid.
30. Lawrence Weschler, manuscript for his "Talks on Toch," 1974, Toch Archive.
31. Lilly Toch, interviews with Bernard Galm.
32. Toni Stolper, transcribed interview with Lawrence Weschler, Los Angeles, 7 Nov. 1972.

Chapter 4

1. Ernst Toch, as quoted in David Ewen's *The Complete Book of Twentieth Century Music* (London: Anthony Blond), 1961.
2. Toch's correspondence with the publishers AMP and Mills Music has been chronicled by his grandson, Lawrence Weschler, whose summaries of the contents are available through the Toch Archive. Similarly, the correspondence with B. Schott from 1933 to 1950 has been organized in the Archive by Barbara Davis Barclay.
3. David Ewen, "Boston Symphony Honors Exiled Modernist," *American, Hebrew and Jewish Tribune,* 1 Feb. 1935, 255.
4. Toch, remarks included in the score of *Pinocchio,* published by Associated Music Publishers, 1937.
5. The Gershwin score, with inscription, is now part of the Toch Archive, UCLA.
6. Paul Pisk, "Ernst Toch," *The Musical Quarterly,* Oct. 1938, 439.
7. Ibid., 438.
8. Franzi Toch Weschler, letter to the author, 27 Feb. 1988.
9. Leslie Halliwell, *Halliwell's Film Guide* (London: Granada, 1985), 761.
10. *Monthly Film Bulletin,* July 1978, 147.
11. Mark Evans, *Soundtrack: The Music of the Movies* (New York: Hopkinson and Blake, 1975), 76.
12. Ibid., 77.
13. Quoted in Halliwell, *Film Guide,* 727.
14. Oscar Levant, *A Smattering of Ignorance* (New York: Doubleday, Doran, 1940).
15. *ASCAP Index of Performed Compositions* (New York: ASCAP, 1978).
16. Halliwell, *Film Guide,* 168.
17. John Baxter, *Hollywood in the Thirties* (London: Tavity Press, 1986), 86.
18. John Russell Taylor, *Strangers in Paradise: The Hollywood Emigrés, 1933–1950* (London: Faber and Faber, 1983), 83.
19. Halliwell, *Film Guide,* 327.
20. Leonard Maltin, ed. *TV Movies* (New York: Signet, 1980), 45.
21. Schönberg did not, as far as is known, compose any film scores in Hollywood, although he was approached by MGM to write music for *The Good Earth* (1937).
22. Letter from Franzi Weschler to the author, 11 Feb. 1988.
23. Jarrell C. Jackman, "German Emigrés in Southern California in the 1930's and 1940's," *The Muses Flee Hitler* (Washington, D.C.: Smithsonian Institute Press, 1983), 108.
24. Letter from Franzi Weschler to the author, 28 Feb. 1988.

25. Letter from Franzi Weschler to the author, 11 Feb. 1988.

26. Gertrude Zeisl, transcribed interview with Bernard Galm, Los Angeles, 1972, Zeisl Archive, UCLA.

27. Lawrence Weschler, "Talks on Toch," 1974, Toch Archive, UCLA.

28. Letter from Franzi Weschler to the author, 11 Feb. 1988.

29. Letter from Toch to Mrs. Coolidge, 21 Feb. 1943.

30. Letter from Toch to Mrs. Coolidge, 11 Feb. 1945.

31. Letter from Toch to Mrs. Coolidge, 15 Nov. 1951.

32. Letter from Albert Schweitzer to Toch, 7 Aug. 1953.

33. Peter J. Korn recalling conversations with Toch. Interview with Lawrence Weschler, Los Angeles, 1972.

34. Letter from Toch to B. Schott Publishers, Dec. 1951.

35. Columbia Records issued *Pinocchio and the Circus Overture;* Sheffield of Los Angeles recorded the *Poems to Martha* of 1942; ALCO, owned by Alexander Copinsky of Los Angeles, recorded *The Chinese Flute* and *The Piano Quintet.* The Louisville Contemporary Series recorded *Notturno* and *Peter Pan* and planned to issue other works.

36. Winthrop Sargent, "Composer Foresees Art of the Future as the Art of Tone Color," *Musical America,* 10 Mar. 1932.

37. Lawrence Weschler, Introduction to *The Shaping Forces in Music* (New York: Dover Publications, 1977), ix.

Chapter 5

1. Paul Pisk, "Ernst Toch," *The Musical Quarterly,* Oct. 1938, 439.

2. Letter from Vagn Holmboe to Toch, Copenhagen, 1 Dec. 1933.

3. David Ewen, "Boston Symphony Honors Exiled Modernist," *American Hebrew Jewish Tribune,* 1 Feb. 1935, 255.

4. Nikolai Lopatnikoff, *The Composer and Conductor Bulletin,* Los Angeles, November 1964, 3.

5. Letter from Lilly Toch to the author, Mar. 1971.

6. Tony Thomas, *Music for the Movies,* (South Brunswick: A. S. Barnes, 1973), 181.

7. As quoted by Lilly Toch in a personal interview with the author, Nov. 1970.

8. Both letters quoted in Charles Schwartz, *Gershwin: His Life and Music* (London: Abelard-Schuman, 1973), 125.

9. Mantle Hood, Foreword to *Placed as a Link in the Chain,* pamphlet containing ten essays by Toch (Los Angeles: UCLA, 1971), 11.

10. Mantle Hood in a personal interview with the author, University of Maryland, Baltimore, Jan. 1982.

11. Ibid.

12. Matthew Doran, as interviewed by Lawrence Weschler and the author, Los Angeles, July 1972.

13. Ibid.

14. John Scott Trotter in an interview with Lawrence Weschler and the author, Santa Monica, California, July 1972.

15. Ibid.

16. Mel Powell in a transcribed interview with Lawrence Weschler, summer 1972.

17. Ibid.

18. Ibid.

19. Ibid.

20. Ibid.

21. Aurelia de la Vega in an interview with Lawrence Weschler and the author, Los Angeles, July 1972.

22. Gerald Strang in an interview with Lawrence Weschler, Los Angeles, summer 1972.

23. Ibid.

24. Toch, in a transcribed interview with Robert Trotter, c. 1962, 12.

25. Toch, "The Teaching of Music Composition is Futile," *Musical Courier*, Mar. 1954, 28.

26. Ibid., 29.

27. Toch, "Ernst Toch Answers his Critics," *Musical Courier*, June 1954, 5.

28. Toch, "Finale," unpublished article intended for the *Musical Courier*, c. June 1954.

29. Toch, "About the Teaching of Music Theory," unpublished article, n.d., c. 1955.

30. Toch, "Blueprint for a demonstration method in the teaching of instrumentation," unpublished article, c. 1950.

31. Ernst Krenek, "America's Influence on Émigré Composers," *Perspectives of New Music* (Spring 1970), 113.

32. Toch to Mrs. Coolidge, 11 Feb. 1945.

33. Franz Neumann, *The Cultural Migration: The European Scholar in America* (Philadelphia: University of Pennsylvania Press, 1953).

34. Toch, *The Shaping Forces in Music* (New York: Dover Publications, 1977), Preface.

35. Thomas Mann, review of *The Shaping Forces in Music,* as presented to the Criterion Music Corporation, c. 1948. Letter in the Toch Archive.

36. Toch, *The Shaping Forces in Music* (New York: Dover Publications, 1977), 3.

37. Ibid., 5.

38. Ibid., 30, 35.

39. Ibid., 24, 58.

40. Ibid., 61.

41. Ibid., 138–39.

42. Ibid., 140–41.

43. Ibid., 141. Toch cites measures 67–75 of Wagner's *Prelude to Die Meistersinger* as an example of fermentative counterpoint and measures 58–67 of Mozart's *Overture to the Magic Flute* as an example of the ornamentative type.

44. Ibid., 116.

45. Ibid., 237.

46. Ibid., 238.

47. Ernst Toch, *Die Melodielehre* (Berlin: Max Hesse Verlag, 1923), Vorwort. Translation by the author.

48. Ibid., 1.

49. Ibid., 6.

50. Ernst Kurth, *Grundlagen des linearen Kontrapunkts* (Berlin: Max Hesse Verlag, 1917).

51. Hugo Leichtentritt, *Musical Form* (Cambridge: Harvard University Press, 1951), 452–53.

52. Letter from W. W. Norton Co. to Ernst Toch, 19 June 1944.

━━ Chapter 6

1. Postscript to Ernst Toch's "Some Thoughts Out of Season," *Notes* (Spring 1966): 1003.

2. The only publication of Toch's writings is the pamphlet "Placed as a Link in This Chain: A Medley of Observations by Ernst Toch." It contains remarks by the composer on eight of his compositions. Published by the Friends of the UCLA Library, 1971.

3. Complete translations of each of the German articles summarized here can be obtained from the Toch Archive: "English Translations of the German Articles, 1923–1932," translated by Diane Jezic.

4. Ernst Toch, "Comparative Points in European and American Music Development," unpublished essay, 1958.

5. Ibid., 2.

6. Ibid., 8.

7. Letter from Toch to Hermann Scherchen, c. 1958. The contents of this letter were later developed into the unpublished essay "Comparative Points in European and American Music Development," Toch Archive.

8. Toch, "The Situation of the Composer in the U.S.A.," *Ars Viva News Bulletin* (Mar. 1953): 2.

9. Toch, "What Is Good Music?" *Musical Courier* (Apr. 1955): 8.

10. Toch, "Some Thoughts Out of Season," *Notes* (Spring 1966): 1006.

11. Toch, "Moderne Komponisten über die Gegenwartsmusik," *Der Tag* (Vienna), (28 Mar. 1929).

12. Toch, "The Credo of a Composer," *Deutsche Blätter* (Apr. 1945): 5.

13. Ibid., 5–6.

14. Toch, "Some Thoughts Out of Season," 1003.

15. Toch, "The Teaching of Music Composition Is Futile," *Musical Courier* (Mar. 1954): 82.

16. Toch, unpublished remarks on modern music, an introduction to a *Pro Musica* concert of Toch's chamber music, 1932.

17. Toch, Radio Speech for "Music of Today," KPEK–FM, Los Angeles, Mar. 1948.

18. Ibid.

19. Toch, "What Is Good Music?" 9.

20. Ibid.

21. Toch, "The Credo of a Composer," 6.

22. Ibid.

23. Nicolas Slonimsky, "Ernst Toch," *Die Neue Zeitschrift für Musik,* (Dec. 1967): 501.

24. Ernst Toch, unpublished remarks on the Piano Quintet, Op. 64, 1940.

25. Toch, "Some Viewpoints of the Composer," unpublished speech given at the Westside Jewish Community Center, Los Angeles, 22 May 1957.

26. Paul Pisk, "Ernst Toch," *Musical Quarterly* (Oct. 1938): 438.

27. Toch, "Some Thoughts Out of Season," 1005.

28. Toch, "What Is Good Music?" 8.

29. Toch, "Credo of a Composer," 12.

30. Ibid., 13.

31. Toch, Introduction to the *Cantata of the Bitter Herbs,* as quoted in the pamphlet "Placed as a Link in This Chain," Toch Archive, UCLA.

32. Toch, Remarks about the Fifth Symphony, as found in the pamphlet "Placed as a Link in This Chain," Toch Archive, UCLA.

33. Toch, Program Notes for the Boston Symphony's performance of the Second Symphony, 12 Dec. 1952.

34. Program notes for the Pittsburgh Symphony's performance of the First Symphony, 2 Jan. 1953.

Chapter 7

1. Ernst Krenek, "America's Influence on its Emigré Composers," *Perspectives of New Music* (Spring-Summer 1970): 115.

2. Nicolai Lopatnikoff, *Proceedings of the National Institute of Arts and Letters,* 1964, 501.

3. Aaron Copland, as cited by Edward Cone, "Conversation with Aaron Copland," in *Perspectives on American Composers* ed. Benjamin Boretz and Edward Cone (New York: W. W. Norton and Company, 1971), 173.

4. Ibid.

5. Roger Sessions, *Roger Sessions on Music, Collected Essays* (Princeton: Princeton University Press, 1979), 321–24.

6. Alfred Einstein, as quoted in Minna Lederman, *The Life and Death of a Small Magazine: Modern Music, 1924–1946* (New York: Institute for Studies in American Music, 1983), 169.

7. Ibid., 170.

8. Igor Stravinsky, *Conversations with Igor Stravinsky* (Garden City: Doubleday and Company, 1959), 129–30.

9. Charles Hamm, *Music in the New World* (New York: W. W. Norton, 1983), 555.

10. For a list of these films, see Jack Docherty's Filmography, Appendix D.

11. Anthony Heilbut, *Exiled in Paradise* (New York: Viking Press, 1983), viii–x.

12. H. Stuart Hughes, *The Sea Change: The Migration of Social Thought, 1930–1965* (New York: Harper and Row, 1975), 1.

13. Charles Hamm, *Music in the New World,* 555.

Selected Bibliography

The Migration: General

Boyers, Robert, ed. *The Legacy of the German Refugee Intellectuals.* New York: Schocken Books, 1969.

Davie, Maurice. *Refugees in America: Report to the Committee for the Study of Recent Immigration from Europe.* Westport, Conn.: Greenwood Press, 1974.

Fermi, Laura. *Illustrious Immigrants: The Intellectual Migration from Europe, 1930–41.* Chicago: University of Chicago, 1968.

Fleming, Donald and Bernard Bailyn. *The Intellectual Migration—Europe and America, 1930–1960.* Cambridge: Harvard University Press, 1969.

Gay, Peter. *Freud, Jews, and Other Germans: Masters and Victims in Modernist Culture.* New York: Oxford University Press, 1978.

_____. *Weimar Culture.* London: Penguin Books, 1974.

Heilbut, Anthony. *Exiled in Paradise: German Refugee Artists and Intellectuals from the 1930s to the Present.* New York: Viking Press, 1983.

Hughes, H. Stuart. *The Sea Change: The Migration of Social Thought, 1930–1965.* New York: Harper and Row, 1975.

Jackman, Jarrell C., and Carla Borden, eds. *The Muses Flee Hitler.* Washington, DC: Smithsonian Institute Press, 1983.

Pachter, Henry. *Weimar Etudes.* New York: Columbia University Press, 1982.

Pachter, Henry, ed. "The Legacy of the German Refugee Intellectuals." Special edition of the review *Salmagundi* (Fall 1969-Winter 1970).

Peyre, Henri, ed. *The Cultural Migration: The European Scholar in America.* Philadelphia: University of Pennsylvania Press, 1953.

Schwarz, Boris. "The Music World in Migration." In *The Muses Flee Hitler,* edited by Jarrell C. Jackman and Carla Borden. Washington, DC: Smithsonian Institute Press, 1983.

Spalek, John. *Guide to the Archival Materials of the German Emigration to the U.S. After 1933.* Charlottesville, Va.: University of Virginia, 1978.
Strelka, Joseph, Robert Bell, and Eugene Dobson, eds. *Protest Form-Tradition Essays in German Exile Literature.* University: University of Alabama Press, 1982.
Taylor, John Russell. *Strangers in Paradise: The Hollywood Emigrés, 1933–1950.* New York: Holt, Rinehart, and Winston, 1983; London: Faber and Faber, 1983.
Willett, John. *Art and Politics in the Weimar Period: The New Sobriety 1917–1933.* New York: Pantheon Books, 1978.

■■■ On Emigré Composers: Their Books

Betz, A. *Hanns Eisler: Political Musician.* New York: Cambridge University Press, 1982.
Carroll, Brendan G. *Erich Wolfgang Korngold: His Life and Works.* Paisley, Scotland: Wilfion Books, Publishers, 1984.
Eisler, Hanns. *Composing for the Films.* New York: Oxford University Press, 1947.
Hindemith, Paul. *A Composer's World.* New York: Anchor Books, 1961.
_____. *The Craft of Musical Composition.* New York: Associated Music Publishers, 1946.
_____. *Elementary Training for Musicians.* New York: Associated Music Publishers, 1946.
Holde, Arthur. *Jews in Music from the Age of the Enlightenment to the Present.* New York: Philosophical Library, 1959.
Jarman, Douglas. *Kurt Weill: An Illustrated Biography.* Bloomington: Indiana University Press, 1982.
Kemp, E. C. *Hindemith.* London: Oxford University Press, 1970.
Klemperer, Otto. *Minor Recollections.* Translated by J. Maxwell Browning. London: Dennis Dobson, Ltd., 1964.
Kowalke, K. H. *Kurt Weill in Europe.* Ann Arbor, Mich.: University Microfilms International, 1979.
Krenek, Ernst. "America's Influence on its Emigré Composers." *Perspectives of New Music* (Spring-Summer 1970).
_____. *Horizons Circled.* Berkeley: University of California Press, 1974.
_____. Letter to the Editor. *Musical Courier* (May 1954).
_____. *Music Here and Now.* New York: W. W. Norton, 1939.
Marx, Henry. "The Americanization of Kurt Weill and Lotte Lenya." Paper read at the Kurt Weill Symposium, Yale University (November 1983).
Newlin, Dika. *Schoenberg Remembered.* New York: Pendragon Press, 1980.
_____. *Bruckner, Mahler and Schoenberg.* Morningside Heights, N.Y.: King's University Press, 1947.

Rózsa, Miklós. *Double Life: The Autobiography of Miklós Rózsa.* New York: Hippocrene Books, Inc., 1982.

Scherchen, Hermann. *The Nature of Music.* Translated by William Mann. London: Dennis Dobson, Ltd., 1946.

Schoenberg, Arnold. *Fundamentals of Musical Composition.* Edited by Gerald Strang and Leonard Stein. London: Faber and Faber, 1967.

_____. *Harmonielehre (Theory of Harmony)* Vienna, 1911, Universal-Edition 3d revised and enlarged ed., 1922; 4th ed., 1949. Abbreviated translation, New York: Philosophical Library, 1948. Complete translation, London: Faber and Faber; Berkeley and Los Angeles: University of California Press, 1978.

_____. *Models for Beginners in Composition.* New York: G. Schirmer, 1942. Revised edition, Los Angeles: Belmont, 1972.

_____. *Preliminary Exercise in Counterpoint.* London: Faber and Faber, New York: St. Martin's Press, 1963.

_____. *Structural Functions of Harmony.* Completed 1948. New York: W. W. Norton, 1954; rev. ed., 1969.

_____. *Style and Idea. Selected Writings of Arnold Schoenberg.* Edited by Leonard Stein; translated by Leo Black. New York: St. Martin's Press, 1975.

Schwarz, Boris. "The Music World in Migration." In *The Muses Flee Hitler,* edited by Jarrell C. Jackman and Carla Borden. Washington, DC: Smithsonian Institute Press, 1983.

Stravinsky, Igor. *Poetique Musicale.* Translated by Arthur Knodel and Ingolf Dahl. Cambridge: Harvard University Press, 1947.

Strobel, Heinrich. *Paul Hindemith, Zeugnis in Bildern.* Mainz: B. Schott Söhne, 1961.

Stuckenschmidt, Hans Heinz. *Arnold Schoenberg.* Translated by E. Roberts and H. Seale. New York: Grove Press, Inc., 1959.

Walter, Bruno. *Gustav Mahler.* Translated from the German by Lotte Walter Lindt. New York: Alfred A. Knopf, 1958.

_____. *Theme and Variations.* New York: Alfred Knopf, 1946.

Twentieth-Century Music

Adorno, Theodor. *Philosophy of Modern Music.* Translated by A. Mitchell and W. Blomster. New York: Seabury Press, 1933.

Austin, William. *Music in the Twentieth Century.* New York: W. W. Norton, 1966.

Bauer, Marion. *Twentieth Century Music.* New York: G. P. Putnam and Sons, 1947.

Bull, Storm. *Index to Biographies of Contemporary Composers.* New York: Scarecrow Press, Inc., 1964.

Cope, David. *New Music Composition.* New York: Schirmer Books, 1977.

Copland, Aaron. *Copland on Music.* Garden City, N.Y.: Doubleday and Company, Inc., 1944.

Deri, Otto. *Exploring Twentieth Century Music.* New York: Holt, Rinehart, and Winston, 1968.

Ewen, David. *Composers Since 1900.* New York: H. W. Wilson Company, 1969.

_____. *The New Book of Modern Composers.* 3d ed. New York: Knopf, 1967.

_____. *The World of 20th Century Music.* 3d ed. Englewood Cliffs, N.J.: Prentice-Hall, Inc., 1969.

Graf, Max. *Geschichte und Geist der Modernen Musik.* Frankfurt: Humboldt Verlag, 1946.

Hartog, Howard, ed. *European Music in the 20th Century.* London: Routledge & Kegan Paul, 1957.

Lederman, Minna. *The Life and Death of a Small Magazine: Modern Music, 1924–1946.* New York: Institute for Studies in American Music, 1983.

Mason, Colin. "European Chamber Music Since 1929." *Cobbett's Cyclopedic Survey of Chamber Music.* 2d ed. Edited by W. W. Cobbett. London: Oxford University Press, 1963.

Myers, Rollo H., ed. *Twentieth Century Music: Its Forms, Trends, Interpretations Throughout the World.* New York: Orion Press, 1968.

Persichetti, Vincent. *Twentieth Century Harmony.* New York: W. W. Norton, 1961.

Peyser, Joan. *Twentieth Century Music: The Sense Behind the Sound.* New York: Schirmer Books, 1971.

Reti, Rudolph. *Tonality in Modern Music.* New York: Collier Books, 1962.

Salzman, Eric. *Twentieth Century Music: An Introduction.* Englewood Cliffs, N.J.: Prentice-Hall, Inc., 1967.

Saminsky, Lazare. *Living Music of the Americas.* New York: Crown Publishers, 1949.

Samson, Jim. *Music in Transition. A Study of Tonal Expansion and Atonality, 1900–1920.* New York: W. W. Norton, 1977.

Schwarz, Elliot and Barney Childs, eds. *Contemporary Composers on Contemporary Music.* New York: Holt, Rinehart, and Winston, 1967.

Searle, Humphrey. *Twentieth Century Counterpoint.* 2d ed. London: Ernest Benn Ltd., 1955.

Shead, Richard. *Music in the 1920s.* London: Gerald Duckworth and Company, 1976.

Stuckenschmidt, Hans Heinz. *Twentieth Century Music.* Translated by Richard Daveson. New York: McGraw-Hill, 1969.

Ulehla, Ludmila. *Contemporary Harmony: Romanticism through the 12-Tone Row.* New York: The Free Press, 1966.

Whittal, Arnold. *Music Since the First World War.* New York: St. Martin's Press, 1977.

Yates, Peter. *Twentieth Century Music.* New York: Pantheon Books, 1967.

▬▬ American Music

Barzun, Jacques. *Music in American Life.* New York: Doubleday and Company, Inc., 1956.

Borroff, Edith. *Music in Europe and the United States, A History.* Englewood Cliffs, N.J.: Prentice-Hall, Inc., 1971.

Chase, Gilbert. *America's Music, from the Pilgrims to the Present.* New York: McGraw-Hill, 1955; 2d rev. ed., 1966.

Ewen, David. *American Composers: A Biographical Dictionary.* New York: Putnam & Sons, 1982.

Hamm, Charles. *Music in the New World.* New York: W. W. Norton, 1983.

Hitchcock, H. Wiley. *Music in the United States: A Historical Introduction.* Englewood Cliffs, N.J.: Prentice-Hall, 1974.

Howard, John Tasker, and Bellows, George Kent. *A Short History of Music in America.* New York: Thomas Y. Crowell Company, 1957.

Mellers, Wilfrid. *Music in a New Found Land.* New York: Alfred A. Knopf, 1964.

▬▬ General

Curjel, Hans. "Donaueschingen Festivals." *Cobbett's Cyclopedic Survey of Chamber Music.* 2d ed. London: Oxford University Press, 1963.

Dent, Edward. "Looking Backward—Recollections of Donaueschingen." *Music Today* (June 1949).

Ewen, David, ed. *The Year in American Music: 1948.* New York: Allen, Towne and Heath, 1948.

Graf, Max. *Legend of a Musical City.* New York: Philosophical Library, 1945.

Haas, Robert. *Handbuch der Musikgeschichte.* 2d ed. Edited by Guide Adler. Berlin: Max Hesse, 1930.

Heinzheimer, Hans. "Music from the Conglomerates." *The Saturday Review,* 22 February 1969.

Kremenliev, R. "Prominent Musicians of the West." *Music of the West* (August 1952).

Leichtentritt, Hugo. *Musical Form.* Cambridge: Harvard University Press, 1951.

McCarty, C. *Film Composers in America: A Checklist of Their Work.* New York: Da Capo Press, 1972.

Prendergast, R. M. *Film Music: A Neglected Art.* New York: W. W. Norton, 1977.

Schorske, Carl E. *Fin-de-Siècle Vienna: Politics and Culture.* New York: Vintage Books, 1981.

Slonimsky, Nicolas. "Chamber Music in America." *Cobbett's Cyclopedic Survey of Chamber Music,* 2d ed. London: Oxford University Press, 1963.

Swan, Howard. *Music in the Southwest.* Los Angeles: Anderson and Richie, 1952.

Zassenhaus, Hiltgunt. *Walls.* Boston: Beacon Press, 1974.

About Ernst Toch

Abendroth, Walter. "Neue Schallplatten von Ernst Toch." *Die Tat* (October 1971): 29.

Anson, George. "The Piano Music of Ernst Toch." *The American Music Teacher* (December 1962).

Barclay, Barbara, and Cole, Malcolm. "The Toch and Zeisl Archives at UCLA" Music Library Association's *Notes* (Spring 1979): 556–70.

Beninger, E. "Pianistische Probleme in Anschluss von Ernst Toch." *Melos* (1928).

Carner, Mosco. Review of *The Third Symphony, Music and Letters,* (October 1957): 406.

Cook, Douglas. "The Composer Tells How." *The Saturday Review,* 26 June 1954, 43.

Dorian, Frederick. Review of *The Third Symphony. The Music Quarterly* (July 1956): 395–96.

Ebert, Carl. "Ernst Toch—Portrait." *The Composer and Conductor Bulletin* (November 1964): 12.

"Ernst Toch." *Signale* (May 1930): 686–87.

Erwin, Charlotte. "Ernst Toch." In *The New Grove's Dictionary of Music and Musicians,* edited by Stanley Sadie. London: Macmillan Publishers, 1980.

Ewen, David. "Boston Symphony Honors Exiled Modernist." *American, Hebrew, and Jewish Tribune,* 1 February 1935.

Goldberg, Albert. "Composer-Philosopher Toch Speaks Out." *Los Angeles Times Magazine,* 2 December 1962.

Harris, Roy. "Ernst Toch—A Portrait." *The Composer and Conductor Bulletin* (November 1964): 2.

Helm, Everett. Review of *The Third Symphony. The Musical Quarterly* (January 1957): 136.

Hood, Mantle. Foreword to *Placed as Link in This Chain—A Medley of Observations by Ernst Toch* (Pamphlet containing ten essays by Toch). Los Angeles: University of California, 1972.

Johnson, Charles. *The Unpublished Music of Ernst Toch.* Ph.D. diss. UCLA, 1973.

Kendall, Raymond. "Composition Teaching, Bay City Postscript." *Los Angeles Times* (1954).

Koenig, Les. "Toch: Giant Composer but Under-rated." *Billboard,* 17 October 1964.

Korn, Peter Jonas. "Ernst Toch, ein vergessener Komponist." *Program Buch, Munich Symphoniker,* 4 June 1970.

Korn, Peter Jonas, and Korn, Barbara. "Ernst Toch, a Tribute." *Musical Courier,* 1 December 1957.

Kristler, Bernard. Review of *The Third Symphony. Notes* (September 1958): 658.

Kroll, Erwin. "Ernst Toch's Opera Capriccio *Der Facher:* Uraufführung in Königsberg." *Die Musik* (July 1930): 757–58.

Leichtentritt, Hugo. "Ernst Toch." In *Cobbett's Cyclopedic Survey of Chamber Music,* vol. 2, edited by Walter Wilson Cobbett. London: Oxford University Press, 1930.

_____. "Ernst Toch." *Reimann's Musiklexikon.* 11th ed. Berlin: Max Hesse, 1929.

_____. "Ernst Toch Proves the Hero of German Tonkünstlerfest." *Musical Courier,* 9 July 1925.

Lopatnikoff, Nikolai. "Ernst Toch—Portrait." *The Composer and Conductor Bulletin* (November 1964): 3.

_____. *Proceedings of the Annual Meeting of the National Institute of Arts and Letters,* 1964.

Malloch, William. "Malloch on Toch." *Pacifica Folio— KPEK-FM* 8(18) (December 1967).

Mason, William. "The Piano Music of Ernst Toch." *Piano Quarterly* (Fall 1962): 22–25.

Monfried, Walter. "Composer Keeps a Promise." *The Milwaukee Journal,* 15 June 1949.

Norton, Mildred. "Toch Remarks on Former Nazi, Walter Gieseking." *Los Angeles Times,* 11 January 1964.

Pasella, Margaret. "The Piano Music of Ernst Toch." Masters thesis, UCLA, 1963.

Pisk, Paul A. "Ernst Toch." *Musical Quarterly* (October 1938):438–452.

_____. Review of *The Geographical Fugue. Notes* (June 1950): 570.

_____. Review of *The Second Symphony,* Op. 73. *Notes* (December 1953): 148–49.

Reis, Claire. "Ernst Toch." *Composers in America.* rev. ed. New York: Macmillan, 1947.

Reisfeld, B. "Ernst Toch." *Musica* (December 1957): 752.

Rosenzweig, Alfred. "Ernst Toch." *Die Musik,* 4 January 1926.

Rutz, Hans. "Ernst Toch." *Melos* (May 1952).

Sargent, Winthrop. "Ernst Toch Foresees Music of the Future as Art of Tone Color." *Musical America,* 10 March 1932.

Slonimsky, Nicolas. "Ernst Toch, a Portrait." *The Composer and Conductor Bulletin* (November 1964): 3.

_____. "Ernst Toch." *Die Neue Zeitschrift für Musik,* 12 December 1967: 499–502.

————. *Music Since 1900.* 4th ed. New York: Scribner & Sons, 1964.

Stone, Kurt. "Ernst Toch." In *Die Musik in Geschichte und Gegenwart. Allegemeine Enzyklopedie der Musik,* edited by Friedrich Blume. Kassel und Basel: Barenreiter, 1968.

Toch, Lilly. Transcribed interviews with Bernard Galm, Toch Archive, UCLA, 1972.

Trotter, John Scott. "Ernst Toch, an Appreciation." *Score* (March 1953): 3.

Weschler, Lawrence. Introduction to *The Shaping Forces in Music.* New York: Dover Publications, 1977.

————. "Talks on Toch." University of California, Santa Cruz. Toch Archive, UCLA, 1974.

■■■ Ernst Toch Speaks

PUBLISHED ESSAYS AND ARTICLES

Toch, Ernst. "Arnold Schoenberg." *Neue Badische Landeszeitung,* 5 March 1932.

————. "Beethoven in der Gegenwart." *Neue Leipziger Zeitung,* 27 March 1929.

————. *Die Melodielehre.* Berlin: Max Hesse Verlag, 1923.

————. "Ernst Toch Answers His Critics." *Musical Courier* (June 1954).

————. "Glaubensbekenntnis eines Komponisten." *Deutsche Blätter* (March-April 1945).

————. "Gluckwuensche und Erinnerungen." *Neue Badische Landeszeitung,* 30 June 1929.

————. "Grenze zur Gegenwartsmusik." *Neue Mannheimer Zeitung,* 5 January 1927.

————. "Klavier als Instrumentkoerper." *Das Klavierbuch* (October-November 1927).

————. "Kompositions Aufzeichnungen auf Maschinellen Weg." *Deutsche Tonkünstler Zeitung,* 5 January 1928.

————. "Kontrapunkt." *Mannheimer General Anzeiger,* c. 1925.

————. "Mechanische Musikinstrumente." *Frankfurter Zeitung,* 28 November 1930.

————. "Moderne Komponisten über die Gegenwartsmusik." *Der Tag,* 28 March 1929.

————. "Musik für Mechanische Musikinstrumente." *Frankfurter Zeitung,* 21 July 1926.

————. "Neue Musik." *Mannheimer Tagblatt,* c. 1925.

————. "Neue Wege der Musik, von neuer Musikform." *Berliner Tagblatt,* 21 November 1929.

————. *Placed as a Link in This Chain—A Medley of Observations by Ernst Toch.* Los Angeles: Friends of the UCLA Library, 1971.

_____. "Revue der Musikinstrumente." *Frankfurter Zeitung,* 28 October 1930.

_____. "Schauspielmusik." *Bühnen Blätter,* 28 February 1928.

_____. "Theremin und Komponist." *Neue Badische Landeszeitung,* 6 December 1927.

_____. *The Shaping Forces in Music.* New York: Dover Publications, 1977.

_____. "The Situation of the Composer in the United States," Part 2. *ARS VIVA News Bulletin* 3(March 1950).

_____. "The Teaching of Music Composition is Futile." *Musical Courier* (March 1954).

_____. "Uber meine Kantate Das Wasser und meine Grammophon Musik." *Melos, Zeitschrift für Musik* (May-June 1930).

_____. "Umfrage, Moderne Komponisten und Gegenwartsmusik." *Der Tag,* 29 March 1929.

_____. "Von Neuer Musikform in Neue Wegen der Musik." *Berliner Tagblatt,* 31 October 1929.

_____. "Was ist Gute Musik?" *Osterreichische Musik Zeitschrift* (January 1955).

_____. "What is Good Music?" *Musical Courier* (April 1955).

_____. "Zur Musik unseres Tages," 4 February 1923. (Clipping without title of newspaper.)

PUBLISHED SCORES

Toch, Ernst. *Burlesken,* Op. 31, für Klavier. Mainz: B. Schott, 1924.

_____. *Capriccetti,* Op. 36, für Klavier. Mainz: B. Schott,1925.

_____. *The Chinese Flute,* Op. 29. Revised version. New York: Associated Music Publishers, 1949.

_____. *Das Letzte Märchen,* Op. 88, English version. New York: Mills Music Company, 1965.

_____. *Das Wasser,* Op. 53, Kantate nach Worten von Alfred Doeblin. Mainz: B. Schott, 1930.

_____. *Der Fächer,* Op. 51, Opern-Capriccio in drei Akten von Ferdinand Lion. Klavierauszug von Franz Williams. Mainz: B. Schott, 1930.

_____. *Diversions,* Op. 78 A, Five Pieces of Medium Difficulty, for Piano. New York: Leeds Music Corporation, 1958.

_____. *Drei Klavierstücke,* Op. 32. Mainz: J. B. Schott, 1925.

_____. *Egon and Emilie,* Op. 56, English Version. New York: Associated Music Publishers, 1948.

_____. Five Pieces for Winds and Percussion, Op. 83. New York: Mills Music Company, 1959.

_____. *The Geographical Fugue.* New York: Mills Music Co., 1958.

_____. *Ideas,* Op. 69, for Piano Solo. Los Angeles: Delkas Music Publishing Company, 1947.

_____. *Jephta, Rhapsodic Poem,* Fifth Symphony, Op. 89. New York: Mills Music Company, 1961.

_____. *Kleinstadtbilder* for Piano, Op. 49. Mainz: B. Schott, 1929.

_____. *Konzert für Cello und Orchester,* Mainz: B. Schott, 1925.

_____. *Konzert für Klavier und Orchester,* Op. 38. Ausgabe für zwei Klaviere vom Komponisten. Mainz: B. Schott, c. 1932.

_____. *Musik für Orchester und Baritonstimme nach Worten von Rainer Maria Rilke,* Op. 60. Mainz: B. Schott, c. 1932.

_____. Nine Songs for Soprano and Piano, Op. 41. English version. New York: Associated Music Publishers, 1968.

_____. *Poems to Martha, A Quintet for Strings and Medium Voices,* Op. 66. Los Angeles: Delkas Music Publishers Co., 1943.

_____. *The Princess and the Pea,* Op. 43. German and English version. New York: Associated Music Publishers, 1953.

_____. Profiles for Piano, Op. 68. New York: Associated Music Publishing Co., 1948.

_____. Quintet for Piano and Strings, Op. 64. New York: MCA Music Publishers, 1930.

_____. Serenade, Op. 25. "The Spitzweg." New York: MCA Music Publishers, 1938.

_____. Sinfonietta for Wind-Orchestra, Op. 97. New York: Mills Music Co., 1964.

_____. *Sonate für Klavier,* Op. 47. Mainz: B. Schott, 1928.

_____. *Sonate für Violine und Klavier,* Op. 44. Mainz: B. Schott, 1928.

_____. Sonatinetta for Piano, Op. 78B. New York: Leeds Music Corp., c. 1958.

_____. String Quartet No. 9, Op. 26. Berlin: Tischer und Jagenberg, 1920.

_____. String Quartet No. 10 on the name "Bass," Op. 28. Berlin: Tischer und Jagenberg, 1921.

_____. String Quartet No. 11, Op. 34. Mainz: B. Schott, 1924.

_____. String Quartet No. 12, Op. 70. New York: MCA Music Publishers, 1946.

_____. String Quartet No. 13, Op. 74. New York: Mills Music, 1961.

_____. String Trio Op. 63. New York: Associated Music Publishers, 1936.

_____. *Symphonie für Klavier und Orchester* (Zweites Klavier Konzert), Op. 61. Mainz: B. Schott, 1933.

_____. *Tanz und Spielstücke,* Op. 40, für Klavier. Mainz: B. Schott, 1926.

_____. The First Symphony, Op. 72. Mainz: B. Schott, 1950.

_____. The Second Symphony, Op. 73. New York: Associated Music Publishers, 1953.

_____. The Third Symphony, Op. 75. New York: Mills Music Co., 1955.

_____. The Fourth Symphony, Op. 80. New York: Mills Music Co., 1957.

_____. The Sixth Symphony, Op. 93. New York: Mills Music Co., 1963.

_____. The Seventh Symphony, Op. 95. New York: Mills Music Co., 1964.

_____. *Zehn Konzert Etüden,* Op. 55. Heft I, Piano. Mainz: B. Schott, 1931.

UNPUBLISHED MANUSCRIPTS

Toch, Ernst. *An mein Vaterland,* Op. 23. Photocopy of the autographed score. Washington, D.C.: The Library of Congress, 1923.

_____. *Cantata of the Bitter Herbs,* Op. 65. Photocopy of the autographed score. Los Angeles: Toch Archive, Music Library of the University of California in Los Angeles, 1938.

_____. *Leaves of Grass.* Photocopy of the original. Los Angeles: The Toch Archive, 1961.

_____. *The Inner Circle,* Op. 67. Photocopy of the original. Los Angeles: The Toch Archive, 1953.

_____. *Valse for Speaking Chorus.* Photocopy of the original. Los Angeles: The Toch Archive, 1961.

UNPUBLISHED ESSAYS AND SPEECHES

Toch, Ernst. "About *The Geographical Fugue,*" 2 pp., n.d.

_____. "About the *Piano Quintet,*" 1 p., n.d.

_____. "About the String Trio," Op. 63, 1 p., n.d.

_____. "About the Teaching of Music Theory," 3 pp. n.d.

_____. Acceptance Speech upon receiving the German Order of Merit, 3 pp., 1957.

_____. "An Extraordinary Experience," 1 p., n.d.

_____. "Autobiographisches," 2 pp., 1961.

_____. Blue Print for a Demonstration Method in the Teaching of Instrumentalization. 2 pp., early 1940s.

_____. "Comparative Points in European and American Music Development," 8 pp., 1958.

_____. "Die Musikalischen Ausdrucksformen im Wandel der Zeiten," incomplete, n.d., c. 1928.

_____. "Ein schoenes Ding ist ohne Spass," 1 p., 1926.

_____. "Feldpost—500," 3 letters to Lilly Toch, 10 November 1916.

_____. "Film Music." The original version of "Sound Film and Music Theatre," published in *Modern Music,* 6 pp., January 1936.

_____. "Ich habe erfahren: Der Einfall ist Alles," 1 p., n.d., c. 1926.

_____. Interview with Frederick Bach, Bremer Sendung, 2 pp., 1959 or 1960.

_____. Introduction to *The Cantata of the Bitter Herbs,* 2 pp., n.d., c. 1938.

_____. Introduction to the *Pro Musica* Concert of Chamber Works by Toch, 3 pp., 1932.

_____. Introduction to the Second Symphony, 2 pp., 1951.

_____. Introduction to the Third Symphony. Radio Speech, 7 December 1962.

_____. "Ironische Kritik der Violinsonate," 1 p., n.d., c. 1948.

_____. "Just What is Good Music?" Speech presented at the University of Minnesota, 11 pp., 9 November 1954.

_____. Letter to Breitkopf und Haertel, concerning J. S. Bach's *The Well-Tempered Clavier*, 4 pp., 27 September 1940.

_____. "Music of Today," 2 pp., 1948.

_____. On the occasion of his 75th birthday celebration, School of Music, University of Southern California, 2 page speech, December 1962.

_____. "On the Origin of The Geographical Fugue," 1 p., n.d., c. 1930.

_____. Radio Speech, Radio Berlin, 3 pp., 1962.

_____. Radio Speech, Vienna, 4 pp., 28 January 1952.

_____. Radio Speech, Zurich Radio, 2 pp., 1962.

_____. Remarks about the Fifth Symphony, 2 pp., 1961.

_____. Remarks about the First Symphony, 2 pp., 1950.

_____. Remarks about the Piano Quintet, 2 pp., 1948.

_____. "So hingedachtes," 1 p., n.d., c. 1950.

_____. "Some Viewpoints of the Composer," Speech for the Westside Jewish Community Center, Los Angeles, 6 pp., 22 May 1957.

_____. "Tiere," 3 pp., n.d., c. 1945.

_____. "Über das Musikleben in Amerika," Letter to Hermann Scherchen, 7 pp., n.d., c. 1950.

_____. "Übergangscharakter der Gegenwartsmusik . . . " 3 pp., n.d., c. 1930.

Toch, Lilly. Interviews with the Oral History Department of the University of California at Los Angeles. Transcribed, 848 pp., August 1972.

Relating to Ernst Toch's Film Scores

The ASCAP Index of Performed Compositions. New York: ASCAP, 1978.

Baxter, John. *Hollywood in the Thirties*. London: Tantivy Press, 1968.

Curtis, David. *Experimental Cinema: A Fifty Year Evolution*. London: Studio Vista, 1971.

Davies, Hugh, ed. *International Electronic Music Catalog*. Cambridge: MIT Press, 1968.

Finney, Brian. *Christopher Isherwood: A Critical Biography*. London: Faber and Faber, 1979.

Fryer, Jonathan. *Isherwood: A Biography of Christopher Isherwood*. London: New English Library, 1977.

Halliwell, Leslie. *Halliwell's Film Guide*. London: Granada, 1985.

Isherwood, Christopher. *Prater Violet*. New York: Random House, 1945.

Kulik, Karol. *Alexander Korda: The Man Who Could Work Miracles*. London: W. H. Allen, 1975.

Le Grice, Malcolm. *Abstract Film and Beyond*. London: Studio Vista, 1977.

Levant, Oscar. *A Smattering of Ignorance*. New York: Doubleday, Doran, 1940.

Low, Rachel. *Film Making in 1930s Britain*. London: George Allen and Unwin, 1985.

Maltin, Leonard, ed. *TV Movies*. New York: Signet, 1980.

Manvell, Roger, and John Huntley. *The Technique of Film Music*. Focal Press, 1957.
Monthly Film Bulletin (July 1978).
Schwartz, Charles. *Gershwin: His Life and Music*. London: Abelard-Schuman, 1973.
Soundtrack: The Music of the Movies. New York: Hopkinson and Blake, 1975.
Thomas, Tony. *Music for the Movies*. South Brunswick and New York: A. S. Barnes and Co., 1972.

▬ Index